· ·

**Retail Power Plays:
From Trading to Brand Leadership**

Retail Power Plays: From Trading to Brand Leadership

Strategies for Building Retail Brand Value

Andrew Wileman and Michael Jary
OC&C Strategy Consultants

NEW YORK UNIVERSITY PRESS
Washington Square, New York

. . . .

First published in the U.S.A. in 1997 by
NEW YORK UNIVERSITY PRESS
Washington Square
New York, N.Y. 10003

Reprinted 1998

This book is printed on paper suitable for recycling and
made from fully managed and sustained forest sources.

Library of Congress Cataloging-in-Publication Data
Wileman, Andrew.
Retail power plays : from trading to brand leadership : strategies
for building retail brand value / Andrew Wileman and Michael Jary.
p.   cm.
Includes index.
ISBN 0–8147–9331–2
1. Brand name products.   2. Retail trade—Management.   I. Jary.
Michael, 1963–   .   II. Title.
HD69.B7W55 1997
658.8'7—dc21   97–14139
                                                                       CIP

Printed in Great Britain

Contents

v

List of Exhibits

Exhibits

List of Case Studies

List of Plates

The following companies have their logos depicted in the plate section:

Marks and Spencer
The Body Shop
Boots
McDonald's
Tesco
Shell
Sainsbury's
Habitat
Laura Ashley
Visa
Conforama
Sears
Texaco
Coca-Cola

Preface

In our day-jobs as strategy consultants, we work for clients across a wide range of industries: information services, telecoms, media, software, financial services, pharmaceuticals . . . and consumer goods, for producers and retailers.

Our clients in those other sectors often raise an eyebrow at consumer goods, and raise it even higher at retailing. Compared with say media and software, they ask, aren't consumer goods and retailing rather . . . limited? Real market growth is low or zero. Industry structures are relatively stable. Technology is having an impact, but not a revolutionary one. Market and competitive trends – for example, consolidation and globalisation – are steady rather than volatile, well understood rather than surprising. In sum, consumer goods and retailing are just, well, 'mature'.

This is a view sometimes shared, explicitly or implicitly, by the management of many consumer goods and retail companies. They come to believe that they work in a 'mature' industry, and start to manage their businesses in a 'mature' way – which in practice means with little imagination.

We don't share that view. We find consumer goods and retailing still to be places of exciting and fundamental change, where imaginative competitors can re-write industry rules and create new futures for themselves.

One of the biggest areas of excitement and change is *retail brand power*, the subject of this book.

What this Book Sets Out to Do

Our intention in the book is to describe what we believe is the biggest opportunity and challenge facing retailers in 'The West' (North America, Europe, Japan) as we move into the new century – namely, building strong retail brands.

We provide an objective context for our arguments, including analysis of industry trends and case examples of brand-building successes and failures that can be documented in the industry today. However, our main focus is on prescription rather than description – on how retail management can develop strategies for shifting the business and the organisation onto a brand-building trajectory.

To make a fundamental shift in the direction and reflexes of a management team and a large organisation, a strategic concept needs to be able to be kept clear and whole in the mind. We have tried to keep the main lines of our argument simple and memorable. We also focus on the principles and strategy of retail brand-building rather than on the detail of implementation and day-to-day operational management.

Our Research Base

The book is drawn largely from our own and our firm's experience of working with leading retailers and consumer goods producers over the last 15 years. This experience embraces over 50 large corporations and businesses, across all major retailing and consumer goods sectors or product categories, in Europe and North America.

Our strategy projects are carried out under conditions of strict confidentiality. Although we draw on experience from our client projects in developing our general lines of argument, all the details in the case examples used in the text are drawn from publicly available information sources such as media coverage, analysts' reports and company filings.

We have supplemented our client project experience with management interviews conducted specifically for this book (with CEOs and senior managers of retailers and producers in Europe and the USA) and with further desk research into companies and market sectors. The management interviews were conducted on a confidential basis; we would like to express our thanks to those executives who gave us generous amounts of their time to debate the issues.

We make extensive use of the UK in our case examples of retail brand development. The UK is, in our view, more advanced than most other countries in the strength and the prevalence of retail brands, particularly in certain market sectors where retail brands are barely off the starting blocks in other countries. The UK situation in this regard was an asset to us as researchers: being based in London, we had a particularly strong familiarity with UK retailing, and extensive access to senior retail managers.

Structure of the Book

In our Introduction, we argue that, given the potential prize in shareholder value and the challenging nature of the retail environment of the twenty-first century, retail Chief Executives (CEOs) need to focus on making the change from *trading to brand leadership*.

In Part I, we provide a *context* and framework for our theme. We describe how and why retailers have seized value–chain power, and why they now need to move on to build real brand power. We address the question of whether retail brands are different from producer brands, and whether there are limits on how far they can build value.

In Part II, we review *brand-building strategies in four retail sectors*: repertoire, proximity, category killers and grocery. We look at each sector in turn and in detail, identifying the potential for brand-building and the key elements of successful brand strategies.

In Part III we turn to the practical issues involved in *managing retail brands*. We look at brand management processes and organisation, and at how retailers can manage investment in brand-building.

In Part IV, we switch our perspectives from that of product retailers and take two *different perspectives*. We look at the relevance of our theme to financial services retailing, and we take the producer perspective on the growth of retail brand power.

Building strong retail brands is one of the top three strategic issues facing product retailers as they move into the next century. The other two are the internationalisation of retailing and the potential growth of interactive home shopping, or the virtual mall. Large retailers will also be facing the temptation and challenge of diversification. Part V addresses each of these issues, *looking forward* to how they might impact retailing in the future.

Finally, we provide a *summary and conclusion* to our argument.

ANDREW WILEMAN
MICHAEL JARY

Introduction: From Trading to Brand Leadership

Great retailers need to be great traders. They need to understand what will sell to their customers, at what price, at what quality, with what service level. They need to be able to deal with their suppliers to get the keenest prices, the best quality product, the most responsive and lowest cost supply chain. They need to be able to react quickly to changes in consumer demand, to competitive activity, to special supplier deals, to changes in supplier economics.

But to build retail brand value, trading ability is not enough. Retailers need to overlay and institutionalise brand management skills, philosophy and reflexes. The trading philosophy focuses on the short-term maximisation of sales and profits. The brand management philosophy focuses on building long-term customer loyalty and customer preference, and thereby on the long-term maximisation of brand and business value (see Exhibit I.1).

The two philosophies need to be in balance – or in a state of constant creative tension. A retail business that loses its trading edge, disregarding the need for short-term sales and profit, is a business at risk that may not survive to reap the benefits of long-term brand-building. But a retail business that has no long-term brand-building strategy and instincts will never build defensible competitive advantage, and will always be very vulnerable to competitive attack.

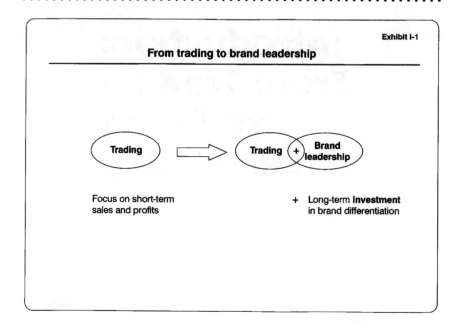

Exhibit I-1

From trading to brand leadership

Trading ⟹ Trading + Brand leadership

Focus on short-term sales and profits

+ Long-term **investment** in brand differentiation

Making the Change

Moving a retail business from a trading to a brand management philosophy requires first a *recognition of the difference*. Many people in the organisation, up to and including senior management, will not accept that it really exists. A retail business that trades well, they will argue, is *de facto* a strong retail brand, and consumers show their appreciation of it by their frequency of visits and purchases.

Once the difference is accepted, the Chief Executive and the senior management team need to make a *commitment to the long-term goal of brand-building*. Building real brand values will take many years, even decades, to achieve.

The business needs to develop its *brand-building strategy*, based on analysis of market opportunity, competitive economics and the business's starting position. Strategy development will focus on target brand positioning, including where and how to segment and differentiate the brand versus competitors. It will also include an evaluation of where and how to allocate funds for investment in brand-building: in-store brand development by category, in the supply chain and supplier relationships, in mass marketing and direct customer relationships, and in establishing a strong brand culture and integrity. Commitment to the long-term brand-building goal requires the *investment mentality* emphasised throughout this book.

Retail brand strategy can be a difficult concept to sell to retail traders. Many get by very well, and build large, successful businesses, without addressing it at all. Many would view it as an irrelevant intellectual distraction from the real business of trading and operations or, worse, as something which can only inhibit the business's ability to respond, quickly and flexibly, to new market opportunities and threats. But all retail businesses and brands have, *de facto*, made choices around strategic positioning – implicit or explicit, by default or by design. The challenge in retail brand leadership is to make sure that all those choices become explicit and by design, and that the choices are the right ones.

The *organisation structure and resources* needed to implement the strategy need to be put into place. A strong Marketing function needs to be created, and its interaction with Buying and Merchandising (B&M) and Store Operations clearly defined. The central B&M function needs to be bought in to the brand strategy – particularly into the trade-offs that will need to be made between short-term trading responses and longer-term brand-building reflexes.

The long-term brand strategy needs *translation into concrete medium-term programmes and priorities*. 'Brand-building' will be an abstract and remote goal for most people in the organisation. They will be unclear as to how it should be incorporated into day-to-day decisions and activities, and into short- and medium-term objectives. The priority should be to make clear, solid progress in a few areas, and to establish brand management principles by practice and example.

Finally, the brand-building Chief Executive will need to spend time *winning over the Board and investors*, convincing them that the long-term investments involved are worth making and will enhance rather than jeopardise financial performance and value. To achieve this, the Chief Executive will need to point both to the size of the prize in terms of potential shareholder value creation and to the broad canvas of threats and opportunities facing retailers in the twenty-first century.

Retail Brand-building and Shareholder Value Creation

Building strong retail brands will be a key to shareholder value creation by retail businesses. In Part I of the book we review the economics of retailing and of retail brands. Based on their track record in the UK (Boots, Early Learning Centre, the UK grocers, Marks and Spencer, Next), in continental Europe (Decathlon, IKEA) and in North America (Loblaw's, Toys 'R' Us, Gap, The Limited), strong retail brands earn *higher operating margins* and higher return on assets than retail traders. The value of brand-building can be seen in bottom-line financial performance.

Successful brand-building creates *higher growth prospects* for a retail business. A strong brand offers greater potential for extension into new geographic markets, into new distribution channels, and into new product categories. Focusing on maximising the potential of a strong brand (McDonald's, M&S, Disney) is more likely to deliver superior long-run results than diversification into new businesses.

Successful brand-building increases the *sustainability* of profits. Brand value accumulates steadily over time, and creates one of the strongest barriers to new competitors entering a market. Without the creation of strong brands, retail businesses are highly vulnerable to next-generation competitors entering on the basis of ever-lower cost, larger-scale formats, or new sites better located against consumer demand.

Successful brand-building also leads to *reduced volatility* of returns. Retail traders' profits can bounce around from one year to the next, as buyers make more or less astute range choices and negotiate more or less well with suppliers. A strong retail brand has a smoother, more resilient demand pattern, based on established consumer preference and loyalty. The higher operating margins of a strong brand eliminate the need for the high operational and financial gearing that is characteristic of many retail traders, further reducing volatility.

The combination of higher growth prospects, greater sustainability and reduced volatility means that the present value of cash flow is greater for a strong retail brand than for a retail trader. The strong retail brand has a much *lower cost of capital*. In Exhibit I.2, we take a hypothetical retail trader and strong retail brand, both with $100 million in sales. With high operational and financial gearing, the retail trader earns the same level of reported Return on Equity (ROE), say 15%, as the strong brand. However, the strong brand's premium generates operating margins and long-run cash flows that are double the trader's: 6% versus 3% of sales. Moreover, the strong brand's cost of capital is lower due to its greater resilience and sustainability, and its growth expectations higher, than the trader's. As a result, the market applies double the multiple to its current cash flows in order to assess the net present value of the business. (In calculating Exhibit I.2 we took a real risk-free rate of 3%; an equity premium of 7%; a beta of 1 for the strong brand and 1.5 for the trader; and

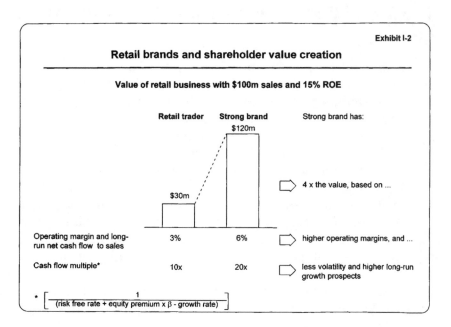

Exhibit I-2

Retail brands and shareholder value creation

Value of retail business with $100m sales and 15% ROE

	Retail trader	Strong brand	Strong brand has:
		$120m	
	$30m		4 x the value, based on ...
Operating margin and long-run net cash flow to sales	3%	6%	higher operating margins, and ...
Cash flow multiple*	10x	20x	less volatility and higher long-run growth prospects

$$* \left[\frac{1}{(\text{risk free rate} + \text{equity premium} \times \beta - \text{growth rate})} \right]$$

long-run real growth rates of 5% for the strong brand and 3.5% for the trader.) Compounding superiority in operating margin and cash flow with superiority in discount rate and market multiple, the strong brand ends up with a value four times that of the trader – $120 million versus $30 million. The shareholder value impact of brand-building is of course not unique to retailing. All businesses with strong brand franchises will have higher value than those without. Fast-Moving Consumer Goods (fmcg) branded producers have operated on this basis for decades.

One final aspect of the value of brand-building deserves a mention. A business that develops a strong culture and set of skills in brand-building may find that it has developed a platform for acquiring a portfolio of retail brands. Other potential platforms for building a multi-business retail portfolio, such as cost-sharing and operational synergy, are becoming less compelling. Brand management skills may prove to be the glue that allows the creation of value-adding portfolio retailers, mirroring the powerful diversified fmcg groups such as Philip Morris, Nestlé, Danone and Unilever.

The Broad Canvas: Retailing in the Twenty-first Century

Shareholder value creation is the prize for successful retail brand-builders. The risk for retailers who do not pursue brand-building is as great as the opportunity. The retail environment in the twenty-first century will bring radical changes and intense competitive pressures.

There will be *intense competitive pressure in mature retail markets*. Population growth in Europe, North America and Japan will be less than 1% a year. The real price of goods in many product retail sectors will continue to decline, while retailers' operating costs (labour and property) will increase in real terms. Consumer spending will continue to switch from physical goods to services, particularly leisure and information.

Retailing growth and profitability has been maintained over the last several decades by the move to ever-larger high volume, low gross margin, low cost formats, and by retailers' seizure of value-chain power. Within the next decade, at least in the more advanced retail markets such as North America and Northern Europe, there will be diminishing returns from these strategies. Category killers and hypermarkets will find themselves facing each other across the same warehouse parks or along the same power strips, in a cutthroat battle for market share. Buying clout and operational efficiencies will have been squeezed out of the supply chain. Retail gross margins cannot go much lower than 10–15%.

Retailing will become an industry of *global competition*. In their search for growth opportunities, and in their attempts to leverage investment, resources, skills and buying clout across as large a volume base as possible, leading retailers will become as international in their outlook and activities as their global suppliers. Regional and national retailers will have to defend their turf against new international competition, and will need to expand their own geographic horizons. The internationalisation of retailing will be given extra impetus by retailers from North America and Europe pursuing growth opportunities in the new consumer markets of Asia and Latin America. In these new markets, the life-cycle of retail formats will be enormously accelerated: markets will leapfrog in one or two decades from a fragmented small-scale family-run sector to a sector dominated by the large-scale, high volume formats of Wal-Mart, IKEA, Carrefour and Toys 'R' Us – as has happened in Spain within the last ten years.

In the advanced consumer markets of the West, and in the wealthier enclaves of the newer emerging markets, the *virtual mall* will become a reality. Interactive home shopping could become at least as significant as mail order within the next decade, and will have a profound impact on many retail sectors. As PC ownership, cable penetration and Internet access climb, and as technology improves to allow full integration of high quality video and audio, the virtual mall could become the preferred shopping medium for millions of high income, pace-setting consumers – reducing the total volume and profit available for physical retail networks.

*   *   *

The next century could be the era of *retail brand power*. The opportunity is there for committed brand-builders. The trends described above make seizing the opportunity a strategic imperative. Developing a strong brand franchise is one of the best defences against the intense competitive pressures of mature retail markets. Rolling out international brands will be one of the most effective forms of global competition. And strong brands provide the best platform for participating in the virtual mall and combating the risk of disintermediation.

Part I
The Context

The Growth of Retail Power and the Brand-building Challenge 1

Producers, and producer brands, have dominated the consumer goods industry for most of this century. These brand producers are major national and multi-national corporations. Historically, they invested heavily in their brands, in R&D, new products, packaging, production technology, advertising, promotional support, consumer research. They alone understood their product categories and their consumers. They sent out their field salesforces to push their brands into thousands of small, independent mom-and-pop stores. The consumers demanded their product, or they would take their custom to another store. Small-scale retailers had almost no clout in the value chain.

This situation is changing, and changing fundamentally. Retailers are seizing power in the consumer goods value chain.

Retailing has become large-scale, concentrated, centralised and sophisticated. The producers' national account managers now deal with professional retail buyers and category managers – many of whom have been poached from the producers' own marketing organisations. The top 3–5 national accounts may control 50% or more of the market. Distribution and shelf-space often have to be purchased as a separate transaction, particularly for new product introductions. Re-ordering is automated. Producers have little or no influence on in-store layout and promotional merchandising; their field salesforce may be even be banned from going into the stores. The retailers have information on consumer shopping behaviour that matches or beats anything that the producers have. Retailer store brands are taking significant market share, and consumers often perceive their quality to be as good as the cherished producer brands. Some market sectors are very advanced along this path of change, while others have barely begun to move along it – but the general direction is common and evident.

This increase in their value-chain power has given retailers a great opportunity. Retailing has always been a highly competitive and volatile industry. Investment levels have been low compared to other industries, and so consequently have been barriers to new entrants, whether nationally, regionally or town-by-town. The move to large-scale, concentrated, centralised and sophisticated retailing raises barriers to entry, and should therefore enable retailers to build more sustainable competitive advantage and earn better long-run financial returns.

The Growth in Retail Value-chain Power

The first, and probably the most important, factor driving the growth of retail power has been an *increase in retail scale and concentration*. Large-scale retailers, with significant regional, national and (recently) international market shares, have strong negotiating and buying clout with even global producer brands. In Europe, the top five chain retailers in packaged grocery in most countries now control access to at least 50% of the market; in the USA a similar concentration is happening regionally, although the national market remains more fragmented. In specialised categories such as toys, sports, electrical and DIY, 'category killers' target 20%-plus market shares wherever they compete; and in certain cases, such as Toys 'R' Us, they already operate on a global basis. Even fragmented proximity sectors such as chemists/drug stores are, where regulation allows, chaining and consolidating.

This development not only increases retailer buying clout and volume discounts. It gives retailers the financial muscle to begin to make investments in people, marketing, technology, quality control and supply-chain management; it gives them access to a broad base of consumers, with close and frequent contact; it also enables the costs and margins of wholesalers to be eliminated.

The *centralisation of retail decision-making*, away from individual store managers and into chain head offices, has enabled retailers to take full advantage of their increased scale and concentration. Producers have less and less opportunity to sell directly into individual stores (with certain major exceptions, for example among French hyper-markets and department store chains); instead they must deal with a well informed professional central buying department, negotiating large volumes from a position of strength.

Reinforcing the benefits of scale and concentration, there has been a structural *shift to large space out-of-town formats*: grocery superstores, hypermarkets, mass merchandisers, warehouse clubs, category killer sheds. These formats become destination stores, pulling consumers long distances for planned rather than impulse shopping. The consumer decision becomes choice of store as much as choice of product or brand in-store.

A fourth key factor has been the development of *retail technology*. While its primary objective has been operational efficiency (check-out, shelf replenishment, warehousing and distribution, stock levels, re-ordering), the side-benefit has been a massive growth in the information available to retailers, and the potential to use that information to manage suppliers and target customers. Retailers now have the ability to track and target, in detail: promotional activity, pricing, in-store layout and range; different segments of their consumer market; and product and supplier performance by category, brand, line and SKU. Producers have already begun to feel the power of this information in their buying negotiations, and retailers have a lot further to go in realising its full potential.

Lastly, increased retail power in the value chain has put enormous *pressure on second-tier producer brands*, with strong retailers rationalising their ranges and pushing for better buying terms. As these brands' market share has declined, their need to fill excess production capacity has provided retailers with sources for high quality private label supply at low marginal cost. The consequent growth of quality private labels reinforces retailers' negotiating strength, not only versus the second-tier producer brands but versus branded category leaders.

The Limits of Retail Value-chain Power

The growth in retail value-chain power has brought enormous benefits to retailers and to consumers. Unit operating costs have declined, gross margins and retail prices have reduced, and range choice has expanded. Successful retailers have expanded to national and international coverage. Successful large chains have pulled away from small chains and independents, in many cases virtually wiping out the independents' presence. The benefits of market leadership and scale have increased, as have barriers to entry.

But . . . retailing remains an industry in which superior long-run profitability is hard to sustain. Aggressive competition continues among the large-scale retailers (fewer, but still many) who have come through the consolidation battle. Competitors quickly copy and catch up with innovations in operations, technology, in-store merchandising and supply-chain management. In most mature markets, capacity growth (stores and square footage) still outpaces demand growth, as retailers fill in their geographic coverage, expand into each other's market areas, and move to larger store sizes. Retailers' key physical assets, their store locations, have become liabilities as consumers have abandoned villages for cities, cities for suburbs, rustbelt for sunbelt, main/high streets for malls/shopping centres, feet for cars. Unit labour cost growth exceeds inflation and volume growth. The 1990s' consumer is highly price-sensitive. Retail price wars continue to break out frequently.

Retailers' focus to date on value-chain power – on scale, operational efficiency and buying clout – can be characterised

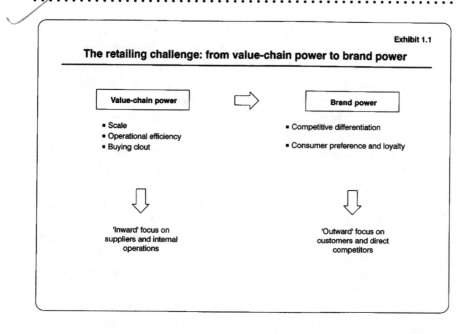

Exhibit 1.1

The retailing challenge: from value-chain power to brand power

Value-chain power	Brand power
■ Scale	■ Competitive differentiation
■ Operational efficiency	■ Consumer preference and loyalty
■ Buying clout	

'Inward' focus on suppliers and internal operations

'Outward' focus on customers and direct competitors

as an 'inward' focus on their own internal operations and on their position versus their suppliers. Although there is still more mileage there (for example, implementation of Efficient Consumer Response), we are starting to see the limits on how far value-chain power alone can take the retail sector.

Value-chain power alone does not provide a retailer with a strong and defensible differentiation versus direct competitors, nor does it generate strong consumer preference and loyalty. Real differentiation, and with it the potential for sustainable competitive advantage and superior long-run profitability, can only come from a 'outward' focus on customers and direct competitors, and on the development of retail brand power (see Exhibit 1.1).

Retail Brand Power: The Next Challenge

Say 'brands', and most people – professional managers and ordinary consumers – think of Coke, Levi, Marlboro, Sony, Nescafé, Mars, BMW, Rolex . . . a list comprised almost exclusively of producer brands. Retail brands don't get much of a look-in. McDonald's would make most Top Ten lists. One or two fashion retailers might make it – Marks and Spencer, Benetton, Gap. In the UK, the leading grocery retailers, such as Sainsbury's or Tesco, might also make it. In the USA, Wal-Mart is a household name, but most people would not think of it as a 'brand' at the same level as Coke or Marlboro. Producer brands have dominated consumer awareness and buying behaviour since their emergence, on a large commercial scale in the industrial countries, in the second half of the nineteenth century.

As we approach the year 2000, there is a sea-change occurring. Retailers, and retail brands, now have the capacity and potential to become as strong a force with the consumer as producer brands. This sea-change is one of the central strategic issues facing both retailers and fmcg producers.

This is already a well publicised issue. Events such as the success of Cott's private label cola (in Canada, the USA and the UK, see Case Study 13.3, p. 207) and major list price reductions for leading producer brands (Marlboro, P&G, Kellogg's) have received extensive media coverage, focusing on the negative implications for fmcg producers. 'The Death of Brands?' is a common headline.

We are less concerned with the implications for producer brands, although we will address them later in the book. While some weaker producer brands may be on their death-beds, the strong ones are still very much alive and will continue to be so, even if they do come under more pressure than they have been used to in the past.

Our primary concern is the building of strong retail brands, which is the next major strategic challenge for retailers.

What is a 'Strong Brand'?

All products and services are 'brands' to some extent, right down to the cheapest third-tier product brand or a discount clothing stall in the local open-air market (see Box 1.1). But some brand franchises are strong, sustainable and valuable, while most are not.

Box 1.1   Retail brands

Throughout this book, when we refer to 'retail brands', we mean the store or fascia brand, not just private label product. High private label penetration, while a characteristic of most strong retail brands, is not a universal or inevitable characteristic.

A 'strong brand' is a product or service that, relative to weaker competing brands, attracts strong consumer preference and loyalty, and extracts a brand premium in return – a price premium and/or volume advantage at price parity (see Exhibit 1.2).

From the *consumer's point of view*, loyalty to a strong brand is often an aspirational act, enhancing self-image and self-esteem; it reinforces a sense of peer group membership, actual or desired; it reduces worry and uncertainty; and it simplifies choice and saves time. The aspirational function is the most glamorous and attracts most attention (Smirnoff, BMW, American Express, Harvey Nichols) but many very

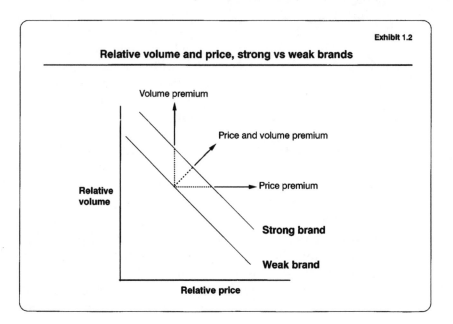

Exhibit 1.2

Relative volume and price, strong vs weak brands

strong brands primarily fulfil the more utilitarian functions (Heinz, Persil, McDonald's).

From the *firm's point of view,* a strong brand should benefit, long-run, from 'super-profits' deriving from a mix of higher volumes/market share and higher $/% margins versus competitors. If the right balance is struck between cashing in and re-investing these super-profits, brand profitability and growth should be more robust and sustainable in the face of periodic competitive attacks and price wars.

In the case of strong producer brands, the brand premium is usually in the form of higher consumer prices versus competing brands. In the case of strong retail brands, the premium is as or more likely to be in the form of higher rates of sale – per store or per square foot – with pricing at parity or often lower than competitors. We will come back to how retail brand premia operate later in the book.

Strong Retail Brands: A Rare Species

With strong producer brands, brand value is created cumulatively over many years, by consistent, high levels of investment in product quality, innovation and marketing. The resulting strength and staying power, and therefore value, of these brands is formidable and well documented. The majority of the leading brands in many major packaged goods categories in the USA and UK in 1925 are still leaders today (see Exhibit 1.3). Held up against that yardstick, there are still very few strong retail brands. Most current market leaders in retailing are young upstarts compared with producer brands. Wal-Mart, now the world's largest retailer, 25 years ago had only 50 stores and sales of $50 million. The category killers taking over leadership in toys, sports, electrical and DIY, in North America and Europe, are generally less than 25 years old, and often much younger. Even in the less fluid competitive environment of Europe, most large retail chains (apart from department stores) date back only to the 1950s or 1960s. In the USA, where chain retailing has a longer pedigree going back to the beginning of the century, former market leaders have not often lasted the

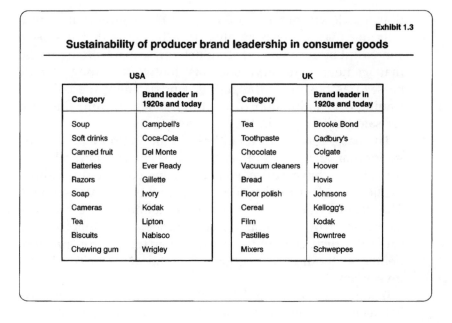

Exhibit 1.3

Sustainability of producer brand leadership in consumer goods

USA			UK	
Category	Brand leader in 1920s and today		Category	Brand leader in 1920s and today
Soup	Campbell's		Tea	Brooke Bond
Soft drinks	Coca-Cola		Toothpaste	Cadbury's
Canned fruit	Del Monte		Chocolate	Colgate
Batteries	Ever Ready		Vacuum cleaners	Hoover
Razors	Gillette		Bread	Hovis
Soap	Ivory		Floor polish	Johnsons
Cameras	Kodak		Cereal	Kellogg's
Tea	Lipton		Film	Kodak
Biscuits	Nabisco		Pastilles	Rowntree
Chewing gum	Wrigley		Mixers	Schweppes

pace: Woolworth's, A&P, Sears Roebuck. All over the world, fashion retailing is a highly volatile sector, where businesses and brands can emerge, peak, decline and vanish in a 10–20-year period.

Problems With Building Retail Brands

Retailers face major problems in building retail brands. Brand-building requires *long-term investment*, in people and skills, in-store brand product development and quality control, in marketing, in consumer research, and in supplier relationships. The need for, and the costs of, such long-term investment are often at odds with the very tight cost management focus of retailing. Retail profit margins, particularly outside the UK, are thin, often only 1–2% of sales, and may not appear to be capable of supporting brand-building investment.

The *organisational culture*, and the philosophy of senior management, may be sceptical of a brand-building orientation, or downright opposed to it. The concept of brand-building may be seen as alien to a business that has been successful by focusing on store network expansion, tight cost management, and aggressive, fast-footwork trading. It may be seen as positively dangerous, undermining the cost and trading orientation and distracting managers from the need for sales and profits in the short term.

The basic concept of retail brand-building may be seen by senior management as of *questionable relevance*. Many successful retailers have survived and prospered to date without explicitly addressing brand strategy and brand management. The retail brand may be seen as nothing more than an aggregation of a format's stores, range, price and service, each of which can continue to be managed fairly independently, without any overlay of brand thinking or brand investment.

It may also be argued that there are *structural differences* between retail and producer businesses that prevent retail brands from operating at the same level as producer brands. Key differences could include: the difficulty of segmentation, a key element of producer brand strategy, when applied to many retail sectors; the necessity for even market leaders in retail to remain very competitive on price; and the problems of defining a retail brand positioning that is clear and distinctive and yet can still embrace thousands of product lines. This is a very real issue, which we will return to in full later in the book.

Finally, there is the *producer perspective* on retail brand development. Producers are, in general, sceptical of retailers' ability to invest in and manage real brands. Until recently they made a point of calling retailers' store brand products 'private label', refusing to dignify them with the name 'brands'. They persistently warn retailers of the risks and costs of taking on the task of retail brand-building, and remind them of the simple advantages of their traditional role as a channel for producer brands. The producers' arguments contain elements of truth, but mainly they are arguing in their own interest. Having had to come to terms with the growth in retail value-chain power, the last thing producers want to do now is to deal with retail brand power.

Differences Across Retail Sectors

Retail sectors appear to vary substantially in their potential for supporting the development of strong retail brands – and they certainly vary in the actual development of retail brand power to date. We find the classification of retail sectors in Exhibit 1.4 useful in defining and evaluating brand-building potential and brand strategies.

Strong brands in the fmcg producer tradition are clearly found today in *repertoire* retailing: particularly in fashion (Benetton, Laura Ashley, Esprit, Next, Gap, The Limited, M&S), but also in 'home lifestyle' (IKEA, Habitat). With repertoire retailing, consumers are accustomed to using a range of stores to fill a range of needs, for style, functionality and price. Repertoire retailers can therefore target specific market segments more easily than in other retail sectors. Repertoire retailing also tends to be predominantly store brand/private label, often with exclusive supplier arrangements. A retailer's private label product is often distributed through a variety of channels, including own stores, depart-

---

Exhibit 1.4

Retail sector classification and main product categories

Sector	Main categories
Repertoire	Fashion Home lifestyle Department stores
Proximity	C-store/CTN Local grocery Drugstore/chemist Petrol
Category killers	Electrical DIY, garden Toys, sports
Grocery	Supermarkets Hypermarkets
Services	Eating out Leisure/tourism Financial

ment store concessions, mail order and international franchising, like a producer brand. Specialty fashion retailers can be seen as producers who have contracted out the manufacturing function. Producer brands, such as Levi in jeans, sometimes forward-integrate into their own flagship retail stores.

Department stores in the USA, UK and much of Continental Europe have generally now become repertoire retailers, with the majority of their sales coming from fashion and home lifestyle products. Their former departmental strengths in electrical, toys, sports and other product areas have been undermined by mass merchandisers, hypermarkets and category killers. Department stores have a particularly tough job of reconciling their historical role as an aggregator of producer brands with their new role as a repertoire retailer.

Proximity retailing occupies the opposite end of the spectrum of retail brand development. By definition, consumers choose stores primarily on the basis of location convenience, and a retailer with sites that are poorly located vis-à-vis passing traffic is dead in the water. Not many names spring to mind as strong brands in proximity retailing. Boots in the UK is a notable exception.

Category killers are large space out-of-town formats, offering maximum range and aggressive prices in their categories, and pulling consumers from a very wide catchment area on planned shopping trips. There are certainly strong market leaders in this sector: Toys 'R' Us in toys; Decathlon in sports; Home Depot and B&Q in DIY; Darty, Circuit City and Dixons in electrical; Tower and Virgin in music mega-stores. IKEA's giant home products stores are a mixture of a category killer and a repertoire retailer. But, in a mature saturated market, there may be little real brand differentiation to offset fierce price competition – as, for example, in the UK DIY market battle between B&Q, Texas, Homebase, Do It All and Wickes. Decathlon, which dominates sports retailing in France, is a rare current example of a category killer that has real brand strength.

We identify *grocery* supermarket retailing as a separate sector because of its sheer size (over a third of all retail product sales) and because grocery retailers have to deal with particularly strong producers of long-established fmcg brands. Its brand development characteristics are a mixture of proximity and category killers (switching steadily towards the latter as consumers polarise their grocery shopping into weekly trips to large supermarkets and top-up purchases from proximity stores). Internationally, retail grocery brands are still generally weak, with the major exception of the UK. Sainsbury's, Tesco, Safeway and M&S have pushed retail brand and value-chain power in grocery up to unparalleled levels, with store brand/private label participation at over 50% of sales.

Some one-stop-shop retail formats combine grocery and non-grocery category killers, including ranges in fashion and home lifestyle: hypermarkets in France, coming from a food/grocery heritage; new Wal-Mart and Kmart supercenters in the USA, coming the other way from a non-food heritage.

Our fifth sector is *services* retailing, where strong global brands can be found in fast food (McDonald's, Pizza Hut, Burger King), hotels (Hilton, Hyatt), and financial services (American Express). In fast food and hotels there is no equivalent of the producer/retailer split and brand tension innate in product retailing: the retail service is the product, consumed at point-of-sale. Retail financial services, which do contain at least the potential for a producer/retailer split, are more analogous to product retailing.

The current status of retail brand development varies widely between these retail sectors: strong brands exist in repertoire and services, but elsewhere there are only a few powerful examples. There are also innate differences between the sectors in terms of future potential and strategies for strong retail brand development, particularly the potential for high levels of store brand penetration.

Differences Across Countries

There are also major differences across countries in the current status of retail development. Retail markets in

Northern Europe – Germany, France, UK, Netherlands, Switzerland, Scandinavia – are generally mature and concentrated. Retail value-chain power is well developed. Space constraints and government regulation also protect existing competitors, to some extent, from new competition and space additions, particularly from large-space out-of-town formats. The *USA* is also a mature retail market on many counts. Retail value-chain power is strong, and leading chains are some of the most cost-efficient and technically advanced retailers in the world. However, the sheer size of the USA, and the size of the consolidation task, has left many sectors, including grocery, still quite fragmented. Barriers to new entrants and new stores are lower: the Robinson–Patman Act of 1936, which prohibits supplier price discrimination, limits the buying clout advantage of large chains, and space is more available, cheap and lightly regulated.

Retail markets in *Southern Europe* – Italy, Spain, Portugal, Greece – are still fragmented, due to competitive immaturity and regulation protecting small stores. Spain is developing rapidly towards the French retail model, driven by the entry of French hypermarkets, but the other countries are changing more slowly. *Japan* is still an immature and highly fragmented retail market, protected by regulation limiting large-space retail competition, and with high cost multiple layers of wholesale distribution. Until quite recently, the only large-scale retail businesses in Japan were the half-dozen leading department stores. Japan is changing – lower cost, larger-space mass merchandise retailers such as Ito Yokado, Jusco and Daiei (see Exhibit 15.1, p. 229) are now larger and more profitable than the traditional department store chains – but regulatory constraints still make the pace of change slow.

For both Northern European and US retailers, development of retail brand power is both a practicality and a strategic imperative. In the less mature markets of Southern Europe, Japan and Asia-Pacific, value-chain power must be the first imperative in most retail sectors – the opportunity for building retail brand power will come later, although retailers can sometimes choose to invest in brand power in parallel.

The UK Model

Retail brand power is most advanced in the UK. In several major retail sectors, leading retailers have not only consolidated very strong positions of value-chain power, they have pushed forward into building strong brand franchises with their consumers: in grocery (Sainsbury's, Tesco, Safeway, M&S) and in proximity (Boots), as well as in fashion (M&S, Next). This is not the case in every sector: category killer markets such as electrical and DIY have consolidated but strong retail brands have yet to be established.

The relative strength of leading UK retail brands can be seen by taking a global look at the market values and financial performance of the world's leading retailers (see Exhibit 1.5). Retailing's share of total market capitalisation in the UK is double that in the USA or Japan (9% versus 4–5%), and retailer p/e ratios are at a premium to the market average, compared with a discount versus the market in the USA and Japan.

12 out of the 55 product retailers that make it into the world's 1000 most valuable publicly quoted companies are UK retailers. The value of the top US retailers is only 3 times the value of the top UK retailers, despite higher p/e ratios and a consumer market that is 7–8 times larger. The contrast between the UK and Japan is even greater: similar equity values for the top retailers despite Japan having p/e ratios 3 times higher and a consumer market 5 times larger.

More importantly, the financial structure and performance of UK retailers is very different from their global peers (see Exhibit 1.6). UK retailers' net profit margins, at 6.1%, are two-thirds higher than the USA, and almost 4 times the levels in Japan and Continental Europe. US retailers almost catch up with the UK at the level of ROE (Return on Equity), by turning their assets slightly faster and by slightly higher gearing/leverage. Japanese retailers' ROE ends up at half the level of the UK, despite much higher gearing. Continental European retailers, like the US, almost catch up at the level of ROE, but only via high gearing/leverage. In fact, UK retailers' financials are more comparable with major branded producers than with retailers in other countries.

Exhibit 1.5a

The world's most valuable publicly quoted product retailers

Equity market value

Equity market value 1995 ($ billion)	USA		UK	Japan	Other countries
> 50	Wal-Mart				
20 - 25	Home Depot	Sears Roebuck	M&S	Ito Yokado	Carrefour (FR)
9 - 12	Mays Albertsons	J C Penney Gap	J Sainsbury GUS Tesco Boots	Jusco Daiei	
6 - 8	Toys 'R' Us Safeway Federated The Limited American Stores	Walgreen Dayton Hudson Kmart Lowes	Kingfisher Safeway	Marui	Pinault-Printemps-Redoute (FR) Ahold (NL)
3 - 5	Winn Dixie Kroger Melville Nordstrom Price/CostCo Circuit City	Autozone Dillard Office Depot Food Lion Tandy	Asda Next Burton Dixons Argos	Mitsukoshi Takeshimaya Nichii Familymart Uny	Promodès (FR) Pryca (SP) Coles Myer (AUS) Kaufhof (GER) Karstadt (GER)

Exhibit 1.5b

The world's most valuable publicly quoted product retailers

Market value and financial performance

	USA	UK	Japan	Other countries
Number of companies in global top 1000	27	12	9	8
Market value ($ billion)	253	92	97	54
% of total stock market value (global top 1000)	5%	9%	4%	n/a

Average p/e ratio
  - retail
  - total market
	23
	25
		20
		15
			60
			85	

Exhibit 1.6

International comparison of top retailers' financial performance

	Number of companies	Profit margin (%)	x	Asset turn (x)	x	Assets/ equity (x)	=	Return on equity (%)
UK	12	6.1	x	1.4	x	2.1	=	18%
USA	27	3.7	x	1.6	x	2.5	=	16%
Japan	9	1.6	x	1.1	x	5.0	=	8%
France + NL	4	1.6	x	2.0	x	4.9	=	16%
Typical FMCG branded producer		6.0	x	1.6	x	2.1	=	20%

This analysis is top-level and simplifying, but its broad direction is correct. In 1995, the year for which data is taken, the UK retail market was still weak, retail competition was intense, and many of the largest retailers had seen profit margins decline from earlier peaks. US consumer spending was relatively robust. Japanese and Continental European consumer markets were weak, but the financial analysis here would be seen as a fair reflection of retail economics over the peaks and troughs of a ten-year period.

Nor, should any reader be tempted to do so, would it be accurate to characterise the UK as a 'soft' competitive market. Competition within sectors between major players is intense. Foreign retailers entering the UK market anticipating a relatively easy time of it have been disappointed, time after time. (Equally, UK retailers have had a tough time in attempting to duplicate their success in other countries.)

Branded producers – particularly in grocery, and including the major global producers of category-leading brands – fear the UK model deeply. The UK multiple grocers have almost doubled their share of the total profit pie from 20% in 1980 to 36% in 1995, through boom and recession. The producers argue, and hope, that the UK is somehow 'unique', and that different retail structures and the greater relative power of producer brands can stop any similar development outside the UK (see Exhibit 1.7).

This is not to argue that UK retailers have got all, or even most, things right, or that there are not very real differences in the characteristics of retailing in other countries. But the UK model does provide evidence that retail brand power is a realistic strategic objective, and gives strong clues as to how to go about achieving it.

Some of those clues can be found by taking a first top-level look at Marks and Spencer, the UK's, and possibly the world's, strongest brand in product retailing (see Case Study 1.1).

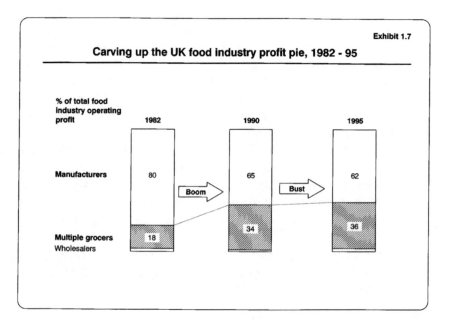

Exhibit 1.7

Carving up the UK food industry profit pie, 1982 - 95

Case Study 1.1   Marks and Spencer: Retail Brand Power in Action

Although our primary interest is in looking at a model of retail brand power, it is worth briefly noting the sheer scale of the M&S business.

In 1995, M&S made a net profit of around $1 billion on sales of around $11 billion, a net margin of 9%. Its equity market value of $20 billion is only materially exceeded, among the world's top retailers, by Wal-Mart, whose market value is around $60 billion on sales of over $90 billion. Relative to the size of the UK market versus the USA, M&S's UK sales are on a scale approaching that of Wal-Mart. Its 15% share of the total UK clothing market is unparalleled in other countries, as is its 5% share of the UK food market with an almost exclusively store brand range. The combination of the two positions in clothing and food, often in the same store, is unique.

Any discussion of the problems and limits of retail brand-building – in Europe, the USA or Japan; with management from retailers and producers – usually at some point gets round to: '. . . oh, except of course for M&S'. Producers and other retailers like and need to think of M&S as an exception – but M&S is really 'just' a model of how retail brands can be built up to the same level and power as producer brands. How has this been achieved? What lessons can we take from M&S in helping us to determine general principles of retail brand-building?

The *post factum* observation can be made that M&S has been around for a long time – as long as the famous producer brands who have been category leaders since 1925. The M&S brand has a long heritage, and has had to time to accumulate in value. This is not an actionable observation for a retailer today, but it does show that long-term retail brand value can be built up over time, just as with producer brands.

M&S has always been *100% store brand*, and one store brand only. (The St Michael label is synonymous in the UK consumers' mind with M&S, and is now being slowly phased down in favour of M&S on the label.) In the clothing sector, M&S's core and initial market, this store brand orientation is far from unique – think of Gap, The Limited, Next, Benetton and any number of fashion specialists – but M&S took it further, earlier, than most competitors. The temptation to create sub-brands to target particular style, product and customer segments has been vigorously resisted; every product in the store is the M&S brand.

Coming from a base business of fashion retailing, with an exclusively store brand product range, M&S's entry into food was radically different from any supermarket. The food range is high quality, value-added, at premium prices, and also 100% store brand. No attempt is made to fill all the consumer's grocery shopping needs. M&S Food fills a role in the repertoire of grocery stores that an M&S shopper uses, just as in clothing. Customer demographics are also different from other grocers, and different from the base clothing business; M&S's food market share is skewed towards the more affluent consumer.

(As an aside, and in the context of our day-jobs as strategy consultants, we cite M&S's entry into up-market food – with a limited, store brand-only range, in the same stores as mass market clothing – as an example of a strategy proposal that would have got us thrown out of most retail boardrooms.)

The second characteristic of M&S worth highlighting is that their philosophy of investment matches that of a branded producer; in particular, *investment in the supply chain and supplier relationships*. M&S has extensive in-house resources for new product design and development, for technical support/ quality control, and for managing supplier relationships. They were the first to invest in a total chilled chain, to bring food product from supplier to consumer with a temperature variance of no more than 1 degree. They also famously invest time, money and management commitment in developing symbiotic relationships with a relatively small set of core suppliers, many of whom end up supplying 80% or more of their output to M&S. This supply chain investment, and these long-term proprietary relationships with suppliers, have proven very difficult for competitors to duplicate. (Note that by 'supply chain' here we do not mean only logistics, EDI, ECR and so forth – although M&S is good at these also – which are vital for retail efficiency but easier for competitors to duplicate.)

The third characteristic is *integrity*, or consistency, of product positioning, product quality, and pricing. Consumers have a very clear understanding of the style positioning of the M&S clothing range and the premium/value-added positioning of the food range, and M&S stays very faithful to that understanding. Product quality is consistently high and never compromised in the interests of fast response to market trends. Consumers know this well, and even the most cash-strapped will pay a premium for M&S clothing basics that wear and last far better than cheaper competing alternatives. Promotions, seasonal sales and mark-downs are minimal compared to most other retailers; M&S applied EDLP (Every Day Low Pricing) well before it became a general retail industry hot button in the 1980s and 1990s.

Fourthly, there is a very strong *brand culture* in M&S. Producers and other retailers will remark that people at M&S talk about the business and the M&S brand (without necessarily using the word 'brand') in a way that is quite exceptional, and again is close to the way brand managers at Coke and P&G talk and think about their brands. This brand culture is transmitted all the way down the organisation, from senior management down to shop floor staff, so that brand 'reflexes' are built into every buying decision and customer interaction. Of course, M&S is not unique in the retail industry in having a strong culture. Companies such as Nordstrom and Wal-Mart in the USA, and John Lewis in the UK, are renowned for their very strong, positive and unifying corporate cultures, and a dedication to customer service.

It is worth identifying what have *not* been important elements of long-term brand-building for M&S. Advertising investment historically has been close to zero. Store environments, even in the Marble Arch flagship in the centre of London, are far from fancy. Stores do not go out of their way to offer a plethora of customer services: even now, they do not accept any credit cards except the M&S store card, a stance which amazes plastic-waving tourists; changing rooms have been provided only recently and reluctantly and are in short supply; and until recently, the Marble Arch store famously had no public toilets – customers were advised to go across the street into Selfridges.

M&S is far from infallible. Despite continual efforts, it has failed to achieve UK leadership in several product areas where its brand strength should be as effective as in general adult clothing: home lifestyle, footwear, children's clothes. Its efforts to take the M&S brand overseas were unsuccessful for a long time, although now, with a steady persistence typical of the company, the M&S store network is starting to perform and expand in Continental Europe and the Far East.

Overall, M&S has built a formidable retail brand, one on a par, in the UK, with the strongest producer brands. The M&S brand today has moved well on from being a clothing/fashion brand: it is now broad and robust enough, as an assurance of consistent high quality, value and consumer-oriented innovation, to embrace consumer financial investments (store-branded, naturally) as well as food and fashion.

Are Retail Brands Different from Producer Brands? 2

We can see today that strong brands can be established in retailing. Internationally, many examples exist in repertoire and service retailing. The UK gives us examples of strong brands in the grocery sector. Examples in the proximity and category killer sectors are harder to find, but we can point to Boots in the UK and Decathlon in France. Retail brands clearly can become 'The Real Thing'.

Many managers, however, would still feel that there are major differences between retail brands and producer brands, which limit retail brand potential and make brand-building innately more difficult – and, for managers coming from an fmcg producer background, very frustrating. Some of these argued differences are real, and some illusory. We will address the main arguments in this chapter.

Can Retailers Apply Classical Brand Concepts of Segmentation and Differentiation?

Classical fmcg producer brand strategy is driven by two core concepts: segmentation and differentiation. Segmentation is about 'where to compete': targeting specific sets of consumer wants and needs, and focusing brand positioning and investment against these 'segments' as closely as is practical and profitable. Differentiation is about 'how to compete', in order to create consumer preference and loyalty and therefore brand leadership – as Ted Levitt puts it, 'Differentiation . . . Of Anything'. Are these two core concepts equally relevant to retail brand strategy?

Segmentation is in theory fully applicable to retailing, along four dimensions: product groups, customer groups, shopping occasions, and price/quality positioning (see Exhibit 2.1). However, the practical relevance of the concept in many retail sectors can be limited. For example, proximity retailers are, by definition, targeted against the convenience shopping occasion. Convenience store chains such as 7-Eleven make no further segmentation of their markets: their objective is to sell whatever mix of products (and services) the c-store shopper needs. Other proximity retailers have core product specialisations – CTNs, petrol, stationery and books, health and personal care, fresh produce – that are largely the result of history or regulation. Segmentation is a relatively unhelpful concept in thinking about Walgreen's strategy versus CVS in the US drugstore market, where both competitors fight for maximum share of total relevant product sales. They cannot exclude any customer group, and they must offer a broad range of price and quality. They may include, exclude or emphasise different sub-categories of product, but only at the margin.

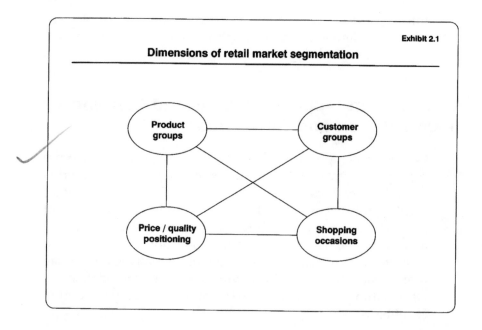

Exhibit 2.1

Dimensions of retail market segmentation

Similarly, the category killers of destination retailing appear to have only one major segmentation choice: which category to kill? Having made that choice, their objective is maximum category market share across all customer groups. The same problem arises in applying segmentation to grocery supermarkets (although there are examples of segmented propositions, such as M&S's up-market food offer and, at the other end of the scale, Aldi's hard discount format). Hypermarkets and US supercenters, which combine category killers and grocery, are the very antithesis of the market segmentation concept. Their objective is to sell everything to everybody.

Among product retail sectors, only in repertoire retailing is segmentation generally applied in brand strategy. Specialty fashion retailers in particular can be very tightly targeted: fashion-forward clubwear for teenage girls at cheap prices, or conservative businesswear for large men, or smart casual-wear for 25–45 year-olds at premium prices. Fashion retailers work hard to develop distinctive fashion points-of-view that consumers can clearly recognise from year-to-year. And segmentation is highly relevant and applied in service retailing: fast food chains major on burgers, pizza or fried chicken, and hotel chains range from the no-frill Formule Un to the luxury Hyatt Regency.

Overall, segmentation is relevant in retail brand strategy, particularly in repertoire and service retailing, but it is less central than in producer brand strategies. While there are examples of segmented propositions in product retailing outside fashion and home, retailers often compete for maximum market share in their categories, across all customer groups within their catchment areas and across a wide range of price positions.

The concept of *differentiation* is far more central and practical in retail brand strategy, and is applicable across all retail sectors. What are the bases of retail brand differentiation?

Retailers would generally break their consumer proposition down into four key elements: *stores, range, price* and *service*. These four elements are fundamental, and any retailer falling behind in any one or more of them will begin to lose customers. However, they do not seem to us to capture the real sources of sustainable brand differentiation.

Good store locations and high quality retail space are obviously critical to retail performance. A retailer that locks up the best sites early, at lower cost than later arrivals, will have a real economic edge over competitors. The retail graveyard is full of businesses whose main problem was a site portfolio of poor quality taken on at too high a cost. However, in the medium term and within reasonable bounds, good space does usually become available for the patient retailer, even if at a moderate price premium. (There are exceptions, where space availability is severely constrained by regulation or supply, such as very crowded city centres or airport terminals.) Moreover, store location is only integral to brand personality in the case of long-established single-store businesses, such as Harrods in London, which is hard to imagine except in its distinctive Knightsbridge location.

Sheer range breadth and in-stock performance, which may once have been a source of differentiation in the early days of department store chains, can now be matched relatively easily by competitors (except for store brands, which we will discuss separately). Low price, where supported by real differences in unit operating costs and asset efficiency, is much harder to duplicate quickly – but yesterday's aggressive discounter can rapidly become today's embattled mid-price retailer (Kmart versus Wal-Mart (see Case Study 2.1, p. 47) and warehouse clubs; Kwik Save and LeClerc versus Aldi), and many retailers can and do adopt a 'never beaten on price or your money back' guarantee. Service initiatives (such as opening hours, bagging, gift wrapping) are probably the easiest aspect of a retail operation for competitors to copy.

We find six different factors more useful in capturing the real essence of brand differentiation, as we observe it manifested in the cases of the few strong retail brands, such as M&S, that exist today. These are sources of differentiation that will create consumer preference and loyalty even if direct retail competitors are facing each other across the same retail park, offering the same breadth of range and in-stock performance, equally efficient at managing their costs and

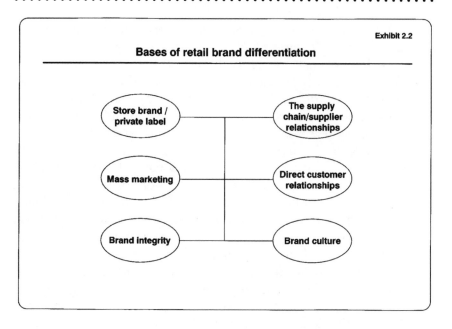

Exhibit 2.2

Bases of retail brand differentiation

Store brand / private label

The supply chain/supplier relationships

Mass marketing

Direct customer relationships

Brand integrity

Brand culture

assets and therefore equally competitive on price, and offering similar services such as opening hours and bagging or wrapping. The producer brand analogy is Nestlé, Maxwell House or Folgers sitting next to each other on the supermarket shelf, or Sony and Philips TVs next to each other on the shelves of an electrical retailer: given equal availability, how can the consumer be persuaded to purchase one over the other? (See Exhibit 2.2)

Investment in the development of a strong, quality *store brand* is the strongest source of differentiation, as the retail brand becomes very like a producer brand. 'Store brands' or 'private label' in the retailing world cover a wide spectrum of price/quality positioning, from very low cost generics through to high quality ranges selling at par or a premium versus producer brands. Generics, at one extreme, clearly have little brand-building value. The further a retailer can invest and push towards the quality end of the spectrum, and the more the retailer puts real innovation into the range, the more brand value is created.

Investment in the supply chain and supplier relationships is the flipside of development of a strong store brand offer. Developing a strong store brand demands investment by the retailer in product development, technical support/ quality control, and close proprietary relationships with long-term suppliers. These supplier relationships require an emphasis on consistent quality, technical innovation, responsiveness and flexibility, supported by an 'open book' information- and risk-sharing relationship between retailer and supplier. This relationship is the opposite of the more traditional 'trading' relationship, which is aggressive, adversarial, and focused on price and short-term dealing.

As with producer brands, *mass marketing* can be a key source of brand differentiation. Many repertoire retailers do invest heavily in differentiating and communicating their brand image; for example, Benetton's highly distinctive and abstract marketing campaigns. However, retailers in general have tended to have low levels of marketing investment. The stores themselves, particularly where in expensive in-town/ high street space, have been considered to fulfil the function of marketing communication. The move to large-space out-of-town formats by category killers, grocers and hypermarkets has increased marketing expenditure, as retailers have needed to pull consumers out to these locations.

There is a powerful potential source of differentiation, complementary to mass marketing, which is still barely exploited even by the strongest retail brands: the building of *direct customer relationships*. Compared with producers, retailers have frequent direct contact with their customers, across a wide range of shopping transactions. With advances in in-store and central database management technology, one of their most valuable assets is the ability to understand shopping behaviour, target marketing investment and build loyalty down at the level of tight customer groups and even at the level of individual customers. Many product retailers now have much of the technology in place and are awash with customer data, but using the data in an effective way is still in its infancy. Store card and customer loyalty schemes remain generally crude, blunt instruments. Financial services retailers have wrestled with a plethora of customer data for years, and are equally far from using the data effectively. The only retail sector which is more mature in this area is mail order, particularly the use of highly targeted credit data: Fingerhut has one of the largest central databases in the USA, and the largest on consumer credit, as does GUS in the UK.

The next factor that we identify is *brand integrity*. Long-term brand positioning and values, as reflected in range, pricing, product quality, promotions and in-store service, must always be the primary consideration, taking precedence over pressure on short-term sales and profits. Many retailers, including several who believe they are in the process of building real retail brands, remain fundamentally traders at heart. Faced with short-term sales and profit shortfalls, they resist only a few weeks before diving into heavy price-cutting or promotions, or cuts in quality specifications to hit gross margin targets, undermining accumulated brand value which will then take years to re-build.

Lastly, brand integrity can be reasonably guaranteed only if a strong *brand culture* has been established from top to bottom in the organisation. Unlike the fairly centralised decision-making processes in producer brand management, retailers have to embed brand values into decentralised decision-making: the hundreds or thousands of range and sourcing decisions made by buyers and merchandisers, the millions of in-store interactions with customers. A strong brand culture creates a set of reflexes in the organisation, such that the CEO or any of the top management team can be largely confident that these decisions and interactions will be consistent with intended brand values.

These six factors capture, in our view, the common and most distinguishing characteristics of the world's strongest and most differentiated retail brands: IKEA, the UK grocers, Benetton, Boots, Gap, McDonald's, M&S, Decathlon, Early Learning Centre. As with segmentation, there are differences between retail sectors in the extent to which these bases of differentiation are practically available to retailers – in particular in the extent to which there are structural limitations on store brand development.

Can Retail Brands Overcome the Problem of Multiplicity?

A real and important difference between most producer brands and most retail brands is the sheer multiplicity of retail brand attributes. We need to recognise and understand this difference, but also to question how far this limits the potential power of a strong retail brand.

A Mars Bar has 16 ingredients (chocolate, sugar, etc.); a few key eating characteristics (taste, texture); a wrapper, with logo and material feel; and a few key brand positioning themes (work, rest and play, etc.), documented in a short brand strategy statement that lives by the Brand Manager's bedside. These two dozen or so tangible and intangible attributes, and the brand strategy statement, constitute the Mars Bar brand and underpin its huge global sales and profit generation for the Mars Corporation over the last 70 years. Changing any one of these attributes will take several years of discussion and will probably go to the CEO. The decision to extend the Mars brand to ice-cream took over five years of debate, research, NPD and trialling, and was a gut-wrenching process for an organisation that for over half a century had kept sacred the notion that each brand name had to have one and only one clear 'slot' in the consumer's brain.

Tesco, in contrast, has 17 000 product lines, 435 stores, and 120 000 front-of-store checkout operators, counter staff and shelf-fillers interacting directly and daily with customers. Simply multiplying out these numbers produces millions of brand attributes, since the Tesco customer's experience of the brand is a combination of all the products she buys there (range, price, quality, etc.), the shopping environment and the service level. Not only that, but 30% of the product lines, or 5000 lines, change every year. Within one key value-added store brand category, ready-to-eat meals, there are 20 new product introductions per quarter. In-store staff turnover runs at around 30% a year.

Many producer brand managers would argue that this enormous multiplicity of brand attributes, and constant high rate of change, make most retail brands innately weaker than producer brands. They cannot stand for anything in the consumer's mind as clearly and consistently as Levi stands for American jeans, BMW for German engineering, or Campari for Caribbean beaches. Retail brands have to embrace too many products, price/quality positions and purchase occasions.

We need to break this argument down. As with the segmentation argument above, repertoire and service retailing are accepted as exceptions: Benetton, Gap, McDonald's and Hyatt stand for something as clearly as Levi and BMW. Category killers, and most proximity retailers with a core product focus such as chemists/drugstores and liquor stores, stand for their core categories: there is no reason why the positioning of Darty or Circuit City as an umbrella brand for electrical goods retailing should be any less clear than that of Sony or Mitsubishi for electrical goods manufacturing. Grocery and hypermarket or supercenter retailers, on the other hand, do face greater difficulties due to their lack of a core product focus, and their need to attract the broadest possible range of consumers and purchase occasions. Retailers in these sectors need to build broader brand positionings based on reassurance of consistent quality and value, innovation in-store brands, and total service. The UK models of M&S, Sainsbury's and Tesco show that this can be done, but it is innately more difficult and the resulting brand positioning is less clear than in other sectors.

It is also worth noting that producer brands are becoming less tightly focused. 20 years ago Mars would not have stretched its brand onto ice cream. The costs of mass marketing, the costs and high failure rate of new product introductions, and the need to 'sweat' the expensive brand asset, are pushing producers to stretch brands over broader product categories and to an increasing use of umbrella corporate branding. Cadbury's chocolate-based brand franchise in the UK now embraces dozens of product categories; Nestlé is using its global corporate brand as a quality reassurance over specific local country product brands; and Richard Branson stretches the Virgin brand, with its rather elusive anti-establishment values, across an airline, a cola, music stores, and personal investment plans. This development is logical for producers, but narrows the gap in clarity of positioning between their brands and those of retailers.

Can Retail Businesses Really be Managed as Brands?

The day-to-day problems and frustrations involved in managing a retail brand, as compared with running a producer brand, stem primarily from the enormous multiplicity of brand attributes and their constant high rate of change. Retail CEOs and senior managers find it hard to achieve a retail brand management process that works as coherently and effectively as the P&G fmcg model. They cannot focus strategic attention on short and simple statements of brand strategy and positioning, that are also powerful, concrete and actionable, and that don't change from month to month. They cannot avoid having to worry about whether the bad attitude of a $6/hour checkout operator has just wiped out 15 years of careful loyalty-building with 100 customers in Dayton or Leeds.

The careful, centralised decision-making and control processes of an fmcg brand do not work in retail. The CEO and senior managers have to find a different day-to-day organisational and operational way of managing the business, so as to preserve the integrity of a brand's intended core values through the thousands of daily de-centralised decisions and customer interactions. Executing retail brand management involves a combination of decision processes and operational controls, embracing a continuous set of 'feedback loops', from store to centre, from customer to retailer, from actual sales to buying and stock management.

The central authority of the fmcg Brand Manager also cannot be replicated in the retail environment. Brand management has to be a team effort between the CEO, Marketing, B&M, and Store Operations.

These differences in brand management processes and organisation are very real. We will come back to their practical implications in full later in the book.

Are There Innate Differences in the Economics of Retail Brands?

Many managers would argue that there are two crucial differences between the economics of retail and producer brands: the extent and nature of the brand premium that can be created, and the ability to invest in brand-building. This is a real and important debate. Before we address it, we need to set out a framework for analysing the economics of retail businesses (see Box 2.1).

Box 2.1   The Economics of Retail Businesses

We can disaggregate retail economics into four main elements. First, *margin structure,* or the conversion of sales into trading margin (see Exhibit 2.3).

Exhibit 2.3

Main components of retail margin structure

	Fashion example: Sales @ full list price	Grocery example: Sales @ net realised price
Sales	100.0	100.0
Full price gross margin	65.0	N/A
Markdown/clearance	(15.0)	N/A
Realised gross margin	50.0	25.0
Store-level costs (labour, property, other)	(30.0)	(15.0)
Store contribution	20.0	10.0
Central costs (logistics, marketing, head office)	(10.0)	(5.0)
Operating profit	10.0	5.0

Store-level scale and volume is one primary driver of margin differences between sectors. Store-level costs (rent, staff, store overhead) are a high percentage of sales for many repertoire and proximity retailers operating out of small outlets with low absolute sales volume; large-scale outlets such as category killers and hypermarkets work off much lower store-level cost/sales ratios. Product risk is the second primary driver of sector differences. Most fashion specialists clear a high proportion of stock at deep markdown prices, and their initial, full price gross margin structure of 60% or more reflects this. While other retail sectors have to manage some level of product risk (for example, perishable fresh product for grocery retailers), it is not as severe and does not require the same gross margin 'cushion'.

Between direct competitors in the same sector there will be enormous differences in margin structure, reflecting competitive strategy and management competence. Store-level scale and volume will vary, as will level of markdown between fashion retailers. Gross margins will be affected by buying clout and savvy and by the level of store brand penetration. Store-level cost ratios will be driven by site cost and quality, and by in-store service levels and staffing efficiency. Central cost ratios will be driven by marketing spend, distribution efficiency and overhead cost management.

Margin structure is then converted into *trading return on assets* (see Exhibit 2.4).

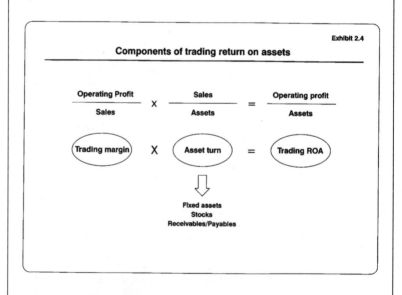

Exhibit 2.4

Components of trading return on assets

$$\frac{\text{Operating Profit}}{\text{Sales}} \quad \text{X} \quad \frac{\text{Sales}}{\text{Assets}} \quad = \quad \frac{\text{Operating profit}}{\text{Assets}}$$

Trading margin   X   Asset turn   =   Trading ROA

Fixed assets
Stocks
Receivables/Payables

Trading margin multiplied by asset turn (sales/assets) equals a business's trading return on assets ('ROA'). A retail business can earn a high trading ROA via high margin and low asset turn or vice versa. Property is the most opaque component of asset turn. Retailers vary in whether they own their land and buildings outright, hold long-term leases, rent, or (most frequently) use a combination of owning and renting. They also vary in whether owned property assets are on the books at market, original or book value, and in how accurately market values are assessed. Stock is the second component of asset turn – and a broader indicator of efficiency. A retailer with a high stock turn (but comparable stock-outs) versus direct competitors will have lower total supply-chain costs, be better at matching stock to consumer demand, and have a lower risk of product obsolescence and markdown. The third component of asset turn is net debtor/creditor balance. Many retailers, notably European hypermarkets and supermarkets, fund cash flow via balancing extended supplier payment periods against immediate cash receipts from consumers.

Trading ROA then needs to be converted into *return on equity* (see Exhibit 2.5).

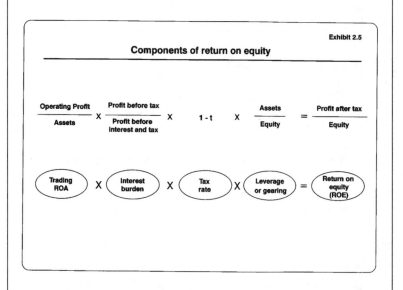

Exhibit 2.5

Components of return on equity

This conversion reflects the financial strategy of the business: tax management and gearing/leverage. Net interest charges and corporation tax need to be deducted from trading profit, and the resulting profit after tax ('PAT') ROA multiplied by the gearing ratio (assets/equity) to arrive at return on equity ('ROE'). A business can achieve a high ROE via a high trading ROA and low gearing or vice versa.

The final element of the economic equation is the creation of *shareholder value* (see Exhibit 2.6).

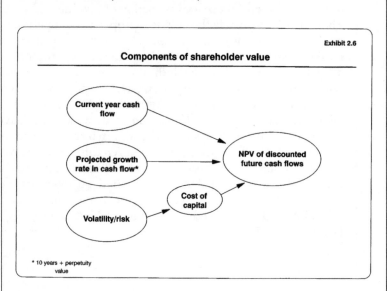

Exhibit 2.6

Components of shareholder value

- Current year cash flow
- Projected growth rate in cash flow*
- Volatility/risk
- Cost of capital
- NPV of discounted future cash flows

* 10 years + perpetuity value

Shareholder value is measured as the present value of discounted future cash flows. This calculation is driven by estimates of future growth rate in cash flow and the business's cost of capital. According to the Capital Asset Pricing Model (CAPM), the gearing decisions that affect reported ROE should not change the value of a business except insofar as they change real tax payments: higher gearing to support a higher short-term ROE should increase a company's beta risk factor, thereby increase its cost of capital and discount rate, and therefore deliver no real change in underlying value.

As retailing has become large-scale and concentrated, moving from small independent mom-and-pop stores to category killer chains, retail economics have changed – and in particular, gross margins have been inexorably reduced. An independent grocery store in the 1950s would have operated off a 60–70% gross margin, based on buying from a whole-saler already taking a 30% or greater markup on manufac-turer selling price. (This economic structure still exists, at least in part, in Japan and Southern Europe.) Very large-scale

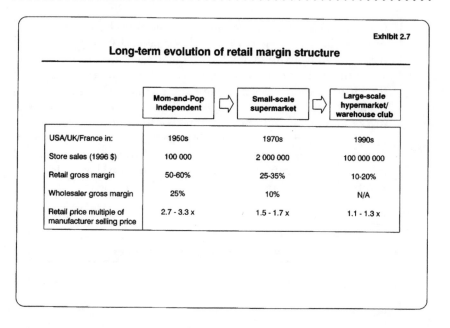

Exhibit 2.7

Long-term evolution of retail margin structure

	Mom-and-Pop Independent	Small-scale supermarket	Large-scale hypermarket/ warehouse club
USA/UK/France in:	1950s	1970s	1990s
Store sales (1996 $)	100 000	2 000 000	100 000 000
Retail gross margin	50-60%	25-35%	10-20%
Wholesaler gross margin	25%	10%	N/A
Retail price multiple of manufacturer selling price	2.7 - 3.3 x	1.5 - 1.7 x	1.1 - 1.3 x

warehouse clubs or mega-hypermarkets in the 1990s, with stripped-down service, are set up to operate on 10–15% gross margins, based off direct distribution from manufacturers (see Exhibit 2.7).

Wal-Mart's historical performance is a good example of the structure of retail economics and of the long-run trend towards lower gross margin, higher volume formats (see Case Study 2.1).

Case Study 2.1   Wal-Mart

Over the last ten years, Wal-Mart has grown total sales from $8.5 billion to $94 billion, and become the world's largest retailer. Total sales have grown at 27% per annum compounded.

Store sizes have become bigger over these ten years. Average sales per store have increased from $10m to $32m. The average size of a domestic Wal-Mart store has increased from 57 000 to 91 000 square feet. The store mix has shifted towards higher volume, larger-scale formats: Sam's Clubs, which have grown from 23 to 433 in the USA, and more recently the supercenter formats, combining general merchandise and grocery, which have grown from 10 in 1992 to 239 in 1996.

For the first half of this ten-year period, Wal-Mart displayed the virtuous economics of large-scale retailing. Gross margins declined by 2.5%, but consumers were won over by lower prices, and higher volumes combined with the lower operating costs of larger stores translated into an improving bottom-line performance: operating margins stayed roughly constant, return on assets improved by 2.1% and return on shareholders' equity stayed well over 30% (see Exhibit 2.8).

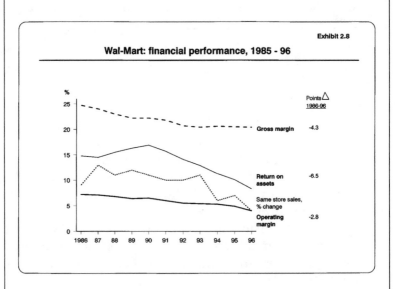

Exhibit 2.8

Wal-Mart: financial performance, 1985 - 96

From 1991, performance started to deteriorate. Gross margins declined a further 1.8% by 1993, but have since remained stable, despite a continuing shift to larger-scale stores and an increasing grocery mix. Operating margins have declined, from 6.5% in 1990 to 4.4% in 1996. Return on assets has halved, and return on equity has plummeted by 14 points. Most worryingly, same-store sales growth, which held up at over 10% until 1994, has crashed to 4% in 1996, little more than inflation. Wal-Mart looks in danger of slipping off the virtuous path of higher volumes, lower gross margins and lower consumer prices supporting high levels of return on assets and return on equity.

We can now return to our main theme. Can retailers build a real *brand premium*? After all, even strong retail brands, in market leadership positions, need to stay broadly price-competitive to keep customer loyalty. Moreover, aggressive discounting and price wars are constantly breaking out in retailing, both reflecting and reinforcing this inability to extract a brand price premium.

Exhibit 1.2 in Chapter 1 showed a graphical representation of a strong brand's ability to achieve a combination of higher selling prices and/or volume advantage at price parity; this is shown in more detail in Exhibit 2.9.

Strong producer brands typically achieve both volume and price advantage. A strong producer brand will be number one or two in market share in its category, and it will also extract a price premium versus weaker brands, in both manufacturer-to-retailer selling price and retailer-to-consumer selling price. With very strong producer brands, the retailer margin can be zero or negative: the retailer has to carry the brand to attract consumer traffic, retail price competition on these leading brands ('KVIs', or 'known

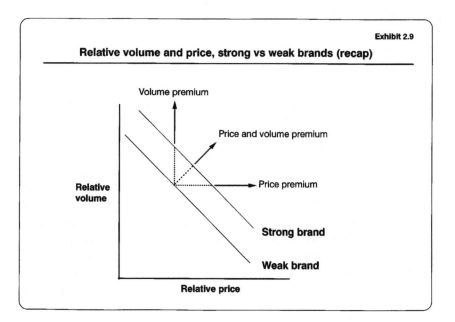

Exhibit 2.9

Relative volume and price, strong vs weak brands (recap)

Volume premium

Price and volume premium

Relative volume

Price premium

Strong brand

Weak brand

Relative price

value items') is intense, and the retailer cannot extract adequate financial support from the producer.

Finding the balance between market share and price premium is a never-ending strategic challenge for producer brands. The temptation is to 'cash in' the strong brand by raising prices, capitalising on short-term volume inelasticity – but that risks limiting the growth potential of the brand, and, if the price increases are seen as exploitative by consumers, risks undermining their long-term loyalty and increasing their incentive to seek substitutes. Coca-Cola's history provides an interesting example of this tension between volume and price premium. By the 1920s, Coke was already market leader in soft drinks in the USA, but got into financial difficulty. Part of its rescue package was an open-ended agreement with its bottlers/distributors that it could not increase the prices charged to them for cola syrup. 'Cashing in' the brand via price hikes was therefore removed as an option for Coke, and the company had to focus on growing category and brand volume, reflected in long-run goals such as making cola as available and more popular than water (their vision is, famously, always to have a Coke 'within arm's reach of desire'), and targeting total 'share of throat' across all drinking occasions. Only in the 1970s was the price freeze negotiated away, and by then the Coke brand culture was firmly established.

The brand premium of strong retailers with high store brand penetration can and does operate exactly like a producer brand premium. A quality store brand extracts a price and volume premium versus weaker retail competitors and often versus leading producer brands, in all retail sectors. As with producer brands, there is a continual strategic trade-off to be managed between volume and price. In the consumer boom of the late 1980s, many retailers were seduced into believing that their brands could extract large and ever-increasing price premiums from their customers. They ratcheted up selling prices and gross margins, and ignored for as long as they could the subsequent decline in traffic and sales volume, until this started to work its way through to a decline in ROA and ultimately a collapse in $ net margin.

However, retailers whose main business is selling producer brands will rarely be able to sustain any material price premium. Consumers will gravitate rapidly to the retailer that offers the most competitive prices. In these instances a retail brand can hope only to extract a volume premium, combined with price parity or price under-cutting versus direct competitors. This volume premium will be manifested in volume per store, volume per line, volume per supplier, sales per square foot, sales per employee – all measures and drivers of relative efficiency and productivity, so that the volume premium can and does still deliver superior financial returns. Retailers sometimes hope that service differentiation can support a price premium, but our experience is that that is rarely true. An electrical retailer may support and increase his volume advantage by offering in-store advice and exceptional after-sales service, but the moment prices become slightly out of line with direct competitors, consumers will gratefully take the service advice and go next door to buy the product.

There are some exceptions, where retailers without high store brand sales are still able to extract a price premium. Flagship stores in tourist destinations, such as the internationally known department stores in New York, Paris or London can achieve this, particularly with their international tourist customers, as can more specialist stores in the same situation, such as Hamleys in toys or the jewellery and fashion stores on Bond Street. (Hamleys provides an example of one often-forgotten component of retail brand value: the ability to extract very favourable rental terms from property owners. Developers trying to fill a new mall – physical and virtual – will offer very favourable terms to get Hamleys in as a prestige, traffic-generating anchor tenant.)

How about the second argument often made, that retailers lack the *ability to invest in brand-building*, owing to their thin margins and high gearing?

It is true that retailers are often highly geared. This high gearing can take many forms. The ratio of debt-to-equity, and therefore the proportion of profit committed to interest payments, may be high. Stores may be on short-term rentals at high fixed cost, rather than freehold or long leasehold.

Cash flow may be funded primarily by extended creditor payment periods. A successful business which is highly geared across all or some of these dimensions typically earns a high ROE via thin margins, low asset and equity investment, and high asset and equity turn. Returns are therefore more volatile and sensitive to minor changes in sales and margin performance, and cash is tight.

This is not, however, a unique characteristic of retailing, but a strategic choice that is open to businesses in any industry sector. Highly leveraged buyouts ('LBOs') were a feature of the 1980s, particularly in the USA, across a wide range of industries. Their premise was that many businesses sub-optimised the return for equity investors by over-conservative gearing, and that the pressures created by the need to service high levels of debt would focus management on cash flow to pay down the debt burden. Productive investment need not be constrained, but unproductive investment would be eliminated.

Nor is it true that all retail businesses are highly geared. M&S has a very conservative financial strategy: it owns freehold or long-term leases on all its property, has a low ratio of debt-to-equity, and has clear and reasonable payment terms with its long-term supplier base. The leading UK grocers are similarly conservative.

Equally, the level of operating margin is the result of success or failure in a retailer's competitive strategy, not the cause of it. A business faced with thin margins has two choices: compete on low cost and minimal investment and try to scratch out survival, or somehow find the funds to invest effectively to create brand differentiation and start to build up higher margins. Tesco in the late 1970s had very thin margins and a low cost, promotional, commodity retailing mentality. Selective investment in value-added product ranges and brand-building steadily transformed the business through the 1980s. Management had the strategy and will to pursue the brand-building route, and found ways to fund the investment out of a thin margin structure.

Summary of Part I:
The Context

The Growth of Retail Power and the Brand-building Challenge

Retailing has become large-scale, concentrated, centralised and sophisticated. Retailers are well down the track of seizing value-chain power. The next major challenge and opportunity for retailers is the development of strong retail brands, that generate long-run consumer preference and loyalty and create sustainable differentiation between direct retail competitors.

The current status of retail brand development, and the future potential for brand-building, varies widely across countries and retail sectors. Strong retail brands are most advanced in the UK, including possibly the world's strongest brand in product retailing, M&S.

Are Retail Brands Different from Producer Brands?

We can see today that strong brands can be established in retailing. Internationally, many examples can be found in repertoire and service retailing. The UK gives us examples of strong brands in the grocery sector. Examples in the proximity and category killer sectors are harder to find, but we can point to Boots in the UK and Decathlon in France. Retail brands clearly can become 'The Real Thing'.

As with producer brands, differentiation is a central concept in retail brand strategy, and applicable across all retail sectors. We identify six key sources of retail brand differentiation: investment in store brands, investment in the supply chain and supplier relationships, mass marketing, the development of direct customer relationships, brand integrity

53

and brand culture. Overall, segmentation is relevant in retail brand strategy, particularly in repertoire and service retailing, but it is less central than it is for producer brands. While there are examples of segmented propositions in product retailing outside fashion and home lifestyle, retailers often compete for maximum market share in their categories, across all customer groups within their catchment areas and across a wide range of price positions.

A real and important difference between most producer brands and most retail brands is the sheer multiplicity of retail brand attributes, and their high rate of change. The problems this creates around clarity of brand positioning are greatest in grocery and hypermarket or supercenter retailing, which need to work hard to create a broad umbrella brand assurance of quality, value and service, overlaid with unique store brands. The multiplicity of attributes of a retail brand also creates practical differences in decision-making, control and organisation relative to classical fmcg brand management.

Two intrinsic differences are often argued to exist between the economics of retail brands and producer brands: the level and nature of the brand premium, and the ability to invest in brand-building. For retailers with highly developed and high quality store brands, there is no fundamental difference in the potential for a volume and price premium; but retailers who mainly sell producer brands cannot extract any material long-run price premium, and must instead focus on volume advantage versus competitors. There is no innate difference between retail and producer brands in their ability to invest in brand-building: the high financial and operational gearing of many non-UK retailers is a choice rather than an inevitability and need not constrain productive investment; operating margins, thin or fat, are the result of strategy, not the cause.

*   *   *

In *Part II* of the book, we take each of our four product retailing sectors – repertoire, proximity, category killers and grocery – in turn and in detail, identifying the potential for brand-building and the key elements of successful brand strategies.

Part II

Brand-building Strategies in Four Sectors

Repertoire Retailing: Fashion and Home Lifestyle **3**

Fashion retail brands often look very like producer brands. They can actively use most elements of both segmentation and differentiation in their brand strategies.

Segmentation in Fashion Retailing

Price/quality positioning, including style, is the primary factor in fashion segmentation. Price points are concrete and objective. So, to a certain extent, is physical quality, as manifested in material, cut and finishing, although how consumers perceive and rate physical quality does change from season to season. Fashion quality (style positioning, or a fashion brand's point of view) is a much softer characteristic, hard to evaluate objectively and hard to correlate with price points. Fashion retailers may have a very recognisable house style that is reasonably consistent from one season to the next: Benetton's bold-splash colours, Laura Ashley's English country patterns, Gap's muted American casualwear. Retailers without such strong in-house styles can position themselves along a spectrum of fashion-forward (rapid and bold incorporation of leading-edge styling) to fashion-follower (slower and toned-down incorporation). Fashion-forward can mean higher priced than fashion-follower, but not necessarily: clubwear for teenage girls can be very fashion-forward but has to be held at affordable price points, while high quality classic fashion such as traditional men's suits can support high price points.

A strong fashion brand, particularly if based on a distinctive house style, can be stretched over many customer and product groups. Gap and Next are good large-scale examples: both have brand franchises that embrace men and women across a broad age range, include strong positions in chidrenswear, and embrace a full range of clothing categories. In Next's case, the franchise extends to footwear and accessories.

However, retail fashion brands are often also targeted at specific *customer groups*. 'Hard' characteristics are sex and age: children, teenage girls, teenage boys, women or men 20–35, older men or women. Size is another 'hard' character-istic: outsize and petite are distinct market segments. 'Soft' characteristics may also come into play – lifestyle (working women), fashion attitude (conservative or risk-taking) – although these tend to blur into questions of style positioning.

Targeting age brackets is not as clear-cut as it sounds. Customers outside the target age range will usually account

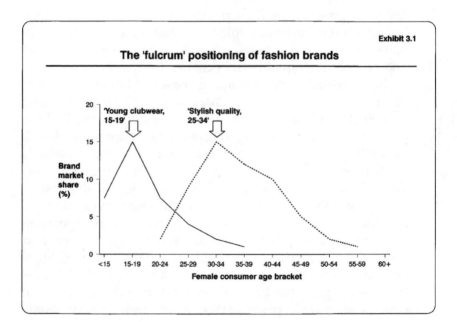

Exhibit 3.1

The 'fulcrum' positioning of fashion brands

for a significant proportion, perhaps 20–40%, of sales. A 45-year-old will frequently want to buy a younger brand targeted at a 35-year-old; a 16-year-old may aspire to an older look and buy a brand targeted at a 21-year-old. Age targeting is better thought of as the 'fulcrum' positioning of a fashion brand: the age range in which market share should be highest, and for which target consumer personality profiles can be sketched out, with market share declining the further out (younger and older) one moves from the fulcrum (see Exhibit 3.1).

Less frequently, retail fashion brands can be targeted at specific *product groups*. Tie Rack and Victoria's Secret are good examples. Footwear has remained a largely specialist sector, with its demands for high stock levels and in-store service acting as a barrier to clothing-based retailers. (See Case Study 3.1 for an example of fashion brand targeting.)

Case Study 3.1   The Burton Group in the 1980s – 1

The Burton Group in the UK built up a portfolio of fashion businesses and brands that were highly targeted against market segments, to a degree that was unusual in UK fashion retailing 15 years ago. The segmentation story was sold hard to the stock market as key to the Group's success and roaring stock price in the mid-1980s (see Exhibit 3.2).

The Burton Group was very successful through the first half of the 1980s. Store numbers, like-for-like/same-store sales and net profits grew at double digit percentages. But in the late 1980s the story turned sour: LFL sales growth turned negative; prices and gross margins were hiked to protect profits, but volumes then declined even further, and stores went into almost constant heavy markdown; profits disappeared altogether in the early 1990s, and the stock price collapsed to under 10% of its peak.

There were many problems with The Burton Group, and brand strategy was certainly one. Only two brands turned out in practice to have defensible target segments.

Evans had and maintained market leadership and a strong consumer franchise in outsize womenswear. The outsize consumer becomes very loyal to a retail brand which over

---

			Exhibit 3.2

Burton Group: segmentation in the 1980s

Brand	Customer groups	Price/quality positioning	Style positioning
Top Shop	Teenage girls	Lower middle	Fashion-forward
Top Man	Teenage boys (+ early 20s)	Lower middle	Mainstream
Evans	Outsize women	Middle	Mainstream
Principles for Women	Women 25-35	Upper middle	Mainstream
Principles for Men	Men 25-35	Upper middle	Mainstream
Dorothy Perkins	Women 20-45+	Lower middle	Mainstream
Burton	Men 20-45+	Lower middle	Mainstream
Debenhams (department stores)	All	Middle	Mainstream

the years shows steady and sensitive commitment to her needs. Moreover, the economics of outsize involve high stock investment (as in footwear) across a wide range of size SKUs with low volumes per line, and these economics deter general clothing competitors from seriously entering the market.

Top Shop continues to battle with Miss Selfridge for leadership in the teenage female fashion market. Although market share and profits can swing wildly from season to season, both competitors have managed to maintain and constantly renew their brand franchise in a very tough market: short and risky product life-cycles, volatile customers who need constant reassurance of freshness and excitement, and a demand for up-to-the-minute product at low prices.

The purported customer group segmentation of the other specialty brands (setting aside Debenhams, which faced the common problems of department store chains) proved to be neither meaningful nor defensible. They all turned out to be competing in a general mainstream fashion market, against strong competitors like M&S, Next and C&A. Relative to those competitors, they had made no clear choice in terms of price/quality positioning; they were all middle market or shades above and below. They had no distinctive style positioning.

Differentiation in Fashion Retailing

Fashion retailers can and do use every potential element of differentiation in their brand strategies.

The most important is *investment in-store brands*. The fashion (clothing and footwear) market is predominantly a store brand/private label market: over two-thirds by retail sales value in Europe and around half in the USA. With the exception of jeans and footwear, the strongest fashion brand names are retail and not producer brands, and these strongest retailers generally do not carry producer brands even in categories where producer brands are the market leaders. Retailers can and do use a variety of own brand strategies, from 100% store brand to a wide range of sub-brands and proprietary labels, but the strongest tend to be exclusively or predominantly store brand, such as M&S, Gap, Next and Benetton.

The fashion supply chain is a complex one. Market trends and consumer demand are far less predictable than in any other sector and create the risk of heavy markdown and clearance on poor selling lines and of frequent stock-outs and lost sales on best sellers. Successful fashion retailers have to make a major *investment in the supply chain and supplier relationships*, trading off cost, responsiveness and quality. They have to have a closer relationship to their suppliers and to production capacity than in other retail sectors. Several still own their own factories, at least for CMT ('cut, make and trim'), supplying at least a proportion of their needs – Zara, the leading Spanish fashion chain, is highly integrated, producing 75% of its range in-house. Fashion chains often have large in-house teams for product design and development and for supplier management. To speed up response times on Far Eastern sourcing, The Limited had its own dedicated planes flying product from Asia into its central USA warehouse.

There are alternatives to a brand-building approach to the supply chain and supplier relationships. A fashion retail trader can choose to make little or no investment in in-house design and development or supplier management; to cherry-pick from ranges offered by suppliers (who often get to know, via trade shows and discussions with other retailers and other suppliers, what the industry is betting on for the next season); to negotiate individual contracts aggressively with those suppliers, as late in the day as possible to get the lowest prices that a supplier will accept to fill up short-term spare capacity; and to switch suppliers from contract to contract to get the lowest possible unit cost.

Certainly fashion retailers cannot afford to let their cost base become uncompetitive, nor make their supply-chain management so structured that they cannot respond quickly to new fashion trends and product opportunities. But we can think of no strong, long-lasting retail brands in fashion that have been built up on the trading approach alone. In the long run the brand-builders' success grows overall volume and volume per line to the point where the cost position, as well as the responsiveness and quality, that they can obtain from their suppliers will systematically beat that of the trader.

Other elements of brand differentiation are used by, and important for, fashion retailers. Mass marketing can be used extensively, as in Benetton's highly distinctive campaigns. The mass marketing mix is often skewed towards print, and towards 'indirect' advertising via placement in fashion articles. Direct customer marketing is also used, particularly by brands with catalogue/mail order distribution.

Brand integrity and a strong brand culture are vital, particularly in the buying and merchandising teams, who must share a common sense of the brand's price/quality/ style positioning. Maintaining brand pricing integrity in the face of heavy markdown pressure on a poor season's range is one of the toughest tests of the strength of a fashion brand and of the management team.

More than in any other retail sector, a store's distinctive look and ambience can reinforce the product brand image (Next, Banana Republic, Miss Selfridge) and become an integral part of the consumer's purchase decision. But product is always the main driver of brand loyalty, and many fashion retailers still prefer a fairly neutral store environment as a backdrop to product display.

Case Study 3.2 The Burton Group in the 1980s – 2

Failure to invest in and develop real sources of brand differentiation was another cause of The Burton Group's collapse in performance at the end of the 1980s.

Although always private label retailers, the poor performing specialty chains (Dorothy Perkins, Burton, Top Man, Principles) had never developed clear brand identities or fashion points of view, and certainly never a consistent, recognisable house style. They proliferated sub-brands within the stores targeted at sub-segments or short-lived trends in the overall market, diluting the potential cumulative value of a single store brand.

In managing the supply chain, the approach was primarily that of a trader rather than a brand-builder. Buyers were aggressive in seeking lowest cost short-term deals and in changing a large proportion of their suppliers from season to season. Investment in in-house design and development was thin at best and often non-existent, as was investment in supplier management. (Although one element of supply-chain management, namely merchandising systems for monitoring and responding to line sales performance, did and does continue to be a real competitive strength.)

The culture was a trading one, not a brand culture, and brand integrity was low. Faced with volume declines, management reflexes were to promote and discount heavily to shore up sales. Shop windows were often completely covered for long periods with brown paper announcing '50% off'. Consumers got the message: they never bought except on sale, and any remaining brand loyalty was eroded. This was in total contrast with Next in the same period, which maintained pricing integrity in the face of difficult trading conditions, despite facing financial collapse itself.

The Burton Group survived. Performance and stock price have recovered, although still far from the heady peaks of the mid-1980s. Building strong fashion brands has been a key element of the Group's successful strategy in the 1990s.

Sales Channels for Retail Fashion Brands

Like strong producer brands, retail fashion brands can be distributed through a variety of channels (see Exhibit 3.3). Leveraging brand value down these potential distribution channels is a real opportunity, but there are trade-offs involved, between volume and exclusivity.

Mail order involves no trade-off . Home shopping is largely complementary to store shopping, involving little cannibalisation of store volume and no dilution of brand exclusivity, and can add 25% or more to own-store volume. There are economic constraints: the need for a minimum volume to break even on the fixed costs of catalogue production/distribution and order handling/fulfilment. For a single brand operation, breakeven UK sales may be around $20 million, which makes mail order economically attractive for specialty fashion brands with own-store sales of at least $100 million. Next Directory, the mail order arm of the store brand, is now a sizeable and profitable business, selling the same

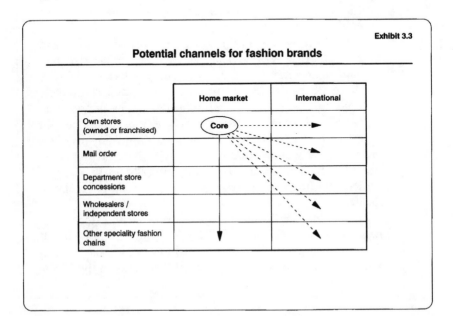

Exhibit 3.3

Potential channels for fashion brands

	Home market	International
Own stores (owned or franchised)	Core	
Mail order		
Department store concessions		
Wholesalers / independent stores		
Other speciality fashion chains		

range as the stores (after a slow start-up in which mail order ran its own, different range).

With *department store concessions*, trade-offs begin to occur, but at a limited and manageable level. For the specialty fashion brand, putting concessions into department stores is not very different from renting own-store space in a shopping mall. Department stores can bring new, often older and more affluent, customers for the brand. Proximity to strong producer brands reinforces the retail brand's claim on the consumer. The overall quality of service and environment in the department store needs to fit with the specialty brand's positioning.

Distributing brand product through *wholesalers into independent stores*, and into *other specialty fashion chains*, involves major trade-offs and is usually dangerous. Exclusivity is destroyed, and the most compelling element of brand differentiation in the retailer's own stores is seriously undermined. Any cost benefits from extra volume are likely to be more than offset by this reduction in core own-store brand differentiation and value. The retailer loses clarity as to whether to manage the business as a retail brand or as a producer brand.

The UK footwear market provides two interesting and contrasting examples.

British Shoe Corporation (owned by the Sears Group), the market leader in the 1980s with a 15–20% overall share, ran several fascia brands theoretically targeted at different segments of the market: Dolcis for young fashion, Saxone for quality, Freeman Hardy Willis for mass market, Curtess for low price, Shoe Express for low price self-service, plus several others. However, in the search for line volume and cost savings, and from a misunderstanding of the kind of real choice that consumers want their retail brands to provide, all product was pushed through all the fascias interchangeably. Any real differentiation, either as retail brands or as producer/private label brands, was destroyed. Consumers became famously incapable of telling one shoe store from another. British Shoe Corporation has delivered poor profits throughout the 1990s, and Sears is rumoured as of early 1997 to be about to sell or close the business.

Clarks, the number two market share player in shoes, faced a similar problem, but has managed to preserve its brand value. It ran a large own-store chain but had a large wholesaling activity selling to independents and other specialty shoe chains. Clarks' history was as a producer more than as a retailer, and it still owns its own shoe production. It invested heavily in its brand like a producer, in product development and innovation, quality control, and mass marketing. Its core brand strength in children's shoes, where it has a 50% market share, gave it a uniquely powerful and differentiated retail franchise with the consumer: mothers knew that the children's departments in Clarks stores provided consistent high service levels and stock availability across a large number of size fittings, and that the product would not damage their children's growing feet.

Expanding into *international* markets, fashion retailers can use a mix of own stores (franchised and/or owned), department store concessions and mail order. Brand positioning may vary from the home market, intentionally or accidentally. A foreign brand may be seen as exotic and innovative even if the home market positioning is mainstream or down-beat. The Gap's mid-market position in the USA becomes an upper-middle market position outside the USA, as consumers attribute chic value to casual Americana. In Japan, Muji was the first major retail format to focus on private label ranges (fashion, homestyle, accessories) that offered Japanese consumers a cheaper alternative to the high priced producer and designer brand ranges of department stores. Exporting its brand to Europe, Muji became Japanese chic, commanding high prices versus local competition, with concessions in the very up-market Liberty department stores.

Airport retailing is an attractive growth opportunity for strong fashion brands. Air traffic volumes are growing at 6–7% a year, and airport managements are realising the profit potential of retail development. International hubs such as Heathrow, Singapore and Schipol are prime sites, with rich sales potential from transit passengers with time to kill between connections, keen to buy duty- and tax-free, and particularly receptive to up-market brands with strong home country associations.

Strong Producer Brands in Fashion

In mass market fashion, there are strong international producer brands in two major product categories: Levi in jeans, and many brands in footwear, particularly in sports shoes: Nike, Reebok, Adidas, Timberland.

On the face of it, jeans looks like a category ripe for store brand/private label capture: a simple, functional product with style continuity from year to year, where quality is relatively straightforward to specify and deliver. Levi has maintained its producer brand leadership by major investment in marketing, and by the American heritage and aspirational associations of the brand in international markets, a characteristic shared with several other global American brand icons such as the Marlboro cowboy, Coke and McDonald's.

Footwear has proven to be a hard category for store brands and private label. Product design, development and production are still fairly complex, and maintaining consistent quality can be difficult. In sports shoes, technical advances in functionality and performance have been made regularly since the late 1970s. Nike built its brand position on these technical advances, then reinforced its brand leadership by transforming itself into a marketing-driven business, making heavy investments in design, new products, advertising and sponsorship.

Other major fashion product categories (shirts, skirts, coats, business suits, underwear, jumpers and sweaters) are now dominated by store brands/private label. However, strong producer brands do still exist in these categories, and their remaining strength in the market is derived from their distribution through department stores.

Department Stores

Certain large, famous department store locations are destination stores, drawing domestic and international customers: Bloomingdales in New York, Printemps in Paris, Mitsukoshi in Tokyo, Harrods in London. These are special cases, to which we will come back later in the book.

The majority of department stores have been under pressure for the last 30 years. Their originally splendid inner-city locations have often ended up in abandoned, run-down city centres. Their historical strengths of high service levels and reasonable choice across a wide range of categories have come under attack, from low cost out-of-town category killers offering even wider choice in a given category, and from off-price branded clothing retailers like TJ Maxx. Despite opening new stores in suburban locations, shopping malls and smaller cities and towns, their aggregate market share has been declining at an undramatic but steady rate.

By default, department stores are increasingly becoming large-space repertoire retailers, focusing on fashion and home lifestyle categories. While a few maintain a strong presence in categories that other department stores have largely abandoned to category killers (for example, Sears Roebuck in DIY hardware, electrical and auto supplies), these are becoming the exception rather than the norm.

In making their new role work, to halt their decline in market share and recover attractive levels of profitability, department stores face two strategic challenges, both centring on building brand value. First they must define and defend their role as high quality showcases for fashion and home lifestyle producer brands. Department stores are the key distribution channel for the majority of these brands, and the channel that reinforces a premium brand positioning. Premium perfume and cosmetics brands reinforce their exclusivity by limiting distribution to top department stores, which gives the stores themselves a strong source of differentiation from other retail outlets. Department stores and premium branded producers in other categories need to work together to build mutually-reinforcing brand value, offering exclusive distribution through high service, high quality store environments. Branded producers that distribute their (non-clearance) product through off-price stores, bargain basements and factory outlets undermine their own brand franchises and offer little long-term value for the department stores. Equally, department stores that show little selectivity in terms of brands stocked, and do not provide consistently high service and high quality environments, will have no long-term relationship with strong producer brands.

Secondly they must find a strong basis of brand differentiation between one department store and another. In the Mall of America in Minneapolis, the largest covered mall in the USA (with its own theme park in the middle!), four anchor department stores (Nordstrom, Macy's, Bloomingdales and Sears) face off against each other at the four corners of the mall. This is a situation replicated in most American malls and retail parks. By and large these department stores sell a similar range of classic producer brands, all in high service, high quality store environments. There are differences in category coverage and weight, and in service consistency but, as with specialty repertoire retailers, the real key to brand differentiation between them is quality store brand/private label development, complementary to their role as a showcase for producer brands. In the same Mall of America, there are over 120 specialty stores in just the apparel, footwear and housewares/furnishings categories. The department stores have to compete with these as much as with each other.

Department stores do face challenges other than these: a high cost base, and older city-centre locations which often need major refurbishment investment and may be simply too big to be filled profitably by fashion and homestyle alone. But getting the repertoire retailing role right, and meeting the challenge of brand-building – as a producer brand showcase and as developers of quality store brands – can lead to a recovery of market position and profitability for department stores, as evidenced by recent sector performance in the USA, where department store stocks have out-performed general merchandisers and the S&P 500 since 1987.

Store brand development in US department stores still has a long way to go. Aggregate penetration of apparel is only around 20%, although JC Penney and Sears are up in the 50% bracket. Compared with the UK, strong fashion producer brands remain dominant, particularly in the better priced categories: Liz Claiborne, St Johns, Dana Buchman and Nine West in womenswear, and Tommy Hilfiger and Nautica in menswear.

Home Lifestyle

Home products occupy a position in the retail market that is a mixture of fashion repertoire shopping and the more functional shopping of category killers.

After fashion, home lifestyle (furniture, soft furnishings, home textiles, tableware and kitchenware, interior design and decoration) is the umbrella category in which consumers can invest most aspirational value and sense of identity. Home lifestyle products represent fashion choices for the home living environment. Consumers will 'repertoire-shop' as they do for clothing and footwear, using different stores to play different roles in creating the wardrobe for the home. There are many retailers focusing on this end of the home products market, offering clear fashion points of view and strong store brand/private label choice to complement the producer brand ranges found in department stores: Williams–Sonoma, Habitat, Pier 1, DFS, Heals. Often fashion retailers can extend a strong house-style brand, particularly if print-based, into home lifestyle 'interiors': Laura Ashley, Eddie Bauer, Next, Liberty. Brand-building strategies are similar to fashion retailers.

There is a more functional home products market, where price and product performance matter as much as or more than style. Retailers such as Bed Bath & Beyond, IKEA and Linens'n'Things are targeted at that market, and are set up to be category killers rather than repertoire retailers, offering a much wider range of lines, styles, prices and quality. They still function, in practice, as part of a repertoire of shops for home products for most consumers. Even in the more functional retailers, store brand penetration is generally high, owing as much to the fragmented nature of the supply base and the shortage of strong producer brands as to retailers' strategic intent to build up retail brand value.

Proximity Retailing 4

At the other end of the spectrum from fashion retailing, proximity retailers face the toughest task in attempting to build up strong brands.

The Proximity Sector

The proximity sector embraces two broad types of retail business: general convenience stores, from c-store chains such as 7-Eleven and Circle K through small supermarket ('superette') chains to independent corner grocery stores and CTNs; and retailers with core product specialisations such as petrol/gas stations, chemists/drugstores, liquor stores/off-licences, stationery/booksellers, and fresh food (fruit and vegetables, bakers, butchers, fishmongers). These specialisations can be the result of regulation protecting retailers from full-fledged competition: examples include pharmacies in many countries, alcohol distribution in the USA, tobacco distribution in France. Where they are not protected by regulation, and even in some cases where they are, these product specialists are blurring into general proximity retailers whose objective is to sell whatever the passing consumer needs. A good example is the development of shops on petrol/gas station forecourts, whose convenience offers include services such as snacking and fast food (many proximity retailers now offer hot and chilled drinks and prepared foods) and video rental.

Retailers coming from historical product specialisations often take many years to understand the needs and objectives of proximity retailing. Petrol/gas station retailers initially thought that the natural product bundle for their forecourt

71

shops revolved around cars (that was why their customers were on the forecourt, filling up) and offered only motoring products and accessories. They then tried selling large bulky items that could be loaded into the car boot/trunk. Only recently have they begun to put together a product offer that fits with the shopping occasion: snacking, grocery top-up/ emergency, gifts, entertainment for the car journey, travel planning, plus a limited range of motoring products and accessories. The offer, merchandising and pricing are still a long way from optimal.

In the mature retail markets in the USA and Europe, proximity retailing is under more structural pressure than other retail sectors, and it is getting harder for chain retailers to earn adequate financial returns. Large grocery stores and hypermarkets have been absorbing many product categories into the weekly major grocery shop: fresh food, alcohol, tobacco, newspapers and magazines, petrol, OTC medicines, health and beauty care. 'Mom-and-pop' independents, while their numbers are declining, continue to be a force in the market, and hard-working entrepreneurs continue to open new shops and try their hand. Barriers to entry and economies of scale are low, and an owner/family-run local store can be lower cost, higher service and more responsive to local needs than a professionally-managed chain, as epitomised by the all-night Korean delis in New York.

In immature and more highly regulated markets the situation is different. The majority of retailing in Japan, Italy and Spain could be characterised as proximity. Compared with the USA and Canada, these countries still have three or four times the number of retail outlets *per capita*, despite a much higher population density (see Exhibit 4.1).

The most profitable, on percentage margin and absolute $ profit, chain retailer in Japan is Ito Yokado, which runs 7-Eleven Japan (and bought out Southland/7-Eleven in the USA when the US parent collapsed). In a market still covered with very small-scale local independents, with regulatory constraints on large-space grocery stores, 7-Eleven Japan's professional retail management systems and distribution efficiencies are enough of a competitive differential to extract premium returns.

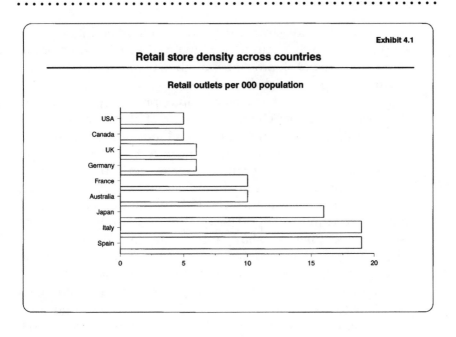

Exhibit 4.1

Retail store density across countries

Retail outlets per 000 population

Problems with Brand-building in the Proximity Sector

The *segmentation* concept does not offer much of practical value to proximity retailers. Their shopping occasion is already a given: convenience. They cannot exclude any customer group, and they must offer a broad range of price and quality. They may include, exclude or emphasise different sub-categories of product, but only at the margin.

Achieving brand *differentiation* is also more difficult than in other retail sectors.

Development of a strong store brand/private label offer, the key source of brand-building in other sectors, can be difficult to achieve. For general grocery products, customers often prefer the reassurance of producer brands when doing a rapid top-up shop, and are more willing to pay the cost premium of convenience shopping for leading producer brands. Convenience retailers' aggregate chain volumes, compared to large grocers, are generally not large enough to support the investment in product quality and innovation and in the supply chain needed to build a viable store brand offer, and are not significant enough to obtain the best buying terms from private label producers.

In contrast, brand extensions into proximity formats by large-space grocery chains can work, if the grocery chains have built up a strong store brand position in their core business. Tesco's down-sized, city-centre Tesco Metro format is a good example. The brand extension works partly because of the main chain's store brand strength in pre-prepared foods and ready meals, which are important in the impulse/ top-up proximity shop. The quality and image of Tesco's store brand (like Sainsbury's and Safeway), particularly in those value-added product categories, is as strong as the strongest producer brands. Without that range and brand strength, extending into small stores would add nothing to consumer choice and would risk diluting Tesco's large-store positioning. With it, the small stores serve to reinforce Tesco's overall brand value.

Mass marketing is rarely economically justifiable for proximity retailers. The stores themselves, with their high rent prime locations, act as the advertising medium. Actively investing in building direct customer relationships is also rarely economic, given the customers' low transaction values and high visit frequency; in-store displays and promotions are more effective ways of generating impulse purchases and cross-selling.

Store location (versus passing/local traffic, and including convenience of access or parking) is of paramount importance to the proximity shopper, and is critical to a retailer's competitive performance. Location does not, however, provide a basis of brand differentiation, such that a consumer has a positive preference for one store over another given equal proximity.

Range, price and service (particularly speed of check-out and opening hours) are important factors in consumer choice, but in small-store proximity formats are hard to turn into a source of sustainable differentiation. Independents, as discussed above, often have advantages over chains in responsiveness and service level.

Petrol/gas station retailing is representative of the problems facing strong retail brand development in the proximity sector. The major oil companies' stores are 100% private label (in fact, vertically-integrated) in the core product category of petrol, and they invest heavily in mass marketing. Yet the consumers' view of the major brands is close to undifferentiated, and loyalty is almost non-existent. Price is the prime consumer criterion for choosing one over another. Consumers will switch for small price differences, and given the 5–15% discount offered by grocers and hypermarkets will abandon the oil company outlets in droves: French hypermarkets now have 50% of the petrol market, and UK supermarkets 25%. If price difference is removed as a variable, consumers will use the first station they come to when they notice that their tank is nearing empty. And if difference in location convenience is adjusted for, the key remaining factor in consumer choice is the absolute number of pumps on the forecourt, which affects actual and perceived queueing time; consumers will drive on if they think they might waste a minute unnecessarily. Not a promising backdrop for building differentiated brand value! In fact, the c-stores on forecourts have now become probably the most important way in which the oil companies can actually differentiate their offers, assuming that they are managing cost/pricing, location and number of pumps to be broadly competitive. In the USA, gas stations now earn 40% of their profits from non-oil products.

However, there are certain cases in which strong brands can be built in the proximity sector. The chemist/drugstore market provides the best platform in the sector for brand-building, and Boots in the UK provides a strong case model (see Case Study 4.1).

Case Study 4.1 Boots and the Chemist/Drugstore Sector

Prescribing chemists and drugstores are different from other proximity markets. Proximity to the prescribing doctor, rather than to passing traffic, is critical. Strong long-term relationships are established between the retailer/pharmacist and his or her regular customers, who use the pharmacist as a source of medical help and advice, complementary to their use of a doctor. Pharmacies are licensed and regulated, their numbers are controlled, they hold exclusive distribution rights on prescription medicines and even certain OTC products, and in many countries (including most of Continental Europe) chaining is still prohibited.

Boots, which is the leader in the UK pharmacy market, has leveraged its core pharmacy position into a strong brand in a more broadly-defined proximity market – and is one of the 3–5 strongest retail brands overall in the UK. The core Boots brand values, stemming from its pharmacy heritage, are care and security. These values have been successfully extended into closely-related areas such as beauty and personal care (where Boots' main retail rival in brand strength is Body Shop), broadly-defined health products including vitamins and healthfoods, baby care, and optician services. Outside the core health and beauty categories which give the brand its overall strength, Boots has focused on extracting maximum value from its huge traffic flow and visit frequency – over 80% of UK households visit a Boots store in any two-month period – and become one of the leaders in other proximity categories such as film processing and pre-prepared sandwiches and snacks, maintaining an image of high quality and brand integrity.

Underpinning Boots' brand strength is its commitment to store brand products. Store brand/private label now accounts for around 50% of sales, and in several major categories is much higher. The high level of store brand penetration stems partly from Boots' history as a significant pharmaceutical producer (ethical and OTC) in its own right. The ethical pharmaceuticals division has recently been sold off, but the business continues to be a major OTC and health and beauty products producer, and its overall commitment to store brands remains as strong. This characteristic of Boots is unique worldwide in the chemist/drugstore sector.

Boots is also an exception to our earlier comment on limited mass marketing investment by most proximity retailers. In 1995 its UK media spend of almost £40 million ($60 million) was on a par with the two biggest grocery spends (Sainsbury's and Safeway) and only exceeded, among the universe of all brands, producer and retail, by Kellogg's at almost £70 million. For comparison, Coca-Cola spent £29 million.

Outside of the chemist/drugstore and health/beauty care sector, there are almost no examples of strong retail brands being built in proximity. Certain specialty wine merchants, such as Nicolas in France and Oddbins in the UK, do offer differentiated expertise and service, but these are small, niche businesses. The next best candidate could be 7-Eleven, which is certainly a ubiquitous brand with high awareness and recognition – there are 14 000 7-Eleven stores world-wide, covering 20 countries – but its collapse in the USA indicates the problems of building valuable and sustainable proximity brands.

Airport Retailing

Airport retailing is a form of proximity retailing. With world air traffic volumes growing at 5% per annum, and a high income, often expenses-paid customer base, this is one of the most attractive segments for retailing and for producers of luxury and fashion brands. The commercialisation of airport management and the development of airport retailing has been surprisingly slow in the USA, and other countries have taken the lead. BAA in the UK, the privatised manager of the London area airports, has been aggressive in developing its retail revenue, which is now close to $1 billion and greater than its revenue from airport charges. Market analysts now treat BAA as a retail stock play.

Category Killers 5

At first glance, category killers would seem to be the antithesis of retail brand-building: warehouse sheds selling on price, range breadth and volume economics. However, as category killer markets mature and look-alike sheds face each other across the same retail parks, brand differentiation and brand-building will become a top management priority.

The Growth of Category Killers

Category killers have been the biggest growth phenomenon in retailing in North America and Europe over the last 15 years.

The retail formula has been fairly consistent. Focus on a product category that is still dominated by a fragmented group of small-scale independents and/or is served poorly by large generalist retailers (department stores, hypermarkets). Aim to offer the widest possible range, minimise out-of-stocks, and under-cut the independents and generalists by 10–25% on price. Open large out-of-town/edge-of-town ('power strips', in the USA) warehouse-type stores with huge parking lots that draw consumers from a large drive-time catchment area of half an hour or more. Aim for a dominant (20%+) share in the catchment area. Become the low cost operator, through a combination of low rents, low cost shop-fits, tight staffing, economies of scale (labour and overhead) at store and chain level, buying muscle, and high asset productivity (space and stock turn).

Consumers are drawn to category killers on the basis of price and range authority. They know that they are unlikely

Exhibit 5.1

Category killer market leaders in the USA, France and the UK

Sector	USA	France	UK
Electrical	Circuit City Best Buy	Darty Conforama	Curry's Comet
DIY	Home Depot Lowe's	Castorama Leroy Merlin	B&Q Texas / Homebase
Sports	Sports Authority	Decathlon	
Toys	Toys 'R' Us	Toys 'R' Us	Toys 'R' Us
Home	IKEA Bed Bath & Beyond	IKEA Conforama	IKEA MFI, DFS
Office Products	Office Depot Staples Office Max		
Pets	PetsMart	Mille Amis	Pet City

to find a cheaper store, that the store is likely to carry what they want, and that what they want is likely to be in stock. The out-of-town locations and easy parking make the planned shopping trip easier than in-town, particularly for bulky or large volume purchases.

This formula has worked across a wide variety of product categories, where category killers either have become or are in the process of becoming the dominant mode of retailing (see Exhibit 5.1). In the list above, retailers such as Toys 'R' Us and IKEA are leaders internationally as well as in their domestic markets. The scale of category killer retailing, at store and at chain level, and the systematic replicability of the formula across different countries, is one of the key factors driving the globalisation of retailing.

New areas for category killers are constantly being explored. PetSmart in the USA is a category killer in pet products, including live pets; it has already spawned imitators in the UK (Pet City) and France (Mille Amis). Circuit City, also in the USA, is experimenting with CarMax, a category killer in used cars, which is probably the largest un-professionalised retail sector left.

The principles of large-scale destination retailing have been applied also in the service industry. Disney is a category killer theme park, changing the scale of the proposition and drawing customers from an international, even intercontinental, catchment area. Very large shopping malls work on a similar basis, combining leisure facilities such as eating out, cinemas and nightclubs with an enlarged shopping choice – and, in the case of Mall of America in Minneapolis, an indoor theme park in the centre of the mall, with rollercoasters and white-water rides. On a different physical scale, Blockbuster Video works in a similar way versus its smaller-scale independent video rental competitors.

The rate of growth of category killers has been phenomenal. In the USA, Home Depot came from nowhere in the mid-1980s to become the market leader in home improvement retailing in the mid-1990s. Market share is now around 12% and is projected to reach over 20% by the year 2000. Sales have grown from zero to over $15 billion in ten years. In the process Home Depot has become the second or third most valuable publicly quoted retailer in the world (see Exhibit 5.2).

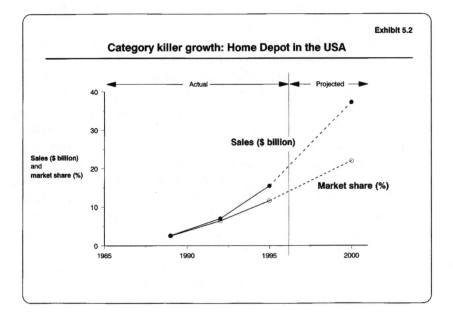

Exhibit 5.2

Category killer growth: Home Depot in the USA

Emerging Concerns Over Category Killers

Category killers have succeeded at the expense of independents and mixed retailers such as department stores and hypermarkets.

Many managers and analysts are now asking what will happen once category killers have reached maturity in geographic coverage and aggregate market share, and have to focus primarily on competition with each other. 'First wave' category killers are often very undifferentiated one from another, as is evident from a visit to any out-of-town retail park: look-alike warehouse sheds, equal emphasis on price and range, and often limited store brand/private label development. There is a tendency towards excess capacity, as competitors follow each other into the best retail parks and out-of-town catchment areas. Consumer preference and loyalty have not been created. There is a big risk of the emergence of cutthroat commodity-like competition, with regular aggressive price wars, as has already happened in the DIY and electrical sectors in Europe.

Outside the USA, planning regulation may give some relief against this threat. France, under lobbying pressure from small shop-keepers, has recently introduced very tight controls on the opening of new large-space out-of-town stores; the UK introduced looser constraints on the pace of retail park development three years ago. But in both cases, although regulation will reduce the dangers of future excess capacity, it is largely too late: major players have already established broad store networks.

Category killers to date have focused on store openings, operating systems and efficiency, and buying muscle. Brand development has been low on their list of priorities until now, even compared with other retail sectors. But looking forward, brand-building strategies, using both segmentation and differentiation tools, will be the only way to avoid the outcome of commodity price-based competition and a long-term deterioration in sector profitability.

Segmentation: Which Categories to Kill?

Most dimensions of segmentation are irrelevant to most category killer propositions. They need to aim for maximum share in their target product categories within a maximum feasible drive-time catchment area. They need to attract as many customer groups, with as broad a range of quality/price/style positionings, as is economically feasible. Customer groups and quality/price/style positionings are excluded only if their potential volumes are too low to merit shelf-space. The shopping occasion is a given: a planned destination shopping trip.

The strategic segmentation choice for category killers focuses on 'which product groups to offer?'. This is a real and crucial brand strategy choice. The destination retailer must be able to offer authority (broadest range, in-stock, at best price) in all sub-categories in which it competes; there should be a logical operational fit across product groups in terms of buying and merchandising skills, supply-chain management, and service requirements; and, most importantly from a branding perspective, the sub-categories must have a logical fit in terms of clear consumer perception and shopping occasion. Category killers wrestle constantly with this question, and the 'right' answer is constantly evolving as markets and technologies change.

To illustrate, a potential product group segmentation map for electrical goods could be as broad-based as in Exhibit 5.3. In this exhibit, a core product group focus common to many electrical category killers is highlighted. The other areas represent product groups where presence is inconsistent, patchy and/or strongly contested by other retail formats, even though there is a potentially logical connection with the core. For example, electrical category killers may be content for light household appliances to slip away to home specialists and department stores: consumer perception of fit is poor, and transaction values are low, without the compensating high gross margins of accessories. Computing and telecoms are natural fits with their core: they should be able to absorb these sectors, as the rate of technology change and the level of consumer need for technical advice and

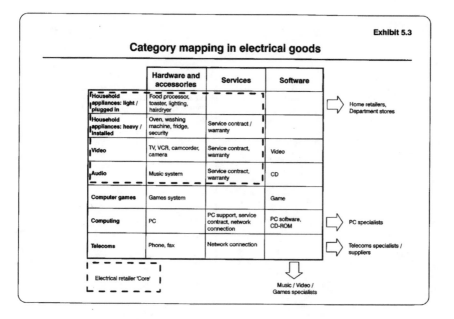

Exhibit 5.3

Category mapping in electrical goods

	Hardware and accessories	Services	Software	
Household appliances: light / plugged in	Food processor, toaster, lighting, hairdryer			Home retailers, Department stores
Household appliances: heavy / installed	Oven, washing machine, fridge, security	Service contract / warranty		
Video	TV, VCR, camcorder, camera	Service contract, warranty	Video	
Audio	Music system	Service contract, warranty	CD	
Computer games	Games system		Game	
Computing	PC	PC support, service contract, network connection	PC software, CD-ROM	PC specialists
Telecoms	Phone, fax	Network connection		Telecoms specialists / suppliers

Electrical retailer 'Core'

Music / Video / Games specialists

service decline and converge with the status of video / audio. Software is more problematic. It represents a major market opportunity, but shopping occasion and shopping frequency, consumer perceptions, and buying and merchandising skills are very different from the core large-ticket hardware product groups.

The boundaries of a target product category have to be defined in a way that fits with consumer perceptions and shopping behaviour, and in a way such that the retailer can deliver a consistent category killer proposition: range authority at best prices. 'Children's goods' is an example of a product grouping that appears logical but in practice does not seem to work as a category killer (see Exhibit 5.4).

Childrens World, a UK out-of-town / destination format (started from scratch by Boots), was based on the idea that 'everything for the child' made a logical bundle of product groups, from toys and books through nursery equipment to clothing and even diapers and baby food and health products. In practice, large elements of that bundle did not fit at all. Most obviously, purchase of consumables (baby food, diapers, medication) is part of the weekly grocery shop.

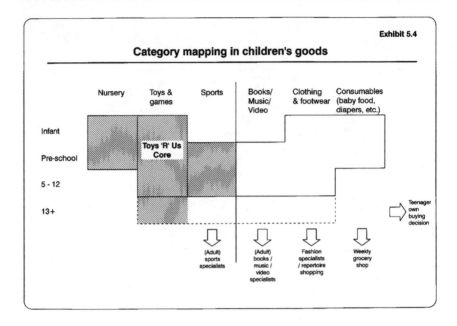

Exhibit 5.4

Category mapping in children's goods

Clothing and footwear require specialist buying and supply-chain skills, and even for children are usually shopped for on a repertoire basis. Nursery equipment was simply a very difficult product group to manage profitably: inefficient suppliers, low volumes per line, high stock investment and very low sales per square foot. In toys, the main competitor was one of the most-focused category killers around, Toys 'R' Us, which out-gunned Childrens World on price and range.

The problems of Childrens World were compounded by being run with Boots' high street chemist retail mentality, which emphasised high gross margin and range editing rather than the high volume, low gross margin, range authority mentality necessary in a destination retailer. Boots has recently sold the chain to Mothercare, which has the advantage of the strongest retail brand name in the UK in the young children's market, and whose core business includes clothing and nursery equipment. The Childrens World outlets are being converted into large-scale out-of-town Mothercare stores.

Toys 'R' Us, in contrast, is focused on a narrow set of product groups that work together well as a unified category killer proposition. It delivers total range and price authority in its core product area of toys and games. That product positioning enables it to extend into certain product areas of good fit – nursery equipment/accessories, and sports equipment for pre-teenagers – and to hold onto teenager (and even adult) purchases in the core area of toys and games. Outside those areas its presence is negligible or non-existent. Children's clothing is offered through the separate Kids 'R' Us format, which may benefit from some brand value crossover and co-location, but fundamentally has to earn its place in the kids' fashion market on its own merits.

Differentiation: How to Tell One Shed From Another

Brand differentiation between category killers is a major challenge. Ranges tend to be equally broad, prices equally competitive, and store environments similar. Mass marketing is used by category killers, to pull consumers in from wide catchment areas, but tends to focus on price and promotions. Several category killer markets are characterised by the dominance of strong producer brands.

Electrical retailing is a good example of the difficulties. In brown and white electrical goods, including 'new' product groups such as PCs and telecoms, there are real barriers against retailers developing strong store brand penetration. Levels of technical complexity and rate of technological innovation, in product development, production processes and quality control, are still high. Production is dominated by a small number of global producers, such as Sony, Philips and Matsushita, investing in large-scale, capital-intensive factories and global brand marketing. The rate of innovation, and the consequent lack of continuity in product lines, is a big barrier: by the time retailers have taken one or two seasons to get product specification, cost and quality up to scratch, the market has moved on. In the face of these barriers, few retailers have tried seriously to develop a strong private label offer. Sears Roebuck's Kenmore range of appliances is probably the strongest to date. Dixons' Saisho private label for brown goods has failed to establish itself.

Electrical retailers have, however, two other strong weapons for brand differentiation: *service* (both in-store and at-home) and, related to service, the ability to build up *long-term direct customer relationships*. Reliability, minimisation of hassle, and total cost-in-use are consumers' priorities at least as much as, if not more so, than a 10% difference in up-front purchase price. Strong service relationships can be developed with customers: from in-store advice on the initial purchase, through appliance installation or set-up, through after-sales repair and maintenance, to advice on the replacement cycle and the next purchase. Creating sustainable differentiation in service is possible in electrical retailing because of the complexity and length of the service relationship, unlike the straightforward purchase transactions characteristic of most retail sectors. Building such service relationships, with the service systems and databases involved, can create tremendous opportunities for managing and marketing directly to individual customers and households over the long-term.

Unfortunately, most electrical retailers operate in exactly the opposite fashion. In-store salesforces are focused on sales volume and high gross margin lines, and rarely give objective, informed and patient advice. High margin warranty contracts are given the hard sell during the hardware purchase. Quality control of installation service is poor. After-sales repair and maintenance, if not covered by warranty, is high priced, low quality, and often contracted out to other firms. Little if any attempt is made to set up and maintain customer databases and records of customer contact, or proactively to contact and market to customers. Electrical retailers tend to be transaction-driven, rather than focused on lifetime customer value and brand loyalty – one reason why the market so frequently turns into an intensive price war.

There are exceptions, even in electrical retailing. Darty, the electrical market leader in France, has made a big effort to differentiate itself on the basis of after-sales service, although it is still a long way from life-cycle customer management. Its 'camionettes' (delivery and maintenance vehicles) generate strong recognition and affection among French consumers. And there is a role model from another industry sector. Automobile dealers used to take a similar stance to electrical retailers but, led initially by Japanese dealerships, are now placing much more emphasis on the total sales-and-service cycle of customer relationship management.

In contrast with the electrical market, the market for *home products* (from kitchens and bathrooms, through furniture, soft furnishings and home textiles, to small household items) is very open to *store brand* penetration, and many leading category killers are already predominantly own brand. The supply base is generally fragmented, production is (surprisingly) local and small-scale, and there are generally few strong producer brands. Home products retailers therefore have a tremendous opportunity to build brand differentiation through store brand development. With big-ticket items such as furniture, they can reinforce their brand values through direct customer relationships and service.

The *DIY/home improvement* market also has few strong producer brands, but the commodities such as timber, bricks and fittings which form such a large part of a DIY retailer's offer are hard to differentiate on any level. In-store service and advice, which UK DIY stores have largely stripped out to lower costs, may be the best long-term source of differentiation, again with an eye on the lifetime value of a loyal customer. Home Depot in the USA, the US retailer with the largest equity market value in 1995 after Wal-Mart, is placing a big emphasis on such services, including ideas for home improvement projects.

The *sports goods* market gives an excellent case study of brand differentiation in category killers: Decathlon in France (see Case Study 5.1).

In the *toy* market, Toys 'R' Us has focused on distributing producer brands, and has achieved an unusually dominant international leadership position and buying muscle with producers. There are good reasons in the toy market for not pushing hard into own label: strong global heavily advertised producer brands such as Barbie, Fisher-Price and Nintendo,

Case Study 5.1 Decathlon: Store Brand Differentiation in the French Sports Market

Decathlon's 130 stores and over $1.5 billion in sales account for over 25% of the French sports goods market, including sports clothing and footwear. It is a classic example of a successful category killer (see Exhibit 5.5).

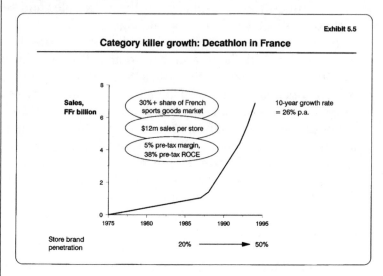

Exhibit 5.5

Category killer growth: Decathlon in France

Sales, FFr billion

- 30%+ share of French sports goods market
- $12m sales per store
- 5% pre-tax margin, 38% pre-tax ROCE

10-year growth rate = 26% p.a.

Store brand penetration 20% ——→ 50%

The sports goods market contains several of the world's strongest producer brands – Nike, Reebok and Adidas – but Decathlon has steadily built its store brand penetration up to around 50% of total sales. In certain major categories, such as bicycles and outdoor clothing, footwear and equipment, store brands account for over 80% of sales, and Decathlon has become the leading brand in the French market. (In bicycles, Decathlon retains Shimano branding on the gear mechanisms, the part of a bicycle in which real technical advances have been made and where Shimano is far and away the leading global producer.) The company employs a team of around 100 research and development engineers to design exclusive store brand sports equipment.

Decathlon also provides a fairly high level of in-store advice, service and facilities. In the superstores, customers can make use of the roller-skating rink, climbing wall and golf practice nets. The cycle shop offers technical support and workshops as well as accessories such as maps, dietary requirements, clothing and shoes.

and often very short product life-cycles. However, opportunities for differentiation on other dimensions such as service are very limited. If strong direct category killer competitors do emerge, Toys 'R' Us will need to develop some store brand offer to create brand differentiation and consumer loyalty, unless it believes it can sustain market position and profitability on volume and cost leadership alone. Based on recent results, the global producers still control the balance of power and profitability in the value chain: in 1995, Toys 'R' Us's net income collapsed by over two-thirds, while Mattel's net income doubled.

Grocery Retailing 6

The grocery sector is at the heart of the debate over the current and potential growth of retail brand power, and on the front-line in the battle with global producer brands for consumer preference and loyalty.

Grocery is central partly because of its size and significance. It is the largest sector in retailing, accounting for 30–50% of all product retail spend, depending on definitions and countries' income levels. Major developments in retailing have often begun in grocery. Self-service supermarkets emerged in America in the 1930s, and crossed to Europe in the early 1950s. Grocery retailers are leaders in the development and application of retail technology, in store and in the supply chain. On the producer side, modern marketing and brand management have grown out of mass grocery markets and the leading fmcg producers. P&G, Unilever, Coca-Cola, Kellogg's, Nestlé, Mars and their peers are world-spanning organisations with enormous resources and investments behind their global power brands.

The grocery sector has therefore been the focus of much of the recent high profile debate, in the press and among stock market analysts, on the growth of retail brands and the possible decline in power and value of leading producer brands.

The UK market provides a working example of how strong retail brands can be built up by leading grocery chains. We will begin this chapter by looking at their brand-building success and strategies.

Retail Brand-building in the Grocery Sector: The UK Model

The first, and most frequently commented on, aspect of the UK grocery market is the high level of penetration by *store brands* (see Exhibit 6.1).

The UK's 39% store brand penetration stands out head and shoulders above the other major country markets. Within the leading UK grocery chains, penetration level is even higher, and has been increasing steadily over the last 20 years (see Exhibit 6.2).

UK grocery store brand/private label ranges are now pitched and perform at a quality level similar to leading producer brands, and often have no price discount (or even a price premium) versus leading producer brands. In several categories, notably in the chilled cabinet, in deli and in fresh produce, retailers are now the primary source of innovation and value-added product development. They have been proactive in widening and developing consumers' tastes and habits, into ethnic cuisines, new types of fresh produce, and

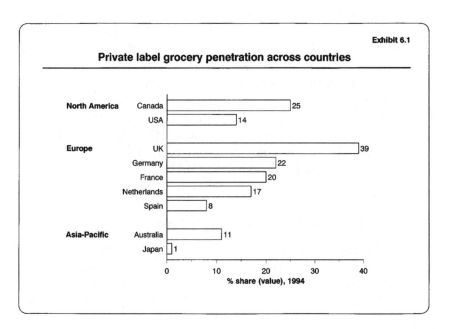

Exhibit 6.1

Private label grocery penetration across countries

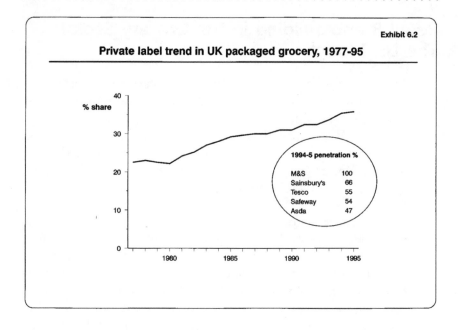

Exhibit 6.2

Private label trend in UK packaged grocery, 1977-95

1994-5 penetration %

M&S	100
Sainsbury's	66
Tesco	55
Safeway	54
Asda	47

new styles of cooking. They have also been active in 're-merchandising' or adding value into whole categories, increasing consumers' frequency of spend and willingness to spend more for quality. One of Sainsbury's tools for this is its in-house magazine, featuring the UK's leading cookery writer and TV presenter Delia Smith, which is comparable in the quality of its recipes and articles with any general distribution food magazine (and is a profitable activity in its own right).

Store brands in the UK have taken on categories dominated by some of the strongest producer brands in the grocery market. Sainsbury's introduction of Classic Cola is a good recent example (see Case Study 6.1).

Case Study 6.1   Sainsbury's Cola

The case of Sainsbury's introduction of Sainsbury's Classic Cola is already famous as an example of the power of UK grocery brands and the consequent pressure on even the strongest producer brands – in this case the symbol of fmcg consumer goods branding, Coca-Cola.

Sainsbury's was approached in 1993 by Cott, the American private label producer (see Case Study 13.3). Cott had already had considerable success in Canada and the USA with a high quality private label cola, produced by the old Royal Crown business, which was sold very successfully by, among others, Wal-Mart in the USA and Loblaw's in Canada. Cott at that time had no activity in Europe, and their representation in the UK was a one-man band. Sainsbury's already had a private label cola, made by a local UK producer, but it was of mediocre quality compared to Coke and Pepsi.

After extensive negotiation and taste tests, Sainsbury's decided to partner with Cott, and to go for a big launch commitment, at a level that surprised even Cott. At the launch in 1994, Sainsbury's created walls of Classic Cola in their stores, far more than the traditional 15–20% of shelf-space given over to private label. A 20–25% discount versus Coke, extensive in-store promotion, point-of-sale material, and 150 ml trial cans stimulated tremendous consumer awareness and trial. Coke themselves, in an atypical marketing error, compounded Sainsbury's efforts by drawing attention to the store brand in media coverage, and by promoting taste test comparisons in which Sainsbury's Cola went on to match and even out-perform Coke.

Two weeks after launch, the Sainsbury's Cola had reversed in-store market share position with Coke, and relegated Pepsi (always much weaker in markets outside the USA) to an also-ran position. The Sainsbury's Cola had achieved a 60% share in-store, and Coke had dropped to 30%. As competition settled down over the next year, and Coke responded with tough marketing and promotional campaigns, the market shares bounced around, but as the dust settled Sainsbury's brand still retained its in-store share leadership.

Building off its success with Sainsbury's, Cott has become the private label cola supplier to Safeway, Gateway/Somerfield, and Tesco (under the Virgin brand label). It now has its own bottling and canning facilities in the UK. (Cott's overall cola market share is still low despite being the supplier to most of the major multiples. Multiple grocers do not dominate cola distribution as they do many packaged grocery sectors: independents, non-grocery retail channels such as petrol stations and off-licences, and food service account for a greater share of the total market.) Sainsbury's has no exclusivity of supply arrangement with Cott; achieving a low production cost in carbonated soft drinks needs higher volumes than can be gained from only one customer, even if the customer is Sainsbury's. With the spread of quality store brand cola across most of the major multiples, cola market shares in the supermarket channel shifted dramatically in one year, and growth of the whole cola category shot up (see Exhibit 6.3).

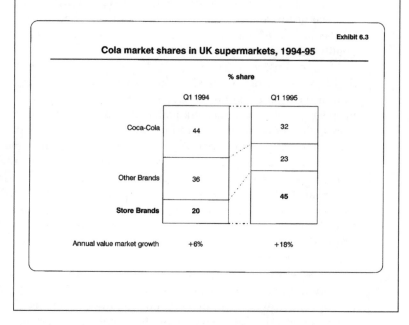

Exhibit 6.3

Cola market shares in UK supermarkets, 1994-95

% share

	Q1 1994	Q1 1995
Coca-Cola	44	32
		23
Other Brands	36	
Store Brands	20	45
Annual value market growth	+6%	+18%

The development of quality store brands/private label in UK grocery has been achieved partly by major *investment in the supply chain and supplier relationships.* For example, Sainsbury's has an in-house staff of 300 buyers and 150 technical support people. They choose their suppliers carefully and then work closely with them in developing product specifications, new products and quality control. They source globally, often pioneering new sources of supply from around the world. These characteristics are equally true of dry packaged goods, chilled prepared foods, and fresh produce. They share risks with their suppliers, encouraging investment in new products and new processing capacity and techniques. They also invest heavily in supply-chain logistics and systems.

Differentiation can be enhanced if a supply base is exclusive, and many of M&S's food suppliers work on an exclusive basis. But even without exclusivity, these investments in the supply chain and in long-term supplier partnerships are very hard to duplicate quickly, as are the ways of working that become embedded in the organisational culture.

Mass marketing has also become a tool of grocery retailers in the UK. Grocery brands (including Boots) now account for four out of the top ten umbrella brand spends in consumer goods, and their levels of spend are still increasing far faster than producer brands' (see Exhibit 6.4).

Advertising is no longer simply focused on price and promotion, but has switched to a balance of value-added messages, often recipe-based, and even lifestyle/image-based, as in several of Tesco's campaigns in the 1990s.

Building *direct customer relationships* is the next major brand-building opportunity open to the UK grocers, and they are pursuing it hard, with store/loyalty cards, micro-marketing programmes and targeted service packages (including self-scanning and pre-ordering). Safeway has one of the more sophisticated customer databases, on its 4.5 million card

Exhibit 6.4

Top 10 advertised UK grocery brands

Brand	1995 spend (£m)	% change on 1994
Kellogg's	69	0%
Sainsbury's	40	59%
Boots	39	23%
Safeway	39	119%
Persil	30	5%
Coca-Cola	29	104%
Tesco	27	-11%
Birds Eye	23	-11%
Cadbury's	22	-27%
Wall's	20	34%

holders, and has 20 people working on identifying, tracking and targeting purchase behaviour by customer segment down to line item by store. The mass marketing and direct customer relationship-building activities are being run by marketing departments of a size and sophistication comparable with the top fmcg producers: Safeway has 150 people in its marketing team, led by a Marketing Director who spent the majority of his career with Unilever and Nestlé.

The net result of this brand-building success for UK grocers (among other factors) has been profit margins far superior to their peers in any other major country market (see Exhibit 6.5). This does not mean that UK grocers do not have a lot further to go in brand-building, nor that their high levels of profitability are invulnerable. In fact, their profit levels have declined in recent years, under pressure from space growth, tight consumer spending and discounters.

The staying power of UK grocery brands has yet to be proven, and how the businesses react in difficult trading conditions will show whether they have really built up the final two elements of brand differentiation: *brand integrity* and *brand culture*. The jury is still out.

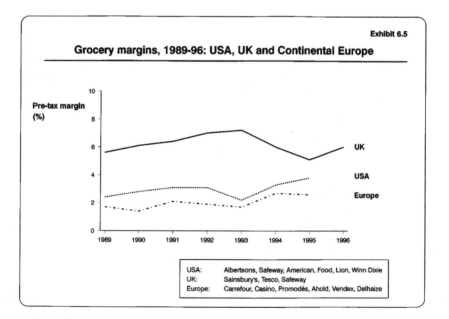

Exhibit 6.5

Grocery margins, 1989-96: USA, UK and Continental Europe

USA:	Albertsons, Safeway, American, Food, Lion, Winn Dixie
UK:	Sainsbury's, Tesco, Safeway
Europe:	Carrefour, Casino, Promodès, Ahold, Vendex, Delhaize

UK grocery brands are still barely out of diapers compared to the long-lived producer brands. Until the early 1980s, Tesco was the epitome of the 'pile-it-high, sell-it-cheap' mentality. Safeway only consolidated its brand in the late 1980s. Asda, which had until then always been positioned as a discount hypermarket chain, almost collapsed in the early 1990s. These are all young brands.

M&S and Sainsbury's have much longer-established retail brands, both positioned around 'quality and value', although M&S only developed its food business significantly in the mid-1970s. Sainsbury's is the only one of the leading grocers that can claim anything like a long-established grocery brand heritage, and even it has wobbled in the face of competitive and margin pressure in the 1990s, being drawn into discounting lines and promotional activity.

Can UK Grocery Brand-building Success be Replicated in Other Markets?

Outside the UK, and particularly in the USA, the future for both producer and retailer grocery brands has been one of the main issues of debate in marketing strategy in the 1990s. Is the UK case a 'model' for the development of other markets, or are there structural reasons why the UK model cannot, or should not, be replicated? Our own answer to this question should, given the central thesis of this book, be predictable: we believe that there are no innate structural reasons why the UK model cannot be replicated, and we believe that the retail brand-building achieved by UK grocers should be a strategic imperative for grocers in other countries. But we will lay out the arguments on both sides: the 'con' lobby, sceptical of retail brand potential, and the 'pro' lobby, our own positive view.

The first argument is based on historical data. Private label penetration in the USA has gone up and down with economic cycles. Although it has grown rapidly in the 1990s, it is still only at the same level it achieved in the 1979–81 recession, and recently growth has slowed (see Exhibit 6.6).

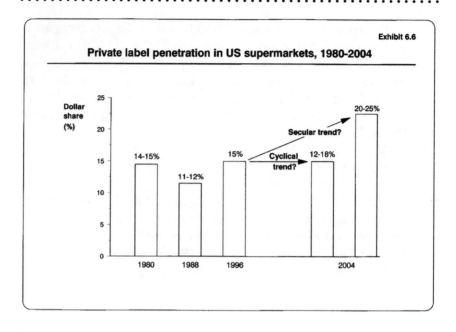

Exhibit 6.6

Private label penetration in US supermarkets, 1980-2004

The 'con' lobby argues that private label share will continue to bounce around within these parameters, and will not break through to a higher level.

Our view is that this historical cycle cannot be extrapolated into the future. In the early 1980s, US private label was at an early stage of development as cheap, often generic, product, and its share naturally slumped back as consumer spending and consumer desire for quality rebounded in the mid-1980s. Quality private label ranges along UK lines, that are now starting to be offered in the USA (and in other markets), constitute a fundamental step-change that makes extrapolation of past cycles invalid.

Private label continues to be viewed in the USA, and in several other markets, as primarily a price play in terms of consumer appeal, with market share entirely a function of the level of discount versus producer brands. This may be true in the early stages of development, but at maturity the opposite is true: private label market share is greatest in categories where it has only a small discount, or even a premium, versus producer brands. (We will return to this issue in Chapter 9.)

A second argument from the 'con' lobby is that the balance of brand power in the USA, and in other markets, is structurally much more on the producers' side than in the UK. In the USA, producer brands work off national economies of scale in production and marketing, while even the largest supermarket chains are still regional. Moreover, because of their high level of accumulated marketing investment, US consumers have been trained to 'need' the reassurance of producer brands, and are innately more loyal to them and sceptical of store brands.

There is some truth to the first part of this argument, at least in the USA. (Outside the USA, grocery retail markets are as concentrated, and sometimes more so, than in the UK.) US grocery retailing is still relatively regional, and these regional chains are facing producer brands operating nationally in the world's largest consumer market. However, even regional chains in the USA are large businesses: California alone is a consumer market as big as the UK, and market share is equally concentrated in the top few retailers (see Exhibit 6.7).

Marketing investments can be made economically on a regional basis. Producer brands' advertising-to-sales ratios

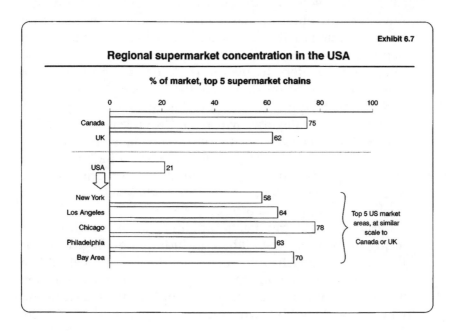

Exhibit 6.7

Regional supermarket concentration in the USA

% of market, top 5 supermarket chains

	%
Canada	75
UK	62
USA	21
New York	58
Los Angeles	64
Chicago	78
Philadelphia	63
Bay Area	70

Top 5 US market areas, at similar scale to Canada or UK

are no higher in the USA than in the UK. Moreover, leading-edge US grocery retailers such as HE Butt and Safeway are already pushing their private label activity up to towards the level of penetration, and quality of offer, characteristic of the UK chains. Wal-Mart, increasingly a major player in grocery via its Supercenter format, is increasing its commitment to its Sam's and President's Choice store brand offer; Sam's Dog Food is the highest line volume private label product in the US market. Outside the USA, in the French market Monoprix and Carrefour are making credible investments in-store brand development. Carrefour created a new sub-category in RTE cereals in the late 1980s, with its store brand chocolate-filled breakfast cereal, which was copied by Kellogg's and Quaker.

The second part of this argument, that US consumers simply 'need' producer brands more than UK consumers, has no factual or logical support. If retailers can generate strong brand values, US consumers will respond to them as much as UK consumers.

A further set of arguments from the 'con' lobby are what we would characterise as 'chicken-and-egg', and run as follows. Retailers outside the UK are unable to afford, and therefore unwilling to make, the investments necessary for brand-building. UK grocers have the luxury of fat profit margins which they can afford to throw at new products and marketing; retailers living on 1–3% net margins have no choice but to be traders. Outside the UK, limited investment in the chilled supply chain and chilled shelf-space removes a whole range of categories which the UK grocers have used as value-added spearheads of store brand development. Outside the UK, private label suppliers are unwilling to invest in joint new product development and long-term partnerships, and are not geared up to deliver high levels of product quality and supply-chain responsiveness.

Certainly these arguments capture some of the difficulties facing grocery brand-builders, including the UK grocers as they have established toe-holds in the US market. When Sainsbury's began working with Shaws, its recent acquisition in New England, it found that the supplier infrastructure and ways of working with which it was familiar in the UK were largely undeveloped in US private label suppliers. The US suppliers were used to working purely on the basis of high volume and low cost, to standard specifications, and from national production centres with long supply-chain lead-times. The idea of a close working partnership with a retailer, focused on value-added quality products, innovation, and responsiveness, was alien to most of them, and had to be slowly built up from scratch.

But the counter to these arguments is that UK grocers have fat profit margins partly *because* they have made investments in brand-building. The UK chilled chain is so well developed because M&S, followed by its competitors, made huge investments in developing it, in order to create a step-change in product quality and differentiation. The quality and responsiveness of the UK private label supplier base (which is not physically based only in the UK, but all round the world) is a result of years of investment in partnerships and ways of working. Investment creates the opportunity for further investment.

The 'con' lobby may also argue that brand-building, and particularly increasing store brand penetration, is the wrong focus for supermarket chains. Retailers' attention should be on store expansion, operational efficiency and systems. Those who push private label penetration too far will alienate many consumers who are still primarily loyal to producer brands, and who require a wide choice of producer brands, not just the top one or two. In several cases retailers have stepped back from aggressive private label strategies that crossed the threshold of consumer acceptance: A&P many years ago, Sears Roebuck more recently, possibly even Sainsbury's today in the UK.

We believe that brand-building can and should go hand in hand with a continued focus on store expansion, operational efficiency and systems. We also believe that, while there are certainly limits to store brand penetration, most grocery markets are nowhere near those limits. Provided the consumer can be brought along, by a private label offer that delivers high quality and real innovation, further store brand penetration is the right strategy, and the cornerstone of building strong retail brands in the grocery sector.

There are other arguments used by the 'con' lobby. One of the least convincing is that the UK market is somehow an uncompetitive cartel. Another is that the major fmcg producers simply will not allow the balance of power in any other market to swing as far in the retailers' favour as it has in the UK. They have now seen the UK model, understand the danger, and will make sure it does not happen again. These arguments are not very convincing.

To summarise our view, there are no innate structural differences that limit the potential application of the UK grocery retail brand-building model in other markets. Producers will undoutedly do their best to see that it does not happen, but the main determinant will be the strategies and investment philosophies of leading grocery chains. We also believe that investing in brand-building, and particularly in developing the quality and penetration of store brands, is the right strategy and a strategic imperative. The UK case provides hard, unequivocal evidence that retail brand-building can be achieved and that the result is worth the effort and risk.

Does This Mean 'The Death of [Producer] Brands'?

The potential growth in retail brand power does not inevitably lead to 'the death of [producer] brands' – a press headline often seen in recent years.

This line appeared around 'Marlboro Friday', when the announcement of deep cuts in the list price of Marlboro caused a massive downrating of stock market values for Philip Morris and many other large consumer goods producers. Marlboro's action in cigarettes has since been followed by other fmcg bastions, including P&G and Kellogg's. In parallel with the growth in private label share in the early 1990s, this led many commentators to argue that we were entering a period of terminal decline in the value of producer power brands.

Several factors could be pointed to as causing or manifesting that decline. Producer brand marketing spend had shifted, from above-the-line media investments that build brand value to below-the-line promotions and discounting that undermine it. Brand power and profitability had been diluted by a proliferation of new products and brand extensions. There was less and less real difference in product quality and innovation between producer brands, and between producer brands and private label. The increased value-chain power of retailers had driven up the difficulty and costs of obtaining retail distribution. Finally, growth in private label penetration was squeezing the share of market available to producer brands – and branded producers are helping the retailers by moving into high quality private label production to fill spare capacity.

All these factors are real, and have led to a downward pressure on the premium that even the strongest producer brands can extract, and therefore a pressure on profit margins. But for strong category leaders they do not mean 'the death of brands'. Strong category leaders still generate enormous consumer loyalty. Their owners are now adjusting their brand strategies and re-investing to make sure that that loyalty does not get eroded. Inflated list prices, which were almost always deeply discounted in practice, corrupted rather than enhanced a brand's position, and recent list price reductions are part of a logical programme for shoring up brand integrity and value. After the panic caused by Marlboro Friday, market analysts and observers have retrenched to this more balanced view of the pressures on producer brands. We will come back to the producer perspective in more detail in Chapter 13.

Segmentation in Grocery Retailing

Traditionally, market segmentation plays little real part in a grocery retailer's brand strategy and brand positioning. As with category killers, each chain and store fights for maximum share of total grocery spend by all consumers within its catchment area, and seeks to maximise that spend and that effective catchment area. (Grocery chains often define their target market as 'middle income family households' or 'family formers', that is families with young children – but this is little more than targeting the centre of gravity of the grocery market.) One of the successes of grocery chains has in fact been to concentrate more and more of consumer spending into a major weekly grocery shop, absorbing product categories that were formerly served by large numbers of small independents (delicatessens, green-grocers, butchers, bakers, fishmongers, wine merchants and liquor stores) or by other retail chains (petrol, drugstores).*

This is not to say that grocery chains do not seek to identify and serve different customer segments in store, nor that they do not tailor individual stores' ranges to fit the demographic composition of different catchment areas.

There are a few well-known exceptions to the unsegmented nature of grocery retailing, and some very successful ones, at both ends of the price/quality spectrum (see Case Study 6.2).

Case Study 6.2   Aldi and the European Hard Discounters

The major exceptions are European narrow-line discounters, of whom the best example is Aldi. Aldi focuses on a narrow range of SKUs (around 1000, compared with a normal supermarket's 20 000 or more), predominantly in dry/ambient packaged grocery with long shelf- and storage-life, and offers a range of cheap, almost exclusively private label products under a range of proprietary labels. Aldi makes no attempt to fill all a consumer's grocery shopping needs. Consumers use Aldi to stock up on basic packaged product that can be kept at home for weeks before a re-stocking trip is needed. Aldi's customer base is very broad: over 90% of German households, across all income ranges, are at least occasional customers. Aldi's total sales in Germany are around $20 billion, more than double the next largest German grocery retailer.

Warehouse clubs in the USA, in terms of their grocery offer, work in a somewhat similar fashion, with an added emphasis on very large package sizes and a large warehouse

---

* In this chapter we are not dealing with proximity retailers, many of whom are largely selling grocery product – for which see Chapter 4 – but only with larger-space supermarket formats.

environment, all to highlight the bulk-buy discount advantage for the consumer. There is, of course, a limit to how many room-sized boxes of cereal even the most avid American bargain-hunter can fit into her garage, and warehouse club growth has tailed off after its racy early years.

The 'hard discount' market is a demanding one, and requires every element of the consumer proposition and business system to be honed down and targeted strictly at the lowest cost/lowest price goal. Hard discounters like Aldi strip out every item of non-essential cost. Locations, staffing and overhead are all rock-bottom. Famous anecdotes include Aldi's cashiers memorising all line codes and prices to avoid the cost of scanners, and of bathrooms without mirrors to minimise staff time spent in them. In total, this can give Aldi an operating cost advantage versus a large conventional supermarket or hypermarket of around 7–9% of sales. In addition, Aldi works hard with suppliers to 'engineer out' non-essential features and costs from its proprietary label products; and concentration on a very narrow range allows them to offer suppliers tremendous run lengths (average annual line volumes are $30–35 million, versus $10 million per line for Carrefour's hypermarket business). The net result is that Aldi, and other hard discounters, can undercut the prices of mainstream supermarket store brands by up to 20%, and producer brands by 40% or more.

Kwik Save in the UK is a interesting halfway house between a full-range supermarket and a hard discounter. It succeeded for many years because the main grocery chains in the UK were focused on building up value-added store brand and full service store networks. But recently, faced with the entry of Continental hard discounters into the UK market, Kwik Save has found itself caught between a rock and a hard place. Its initial response has been to add value into its offer, with fresh produce, a wider range and improved service, thereby compromising and undermining its discounter economics.

In conclusion, Aldi is a segmented grocery brand. The word 'brand' may seem inappropriate when applied to a retail proposition built entirely on low cost and low price, but Aldi also differentiates itself from other hard discounters by its commitment to almost 100% own label product. Brand differentiation can be compatible with a hard discount positioning.

At the other end of the price/quality spectrum, M&S Food has carved out 5% of the UK food market with a proposition emphasising value-added prepared foods and high quality fresh produce, all 100% under the M&S/St Michael brand. Whole categories of packaged grocery are not offered at all; M&S makes no attempt to fulfil all the needs of the weekly shopping basket.

These examples show that, although most chains will continue to address the unsegmented general market, segmentation is possible in grocery retailing. As store networks are duplicated and reach saturation, with chains facing each other on the four corners of major road junctions, more retailers may find it more attractive to pursue a segmented strategy, with high market share in a limited set of customer or product groups and a clear position on the price/quality spectrum, rather than to continue to go for maximum share of aggregate catchment area grocery spend.

Hypermarkets and Supercenters

Continental European hypermarkets (Carrefour, LeClerc and the like) and their recent supercenter equivalents in the USA (run by, among others, Wal-Mart and Kmart) are combinations of grocery stores and category killers, with some functional fashion thrown in for good measure. Their most striking feature is their sheer scale: 100 000 square feet is a modest new store, 200 000 square feet is increasingly common, and some stores hit the 300 000 square feet mark. Sales per store average $100–150 million, and giant stores can top $300 million.

However, the brand-building challenges faced by these mega-stores are different from and greater than that of either grocery stores or category killers. Food (in its broad grocery sense) is a regular weekly shop, while the buying of major non-food items such as electrical or DIY is a distinct, planned purchase occasion, where consumers will seek out the authority specialist. Category killers work by delivering total authority and clarity of positioning. Hypermarkets rarely succeed in matching category killers in any particular category, as they have to allocate resources, attention and shelf space across so many product groups.

Hypermarkets are also drawn into spreading their store brand/private label efforts too wide too early, before they have built up real differentiation in any one particular category. In many non-food categories the challenge of building quality private label is greater than in food, and inferior product performance risks undermining overall brand image.

Also, compared to grocery stores, US supercenters require a massive catchment area for their economies of scale to work. The majority of consumers on their regular weekly grocery shop are unlikely to trade in their smaller, closer-to-home supermarkets for remote supercenters.

We should also note that the hypermarket/supercenter proposition is fundamentally supply-driven rather than customer-driven. French hypers, coming from a grocery base, have simply added in more new categories as they have found it marginally profitable to do so, initially in very limited ranges. US supercenters, coming from a general merchandise base, added in grocery because they were envious of the visit frequency of grocery store customers, which is 80 times per year versus 30–40 times for general merchandise stores.

Hypermarkets and supercenters represent the end of the last wave of retail development, focused on scale and operating efficiencies, rather than the new wave of brand-building and differentiation. Faced with effective category killers, French hypers have been steadily losing share in non-food categories (including commodity fashion, where out-of-town or edge-of-town self-service formats like Halles aux Chaussures in shoes have become market leaders). Faced with effective, brand-differentiated supermarkets closer to and focused on their local customers, US supercenters will have a hard time in grocery.

Summary of Part II: Brand-building Strategies in Four Sectors

Repertoire Retailing: Fashion and Home Lifestyle

Brands in repertoire retailing, both fashion and home lifestyle, can be as strong as the strongest producer brands.

Fashion retailers can use the full range of segmentation and differentiation approaches and tools in their brand-building strategies. The most important and powerful is the development of a strong and distinctive store brand range, supported by investment in managing the complex fashion supply chain. Like producer brands, they have the opportunity of distribution through a mix of sales channels, although they must retain some exclusivity and competitive distinction for their core own stores.

By default, department stores are increasingly becoming large-space repertoire retailers, focusing on fashion and home lifestyle categories. They need to make this repertoire retailing role work, by meeting the challenge of brand-building as both a producer brand showcase and as a provider of quality store brands.

Home products occupy a position in the retail market that is a mixture of fashion repertoire shopping and the more functional shopping of category killers. Home lifestyle products can represent fashion choices for the home living environment, and brand-building strategies can be similar to fashion retailers.

Proximity Retailing

The chemist/drugstore market is unusual in proximity retailing: the health and beauty product core provides a strong platform on which to build brand loyalty and differentiation. Elsewhere across the sector, brand-building is a particularly hard challenge, unless a retailer is leveraging a strength in store brands/private label from a core position in another, large-scale retailing sector, such as Tesco with its Tesco Metro format.

Category Killers

Strong retail brands can be developed in category killer destination retailing, and will become the central driver of competitive performance and profitability as category killer markets mature. Defining the target product market, or 'which category to kill', and sticking to it, are key elements of a successful brand strategy. Developing a strong store brand/ private label offer is also key, and has been achieved by retailers of home products and sports goods.

Where destination retail sectors are dominated by producer brands, and there are real barriers to store brand development, category killers may have to depend on other sources of brand differentiation, particularly service and the creation of long-term direct customer relationships.

Grocery Retailing

The grocery sector is at the heart of the debate over the current and potential growth of retail brand power, and on the front-line in the battle with global producer brands for consumer preference and loyalty.

The UK provides a concrete case of how grocery retailers can become very strong differentiated retail brands. Their key differentiation strategy is based on the development of quality store brands/private label, supported by investment in the supply chain and supplier relationships. Another key weapon is the building of strong direct customer relationships, which supermarkets are in a unique position to be able to do, and which should prove even more effective long-run than investments in mass marketing.

There are no innate reasons why the UK grocery model of retail brand development cannot be replicated in other markets, including the USA, if leading grocery retailers make the necessary commitment to long-term brand-building investment. Arguments that the UK is somehow 'different' do not hold water. Several US grocers are making good progress in building their brands, and the recent growth in store brand/private label share will prove to be a secular rather than a cyclical trend.

Although most chains will continue to address the unsegmented general market, segmentation is possible in grocery retailing. As store networks are duplicated and reach saturation, more retailers may find it more attractive to pursue a segmented strategy, targeting limited sets of customer or product groups with clear positions on the price/quality spectrum, than to continue to go for maximum share of aggregate catchment area grocery spend.

Hypermarkets and supercenters face particularly tough brand-building challenges, caused by their combination of non-food (competing with category killers) and food (competing with local, close-to-customer supermarkets).

*   *   *

In *Part III* of the book we turn to the practical issues involved in managing retail brands. We look at brand management processes and organisation, and at how retailers can manage investment in brand-building.

Part III
Managing Retail Brands

Managing Multiplicity: 7
The Detail in Retail

In Chapter 2 we argued that one of the primary differences between retail brands and producer brands is the sheer multiplicity of retail brand attributes, and the difficulty that this multiplicity creates for retail brand management. We compared the two dozen or so attributes of the Mars Bar brand with the millions of attributes of the Tesco brand – the customer's experience of Tesco being a combination of all the products she buys there (range, price, quality, etc.), the shopping environment and the service level. We also observed the very high rate of change in attributes of a retail brand, given line and staff turnover.

A producer brand can be managed in a very centralised and tightly controlled way. Brand strategies can be committed to paper in half-page memos that will capture the essential decisions for the brand and will not change materially from month to month, or even year to year. Senior management will be involved in, and can determine, every material change to any of the 10 or 20 key attributes that make up the brand, and those changes will be the subject of extensive research, analysis and debate. Systematic quality control at the point of production can provide a reasonable guarantee of consistent brand delivery.

The contrast with a retail brand is enormous. Half-page strategy statements can provide broad guidelines on brand positioning, but will not capture any of the actual detailed decisions (on range, pricing, promotion, service) that make up the retail proposition as experienced by the consumer. These detailed decisions are being made constantly, at all levels up and down the organisation, and the brand proposition is constantly evolving. Senior management cannot hope to be involved in even a significant minority of these decisions. Centralised quality control is not an option: customers experience and rate the brand based on their most recent visit to their local store, on the attitude of the check-out operator or the on-shelf quality of fresh produce.

Managing the Detail in Retail

The day-to-day problems and frustrations involved in managing a retail brand, as compared with running a producer brand, stem from this enormous multiplicity of brand attributes and their constant high rate of change.

Retail CEOs and senior managers find it hard to achieve a retail brand management process that works as coherently and effectively as the P&G fmcg model. They cannot focus strategic attention on short and simple statements of brand strategy and positioning, that are also powerful, concrete and actionable, and that don't change from month to month. They cannot avoid having to worry about whether the bad attitude of a $6/hour checkout operator has just wiped out 15 years of careful loyalty-building with 100 customers in Dayton or Leeds.

It is here that the fmcg-experienced manager has to make the greatest changes in mindset. The careful, centralised decision-making and control processes of an fmcg brand don't work in retail. Somehow the CEO and senior managers have to find a different day-to-day organisational and operational way of managing the business, so as to preserve the integrity of a brand's intended core values through the chaos of thousands of daily de-centralised decisions and customer interactions. Executing retail brand management involves a combination of decision processes and operational controls, embracing a continuous set of 'feedback loops', from store to centre, from customer to retailer, from actual sales to buying and stock management.

We have observed two key characteristics of successful management practice on the part of a retail business's Chief Executive and his senior management team, particularly the three market-facing functional heads of B&M, Marketing and Store Operations: getting into the detail and out into the field; encouraging experimentation within the brand strategy; and developing effective head office decision support systems.

Getting into the Details and out into the Field

The old maxim that 'retail is detail' holds true. Retail management has to lead by example in mastering and managing the details of the business, and in 'getting their hands dirty' out in the field. Although the number of decisions involved are too many to be made by senior management alone, they must be informed about and involved in a large proportion of them, to provide a decision-making role model for junior staff and to establish the principles of quality control over those decisions. A brand strategy only becomes real for a retail organisation insofar as it is manifested in small, specific concrete instances.

There are five key components of 'managing the detail in retail' (see Exhibit 7.1).

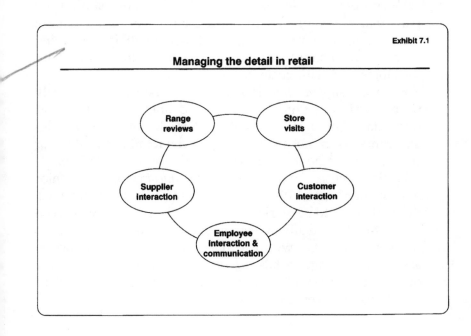

Exhibit 7.1

Managing the detail in retail

Range reviews

Store visits

Supplier interaction

Customer interaction

Employee interaction & communication

First, *range reviews*. Detailed, hands-on range reviews, at item- and category-level, and including competitors' as well as own products, are the cornerstones of retail decision-making. The Chief Executive and the senior team must be involved deeply and frequently in these reviews, which can easily take a day per category every few months.

Secondly, *store visits*, to own and competitors' stores. Senior management must be able to 'walk the store' and comment on the in-store effectiveness of ranges, display, layout, category management, promotions and service standards, and compare best practice across own stores and competitors' stores. Senior management's ability to do this effectively sets the standard for junior management and shop floor staff, and is one of the most powerful ways of generating respect, commitment and a common brand vision down through the organisation.

Thirdly, *customer interaction*. Senior management must actively seek frequent, no-holds-barred dialogues with customers, via store visits and consumer panels. The latter cannot be delegated to a market research function: there is no substitute for personally hearing customers' views on own and competitive stores. The B&M function should be particularly encouraged to participate in consumer panels; there is often a temptation for B&M to 'hole up' in the buying office, or with suppliers, and not risk direct interaction with the stores and with customers.

Fourthly, *supplier interaction*. Retail managers, particularly from B&M, must go to their store brand suppliers and understand the details of the supplier's business, economics and concerns, rather than waiting in the retail head office for suppliers to come to them with slide-show presentations.

Lastly, *employee interaction and communication*. Even if senior management gets fully involved in the first four elements, this still needs to be worked on separately. Range reviews can be confined to relatively senior management, store visits to 'walking the store' with just the store manager. Interaction and communication has to occur with all levels of the organisation, down to the most junior shop floor staff or warehouse worker.

One of senior management's priority goals must be to develop a set of 'reflexes' throughout the organisation, down to the trainee buyer and checkout clerk, that manifest as consistent as possible an interpretation of how the brand is intended to be positioned with its customers. The key to developing these reflexes is *clear, persistent communication* right down through the organisation. Getting into the details and out into the field is in itself a powerful way of communicating brand values and connecting with the organisation: it sets standards and sends the right signals to employees. Public recognition of excellence, such as out-standing in-store customer service or a runaway new product success developed by a junior buyer, are a powerful way of making brand objectives real and concrete for everyone in the organisation. Interaction and communication must also be regular and persistent: as with brand value itself, the creation of a consistent brand culture is the result of cumulative effort over time. Many retailers now use 'Monday morning videos', sent out to every store weekly, as a way of communicating values and exciting new developments in the business to every employee across the store network.

Getting into the details and out into the field should take up a large proportion, possibly the majority, of senior manage-ment time. This is particularly true for very large businesses where the sheer size of the management task can lead to senior management spending most of their week preparing for and holding head office meetings.

Finding the right balance for this involvement is critical. Junior management must still take responsibility for the individual decisions. They must be encouraged to learn through trial and error, and allowed to try and fail. There must be a balance of challenge or criticism with praise and recognition of achievement, and clear feedback must be given. Senior management is involved in the detail in order to institutionalise a set of decision-making reflexes and cap-abilities, not to make the organisation dependent on their individual retailing abilities. The involvement must also be clearly structured in order to be productive, and senior management must have a clear agenda and checklist for the range reviews and store visits. Random and incoherent interventions are often as dangerous as total delegation.

Sam Walton epitomised this characteristic of successful top-level retail management. Right up to his death he was still involved in extensive range reviews at Wal-Mart, and visited several stores every week, where he showed detailed knowledge of sales performance down to item level. M&S is another well known example, with board meetings given over to detailed merchandise reviews.

There is no substitute in retailing for this familiarity with and attention to detail. The retail Chief Executive who believes his job is to set policy, direction and structure and to delegate details and execution to his staff will most likely fail, as will the B&M Director, and so on down the organisation. In a similar vein, the retail Chief Executive who concentrates his attention, and that of his top team, only on top-level brand strategy issues and statements (which are so central in fmcg producer brand management) will have difficulty in succeeding with retail brand management.

Encouraging Experimentation Within Brand Strategy

More than in many industries, strategy in retail businesses is evolutionary. Senior management can begin with a clear but general idea of brand positioning and objectives, but then has to let that idea evolve in response to actual events out in the stores. Given the diversity of what makes up a retail proposition, a top-level strategy statement has no chance of capturing all the possibilities opened up in actual trading. Many of the most effective innovations in McDonald's came from experimentation by local franchisees, trying out a new product idea, a new way of improving quality or customer service, or a new marketing initiative in their local community. Failure to be open-minded and flexible, encouraging experimentation and responding to what sells and does not sell, will limit a retail brand's potential.

Moreover, compared with the lead-times and costs of experimentation in producer brands, experimentation in retail is cheap and quick. New products or store initiatives can be tested in a few stores without large investment or risk of hurting the brand, and consumer feedback is direct and immediate. This does not mean that experimentation can be sloppy: tests need to be rigorously set up, with objectively-selected control stores against which to measure results. Nor can experimentation be allowed to run wild, out of the control and oversight of head office.

Developing Effective Head Office Management and Decision Support Systems

Given the mountain of detail involved in retail management, and the obligation to work at a detailed level, effective management and decision support systems ('DSS') are an absolute necessity.

The twin cornerstones of retail management information systems are sales and stock tracking, and the management accounts. In combination, these can provide internal data that track performance (revenue, cost, profit and assets) down to store and line level and back up to region and category level. Most retailers rely on this combination for 99% of their head office monitoring and control. Within these cornerstones are several key performance indicators ('KPIs') of trend in brand strength or weakness: like-for-like ('LFL') same-store sales trends; trends in real price levels; mix changes between categories and in-store brand category share, and trends in gross margin before and after discount/markdown/clearance costs.

Our objective here is not to provide a comprehensive review of retail MIS/DSS, but to highlight where the internal focus of most retailers' information systems needs to be supplemented or fine-tuned to provide a more effective set of tools for retail brand management. In the main, this involves supplementing existing internal data with external data and combining the two to track brand performance.

Exhibit 7.2

Brand sales performance KPI

	% Annual change		
	Own Stores	Competitors	
		A	B
Total sales (nominal)	+10.0	+ 5.0	+12.0
LFL/Same-store sales (nominal)	+ 5.0	+ 7.5	+ 2.5
Relevant category RPI	+ 3.5	+ 3.5	+ 3.5
LFL/Same-store sales (real)	+ 1.5	+ 4.0	(1.0)
Relevant category market volume	+ 2.5	+ 2.5	+ 2.5
LFL/Same-store volume vs market	(1.0)	+ 1.5	(3.5)
Retail capacity (sq. ft.)	+ 1.5	+ 1.5	+ 1.5
Capacity-adjusted LFL/same-store volume vs market	+ 0.5	+ 3.0	(2.0)

For example, internal nominal sales performance needs to be set in the context of inflation, aggregate market performance, the sales performance of key competitors, and the rate of growth in retail capacity. The resulting KPI provides a true indicator of *brand sales performance* (see Exhibit 7.2).

Sales performance information needs to be supplemented with disaggregated detail on *consumer purchase behaviour.* Point-of-sales data can provide information on changes in the mix of average items purchased, average item value, and average transaction value. Combined with store card information, changes in sales mix across different customer groups can be tracked. This internal data needs to be regularly fleshed out with surveys that track changes in the catchment area of a store, in consumer visit frequency, and in stores' share of total consumer spend in relevant categories (see Exhibit 7.3).

Internal data needs to be regularly supplemented with *external competitive monitoring.* Regular checks need to be made of competitors' basket and KVI pricing, of range breadth and depth, and of the mix and positioning of store brands. Consumers need to be regularly surveyed to track

Retail Brands . . .

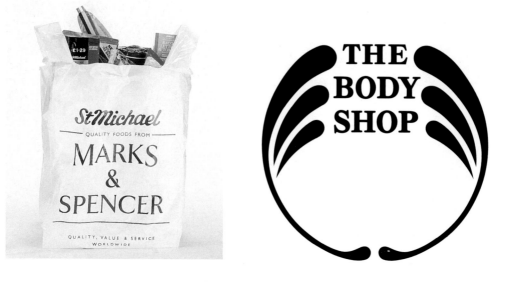

habitat

VISA

CONFORAMA

Le pays où la vie  *est moins chère.*

SEARS

. . . can they become 'The Real Thing'?

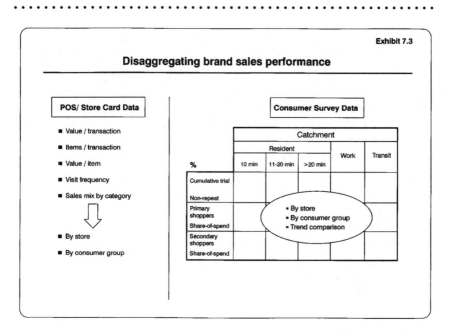

Exhibit 7.3

Disaggregating brand sales performance

changes in their attitudes and behaviour *vis-à-vis* the key competitors, and the reasons for those changes. Finally, the financial performance of key competitors needs to be reviewed and analysed, for comparison with a retailer's own business and to understand the reasons for positive and negative changes.

One final external information monitor is the tracking of *supplier base and supplier performance.* There needs to be a regular review, at least annually, of the composition and concentration of the supplier base, and the rate of turnover of suppliers, particularly suppliers of store brand product. For all suppliers, financial performance also needs to be reviewed, as does individual sales and service performance for the retailer.

Internal MIS and DSS need to be structured around *exception reporting of line, category and store performance.* Too many systems are comprehensive in their coverage of the enormous detail of the retail proposition. Management needs to be able to focus in quickly on unusually good or bad performance, to take corrective action and/or to learn lessons (negative and positive) to apply broadly across the business.

This need for exception reporting is particularly acute with B&M, which can otherwise drown in detail and be slow to identify and respond to problems and opportunities.

The internal MIS/DSS of a retail brand-builder needs to provide a particular depth of coverage in *monitoring store brand performance*. A brand-building management will be very interested in short- and long-run trends in relative price and relative rate-of-sale of store brands versus producer brands, at product and category level.

As retailers increasingly invest in brand marketing at the same level as producer brands, they need to add certain DSS tools commonly used by those producer brands to monitor *advertising spend*. In analysing share-of-voice versus share-of-market, market leaders will expect to gain some economies of scale in advertising, while market followers will need to invest at a higher ratio to sales.

Lastly, we would propose a periodic monitoring and review of *overall brand investment*. This would include the investments in brand differentiation discussed later in Part III: store brands, the brand–customer relationship, and brand integrity. Some of these areas involve subjective judgement rather than hard, objective data, but the review process will focus senior management attention on the brand-building goal, on maintaining a commitment to long-term investment, and on tracking the progress achieved.

Organising for Retail Brand Management 8

In fmcg producer organisations, the Marketing function, and specifically the brand manager, has been and continues to be king or queen. The brand manager drives brand strategy and marketing execution. The sales and production functions, while they work as a team with the brand manager and are equally essential to business results, at the end of the day carry less weight. This organisational structure, with its clear centre of authority, is simple and effective.

In retail brand management, organisational structure and authority are more complex. In most retail organisations, the centre of organisational power under the CEO has usually been the trading, or buying and merchandising (B&M), function. A marketing function often does not exist. If it does, it is likely to be subordinate to the trading function, whether reporting to the Trading Director or to the CEO, and more likely to focus on promotional execution than on brand strategy. The fmcg role of 'brand manager' does not exist today in retailing; at the end of the day, the CEO resolves brand management debates.

Moreover, because of the decentralised nature of the retail brand management process, the role and supremacy of the fmcg Brand Manager cannot be transplanted into the retailing environment. Retailers committed to brand-building need to find new organisational solutions for brand management.

The Conventional Retail Organisation

In the mid-1980s, most retail organisation structures typically looked like that in Exhibit 8.1.

123

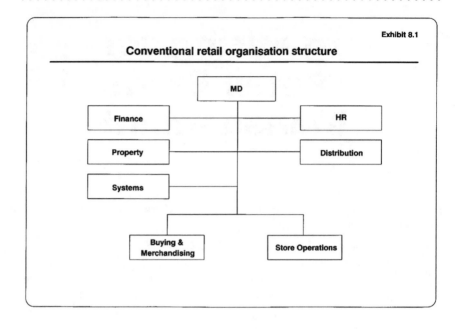

Exhibit 8.1

Conventional retail organisation structure

In this conventional organisation, the key centre of authority beneath the Chief Executive or Managing Director is B&M (or 'Trading'). B&M controls most of the decisions determining the retail proposition: range, pricing, sourcing and supplier relationships, buying terms and gross margin, promotional activity, planogramming.

The next strongest centre of authority is Store Operations, which runs the stores and in-store service levels. Store Operations will have an input into promotional programmes and in-store layout including planogramming, and into store look and ambience, but essentially acts as a service function relative to the authority of B&M, similar to the balance of weight between production and marketing in an fmcg producer organisation. Store Operations will have more organisational weight when a chain is expanding rapidly, and business performance is more dependent on new site selection, on store openings and on ramping up new-store sales volume over the first two or three years.

This organisational model is of a centralised, sophisticated retail business. There are still retailers operating with an older model of decentralised, store-level management and decision-making, where store managers continue to make the majority of the B&M decisions. Several large hypermarkets in France are still surprisingly decentralised, despite being very large businesses (as chains and as individual stores): local store managers make most of the range and pricing decisions, and central buying is a subsidiary service function, providing lists of approved vendors and negotiating overall volume-based buying terms. One of the leading French menswear fashion chains, Armand Thierry, left range selection, buying and pricing up to local store managers until only a few years ago. Several department store chains also still place much B&M authority and decision-making in the hands of individual store managers.

However, the majority of large retail businesses in Europe and North America have moved on to the 'conventional' centralised organisation model, with authority centred in the B&M function. As strategy consultants, when we work with a retail client our key 'constituency' beneath the CEO is the B&M Director and the B&M organisation; if they do not get behind our conclusions and recommendations, there is little chance of successful implementation, even with the full support of the CEO.

The Conventional Retail Organisation Under Attack

Today, this conventional structure is everywhere already under attack and evolving. The B&M function is being unbundled into different skill blocks, such as 'product and supplier selection' versus 'supply-chain management'. The discretion and autonomy of buyers is being challenged by the need for more systematic approaches to range/price architecture and category management. The growth of store brands demands customer-focused product development as well as supplier-focused negotiation of buying terms. Store Operations has already had to go through enormous change in the shift from decentralised to centralised organisations, and store managers have had to come to terms with a major reduction in the scope of their authority. Central IT is being decentralised into user applications. Distribution and ware-housing is having to develop into 'total supply-chain management'.

The demands of retail brand management will bring further pressures for change. The main organisational impact will be in two areas: further changes in the role of the core B&M function, and the creation of a new strong Marketing function. How the new B&M and Marketing functions operate, and how they interact with each other, will be critical to successful retail brand management.

The Need for a New Strong Marketing Function

Many large retail businesses still have no Marketing function, or have only a token one with limited resources and authority. Retail Chief Executives and Operating Boards are still asking themselves: 'Should there be a Marketing function at all? If yes, what should it do, what should it not do, and where should it report? What conflicts will arise with the rest of the organisation, particularly B&M, and can they be managed?'

The short answer is that any retailer committed to brand-building needs to have a strong, professional, dedicated Marketing function.

The Marketing function is needed partly to manage the large investments that a retail brand-builder needs to make in marketing its brand. Advertising budgets for retail brands are now significant and growing fast in real terms. Database technology that enables the development of direct customer relationships and individualised marketing is expensive to acquire and to run effectively. The level, frequency and complexity of promotional activity has grown in the price-sensitive competitive environment of the 1990s.

Over and above the sheer management task, a strong Marketing function is needed to help move a retail business from a 'trading' to a 'brand management' mentality. Brand stewardship has historically been left, largely by default, up to the B&M function. This can work, if the senior B&M team shares an understanding of and commitment to the long-term brand-building process. But often B&M bears the brunt of short-term pressure in sales volume and margins, and finds it difficult to combine the short- and long-term perspective. A strong Marketing function should 'carry the flame' for the long-term brand-building goal, and act as a counter-weight to the temptation to over-react to short-term trading problems.

A better way to phrase the question posed above might be: 'Are there any types of retail business which could logically justify the absence of a Marketing function in the mid-1990s, apart from small businesses where the MD or B&M head can personally perform the Marketing function without the cost of a separate manager or department?'

The most obvious candidates would be businesses with little marketing investment to manage and little prospect or intention of long-term brand-building. Characteristics could include: low or zero store brand penetration, and no plans to develop private label; prime in-town high street locations which 'advertise' the business by themselves; immaterial media spends, say less than 1% of sales; consumer shopping behaviour which will not respond to, and therefore will not justify investment in, building long-term direct customer relationships; and, possibly, a marketplace or competitive positioning based single-mindedly on low price.

Several proximity retailers might fit this bill. Their retail proposition is highly functional, based on location convenience rather than brand–customer relationships, and a Marketing function might find it hard to add any value. Some hard discount businesses in other retail sectors could also match these characteristics, and the overhead cost of a Marketing function could be an unnecessary luxury.

But the vast majority of large-scale retail businesses would not have a strong rationale for the absence of a Marketing function. Even very price-driven businesses such as out-of-town category killers in electrical or DIY have large advertising budgets to draw consumers to their destination locations, the opportunity to create long-term direct customer relationships, and the possibility of developing store brand penetration.

We would argue that the onus should be on a business to demonstrate why it does *not* need a dedicated, professional Marketing function, not the other way round.

What Should the Marketing Function do and not do? Where Should it Report?

The retail Marketing function should manage the *classic fmcg marketing activities*: advertising and media; image communications and PR; promotions; and non-product-specific consumer/competitive research, such as competitive usage and attitude (U&A) surveys. It should also manage all activities relating to the *development of direct customer relationships*, including store cards, loyalty schemes, and customer sales and service databases. (Operational execution of these activities may be 'contracted out', to in-house or external groups – execution of store card programmes, data processing and database management, after-sales service for electrical retailers – but Marketing should be responsible for overall planning and coordination.) In the case of fashion retailers with a strong style point of view, where window look and store ambience are crucial elements of the brand statement, Marketing should also take on responsibility for '*store look*': front store design, window display, and visual merchandising. (In other retail businesses, physical store design should rest firmly within the remit of Store Operations, and product layout and planogramming within B&M.)

Equally important to define is what the retail Marketing function should *not* take on and *not* be – particularly in terms of its role relative to B&M. It should not become an alternative B&M planning department: it should not take on the responsibility for category and space planning, including DPP analysis. This must remain clearly within B&M's remit – or, more precisely in the modern retail management structure, within the 'Product and Supplier Selection' group in B&M. If these planning skills are not adequately present today, they should be built in to the B&M organisation. The intersection of B&M and Marketing's roles in driving overall brand positioning occurs in *category management*, which we will deal with fully later in this chapter.

In assessing where the Marketing function should report, the onus should again be on the business to demonstrate why it should not report directly to the CEO/MD, on a level with the other key line and support functions. In the proximity or hard discount businesses mentioned earlier, where the Marketing role is extremely limited and its main focus is short-term promotional activity, it may be more practical and efficient to have Marketing as a sub-function within B&M. But in most cases Marketing will warrant a direct report to the MD.

Unbundling the B&M Function

Quite apart from the changes involved in moving to retail brand management, the conventional B&M organisation is already under pressure and facing structural change.

Conventionally, B&M has been organised around categories or product groups. Within a particular category – say electrical brown goods in a hypermarket – the senior B&M manager is the Buyer. Underneath the Buyer are Buying Assistants and Merchandisers. This B&M sub-team handles the whole spectrum of decisions and tasks relating to product range, pricing, supplier selection and management, stock management, and space planning.

The strains on this organisational model are most apparent in businesses with a high proportion of private label product, of which fashion retailers are the clearest example. A young fashion buyer is expected to handle a wide range of skills and activities: range design with a strong style point of view, finding suppliers (domestic and overseas) and negotiating buying terms, overseeing product delivery and stock allocation to stores, and directing pricing policy including markdown and clearance. In practice these skills are hard to find in one person. A talented fashion designer may be very poor at supplier negotiation, and vice versa. A good merchandiser, effective at stock management and pricing/markdowns, may be out of his or her depth if asked to take on range design and buying responsibilities.

Fashion retailers are now beginning to 'unbundle' the B&M function, recognising three distinct skill sets. First, range planning and range design, which requires a talent for leading, or quickly picking up on, fashion trends. Secondly, supplier selection and supplier management, which requires hard-nosed negotiating skills, an understanding of supplier production economics, and an ability to manage quality control and supplier service levels. Thirdly, stock management, which requires an analytic capacity to manage store allocation and replenishment, stock levels and delivery cycles throughout the supply chain, and optimisation of pricing policy to maximise revenue from existing and committed stocks.

These principles from fashion retailing can be generalised to many other retail businesses, particularly ones with high store brand penetration or the strategic intention of developing store brands. We use the following three classifications for the 'unbundled' elements of B&M.

Range Management is the primary sub-function, determining the shape of the retail proposition. It includes specifying range and price architecture, and space planning and space allocation. Importantly for retail brand development, it includes responsibility for store brand strategy and consequent product range design and development.

Supplier Management is the secondary sub-function, servicing but working very closely with Range Management. In initial sourcing of new suppliers, or in the development of whole new store brand categories, the two functions will work hand in hand, making joint visits to suppliers to understand quality and economics and select suppliers. As category strategies and supplier relationships mature, the supplier management function should take over most of the day-to-day responsibilities for maintaining strong supplier relationships: quality control, reviews of supplier service levels, negotiation of supplier contracts.

The third sub-function we call *Stock Management*, and it services both the Range Management and Supplier Management sub-functions. Its responsibilities are to monitor and control the flow of stock through the total supply chain, from supplier through central warehousing to in-store; and to maximise the revenue potential of that stock via store-level replenishment and markdown management. This sub-function should be the 'data warehouse' within B&M, being the central source for collection and analysis of point-of-sale and stock information. As a data warehouse, it services Range Management in periodic range planning reviews with information on rates-of-sale and realised gross margins by product line and product group, and with DPP analysis incorporating returns on space allocation; and it services Supplier Management with information on supplier performance, both line sales and profitability and service levels. It also manages the liaison between B&M and in-house or contracted logistics operations (see Exhibit 8.2).

Although we call this process the 'unbundling' of the B&M function, in practice these sub-functions continue to work as a closely integrated team within their respective product categories. They will physically share the same open-plan office space, with desks right next to each other, total transparency of information, and pooled performance-related compensation.

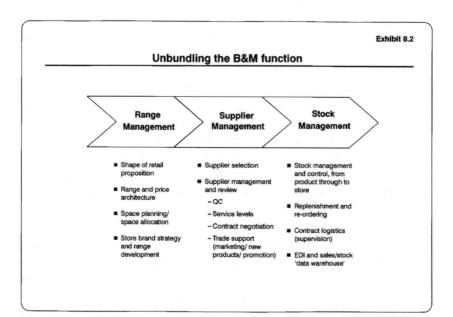

Exhibit 8.2

Unbundling the B&M function

Range Management	Supplier Management	Stock Management
▪ Shape of retail proposition	▪ Supplier selection	▪ Stock management and control, from product through to store
▪ Range and price architecture	▪ Supplier management and review	
▪ Space planning/ space allocation	– QC	▪ Replenishment and re-ordering
	– Service levels	
	– Contract negotiation	▪ Contract logistics (supervision)
▪ Store brand strategy and range development	– Trade support (marketing/ new products/ promotion)	▪ EDI and sales/stock 'data warehouse'

The Strategic Intersection of B&M and Marketing: Category Management

The intersection of B&M and Marketing is the heart of retail brand management, and its focus is category management. Line accountability and day-to-day responsibility for category management must continue to rest within B&M. However, Marketing needs to be an equal partner in setting the broad parameters within which category management occurs, in the context of the long-term objectives of brand-building. Marketing's involvement should centre on two key elements of brand strategy.

First, *overall category strategy*. For each category, the business needs to determine its top-level strategy versus competition: what role the category should play in the overall retail proposition (from core to ancillary, and from traffic-builder to profit-earner); what space to allocate to the category; what breadth of range and price points to offer; where to beat, match or not take on the main competitors; and how to establish price positioning with customers, via basket pricing, KVIs and promotions.

Secondly, *store brand strategy*. The business needs to determine which categories should be the focus for store brand development, and what the strategic objectives of store brand development are within each category. Strategic objectives could include: offering value alternatives to producer brands; offering quality alternatives to producer brands; and innovative development of new products and the 're-merchandising' of a category. Marketing also needs to make a strong input into product branding decisions: should all private label, across a wide range of price and quality, be packaged under one store brand, or should there be proprietary sub-brands targeted at different categories or at different price/quality points?

These two elements of brand strategy need to be formally reviewed between Marketing and B&M – specifically, the Range Management team within B&M – around every six months. If reviewed any more frequently, decision processes will become too bureaucratic and over-managed, and B&M

will lose its ability to respond to the marketplace and its accountability for trading performance. If reviewed less frequently, trading execution will be in danger of diverging from brand strategy.

Who is the 'Brand Manager' and 'Brand Champion' for a Retail Brand?

In fmcg producer businesses, the answer to this central question is usually straightforward. The Marketing function is dominant in the organisation. Within Marketing, the brand manager is king or queen. The answer in retail is rather more complex.

The ultimate strategist for the brand, determining long-term direction and top-level policy, must be the Chief Executive or Managing Director. He or she is also arbiter of last resort when major differences of opinion arise among functional heads as to how to interpret and apply, on a practical day-to-day basis, the long-term brand strategy.

On a day-to-day basis, however, retail brand management is a complex team effort. The core senior team is the 'four-hander' of the Chief Executive, the B&M Director, the Marketing Director, and the Director of Store Operations. This team represents the market-facing elements of the retail proposition, and forms the 'inner circle' of brand strategy and brand management. This team is supported by an 'outer circle' of the heads of the key support functions: logistics (distribution and warehousing), IT, property, finance, human resources, and technical/after-sales support.

For the business to run well, and for the brand to develop consistently in the right direction, the long-term brand strategy must be as concrete as possible and clearly articulated; the functional heads must have a deep shared understanding as to how that strategy converts down into individual tactical decisions; and they must be able to push that understanding down into their own functional organisations.

Investing in Store Brands 9

One of the key characteristics of brand-building retailers, compared to retail traders, is an investment mentality: a willingness to make consistent, patient investment in building the brand franchise over the long term. This characteristic is what producers argue is lacking in many retailers.

In the balance of this section we explore three key dimensions of brand-building investment. We begin with investment in store brands, particularly store brands that deliver quality comparable with producer brands, and even go on to take on a market leadership role. High penetration of high quality, differentiated store brands is perhaps the most common and distinctive characteristic of the world's strongest retail brands today. While strong retail brands can be built up without high store brand penetration, these are very much the exception, and are likely to be far more difficult to sustain in the long run (see Box 9.1).

> ### Box 9.1 Store Brand Terminology
>
> A brief word on terminology. Retailers, producers and industry observers use many terms to describe store brands. 'Private label' and 'own label' are synonymous. 'Store brand' is also often used synonymously, but many commentators are now coming to distinguish the latter term, using it to refer to product ranges branded exclusively with the store or fascia brand and of a higher quality than early, cheap private label offers. 'Private label' sounds intrinsically rather pejorative, denying retailers the endorsement of the word 'brand'. We generally use 'store brands' throughout as a catch-all term, embracing all variants of 'private label', 'own label' and 'store brands', whether fascia-branded or using other proprietary brand names.

Store brands embrace a wide range of quality and price positionings. We need to begin by looking at the different stages and levels of store brand development.

The Stages of Store Brand Development

There are five stages in the development of store brands, roughly matching the stages of maturity and power of the retail brand (see Exhibit 9.1).

Generics, typically in plain white or brown packaging labelled 'CIGARETTES' or 'SOAP', are commodity offers based on simple product functionality and very low prices. In certain cases they can acquire a kind of inverse chic appeal in their deliberate eschewal of normal brand values, as with Muji's generic stationery.

Cheap store brands are a step above generics, but still offer inferior product quality at large discounts off producer brand prices. They often use innocuous proprietary brands ('Mother's Favourite' cooking sauces) and/or packaging that draws on associations with the leading producer brands.

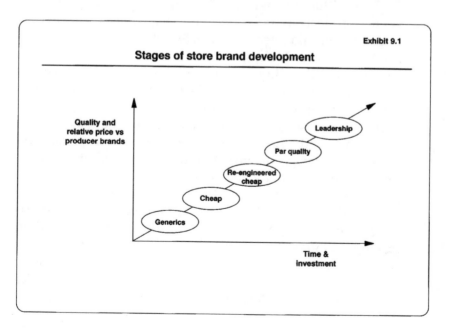

Exhibit 9.1

Stages of store brand development

Producers will fight such packaging similarities hard. Grand Metropolitan, the global food and drinks group, is taking legal action against one of the leading UK grocers, Asda, over several of Asda's private label drinks range. The packaging and labelling of Asda's Deep South, Windward rum and Daniel Boone's bourbon do bear striking resemblances to Southern Comfort, Malibu and Jack Daniel's. Retailers have to tread a fine line in how closely they can imitate the look of leading producer brands.

These first two stages require little or no investment. The retailer puts out a contract tender to third-tier producers with spare capacity. Little effort needs to be put into product or packaging design and development, and quality control can be kept to a bare minimum.

At the third stage, *re-engineered low cost* store brands are still cost- and price-based, but do require some level of proactive management and investment. Aldi is probably the best example of this approach. Elements of product and packaging are carefully disaggregated and analysed to see where costs and quality can be reduced while still delivering basic functionality to consumers. The retailer works with suppliers to deliver this 're-engineered' product, at a deep discount versus producer brands, but with clear quality and feature trade-offs and no attempt to pass itself off as a copycat of a producer brand. Interestingly, suppliers like working with Aldi despite their tough stance on cost and price, because Aldi will work with them to re-engineer products, rather than simply put the problem into their laps.

The last two stages of store brand development move from being cost- and price-based to being based on quality and innovation. *Par quality* store brands are pitched at matching producer brand quality and performance every way, but at a price that is 10–25% lower. The price advantage is possible because of the retailer's elimination of much of the product- or category-specific marketing overhead of the leading producer brands (the 'brand tax'), and because the retailer can negotiate attractive contract prices from high quality second-tier producers with excess capacity. Although quality is comparable, the store brand is unlikely to take on real innovation.

In the final stage of development, *leadership* store brands take on a real market and brand leadership role, driving innovation and re-positioning of product lines and whole categories. The leadership role enables these store brands to extract at least price parity, and often a price premium, versus producer brands and versus other retailers. In several cases, there may be no strong producer brands in categories primarily developed by strong store brands.

These last two stages require extensive investment by the retailer, in design and development, quality control, and close long-term supplier relationships. They may also start to require directly-allocatable marketing investments, particularly if product- or category-specific sub-brands are offered.

There are variations on these stages of store brand development. One common in the fashion sector is 'producer exclusives' ('Chester Barrie for/in Austin Reed').

The Strategic Purpose of Store Brands: Margin Enhancement or Brand-building

Retailers can view the strategic purpose of store brand development as either short-term margin enhancement or long-term brand-building.

Retailers who concentrate on generics and cheap store brands usually focus on margin enhancement. Gross margin percentages can be higher than on strong producer brands, even with deeply discounted consumer prices. But focusing on the margin enhancement benefits misses the main long-term opportunity of brand-building, and even on its own terms may be downright wrong. As producers are at pains to point out, cheap store brands may deliver higher percentage gross margins, but rates-of-sale per line and per square foot are usually much lower than for producer brand alternatives, so that the critical measure of $ contribution per square foot of selling space is lower than on the low gross margin producer power brands.

Long-term brand-building is by far the greater opportunity offered by store brands. Short-term margin impact, positive or negative, needs to be understood and taken into account, but is a secondary consideration and is of secondary value. A retailer whose strategic purpose is long-term brand-building will behave and invest in a very different way, even in the early stages of store brand development. As such retailers progress to the 'par quality' and 'leadership' stages, the margin versus rate-of-sale trade-off between retail and producer brands may even be reversed: a strong store brand that is a category market leader in-store may end up achieving lower gross margins but higher rates-of-sale and therefore higher $ contribution per square foot than competing producer brands.

Targeting and Prioritising Categories for Store Brand Development

Retailers cannot hope to develop strong store brand positions across all categories simultaneously. They must target and prioritise their effort and investment. Broadly, there will be two kinds of situation that create store brand opportunity.

First, *targeting weak producer brands*. Whole categories may be characterised by fragmented competition and poorly developed producer brand positions. Other categories may be dominated by a few leading producer brands who are resting on their laurels and under-investing or milking their market position, with low levels of above-the-line marketing support or low rates of innovation in product and production processes. Both situations create store brand opportunity, which is enhanced if categories are also characterised by relatively stable technology, longer product life-cycles, and spare capacity among second- and third-tier producers. Retailers will often be starting with some store brand presence in a target category, even if only a generic or cheap

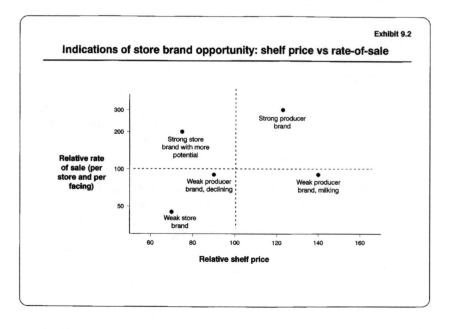

Exhibit 9.2

Indications of store brand opportunity: shelf price vs rate-of-sale

offer, and can begin to gauge category opportunities by looking at current relative prices and relative rates-of-sale between producer brands and existing store brands (own or competitors'). If the producer brand has a large price premium but only an average actual rate-of-sale performance, and if that price premium is not being supported by adequate investment in marketing and innovation, there could be an opportunity for quality store brand penetration (see Exhibit 9.2).

Secondly, there may be an opportunity for *re-merchandising a category* – re-defining it and/or adding value into it, such that consumer volume and value spending on the category is shifted upwards. This situation provides the most powerful platform for quality and leadership store brand development, and for creating real store brand differentiation. We will look at several examples in Case Study 9.1. In each case the result has been the strongest possible development of retail brand power and competitive differentiation.

Case Study 9.1   Re-merchandising Categories

Our first example is *wine*, in the UK grocery sector. Through to the late 1970s, UK consumers' *per capita* consumption of wine was low relative to Continental Europe. Most wine consumed was cheap and low quality. Consumers were intimidated by the complexity of choice involved in selecting a bottle of wine, and found it impossible to remember differences between grape varieties, countries of origin, appellation contrôlée labelling, and producers/vineyards. The majority of wine was sold through specialist high street shops, 'off-licences', which were generally tied to major drinks producers.

In the 1980s the leading UK grocery chains initiated a revolution in the merchandising and selling of wine. They 'de-mystified' the category with clear presentation and labelling of consumers' options, by colour and dry–sweet taste, price point, country of origin and producer. They reduced purchase risk by developing their own high quality store brand ranges. They found and developed new sources for their ranges, particularly the lesser known European regions such as Fitou and Minervois in France and New World producers in Australia, New Zealand, California and Chile, whose quality and value soon exceeded that of most old world producers. They encouraged consumer interest and knowledge by stimulating greater wine coverage in national newspapers and magazines, with weekly and annual competitions for best purchases and best wine merchant.

This effort has transformed the UK wine market over the last 15 years. *Per capita* consumption of wine has doubled, and the real average price paid per litre has increased by over a third as consumers have traded up to higher quality. Consumers themselves have lost much of their fear of the category, and can be heard talking knowledgeably and comfortably in the wine sections of supermarkets over their choice of a French Bordeaux or an Australian cabernet. For the UK grocers, the sales and profit payback has been tremendous: they have become the leading distribution channel for wine, and accelerated the long-term decline in off-licences (see Exhibit 9.3).

Another interesting example, from the home products sector, is the unlikely category of *storage and containers*. 'Storage and containers' embraces a range of products, from laundry

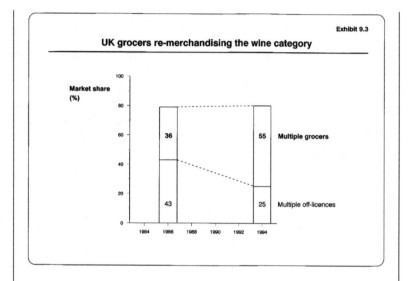

Exhibit 9.3

UK grocers re-merchandising the wine category

baskets and linen chests through to filing boxes and waste bins. In most furniture and home products retailers, storage and containers were merchandised almost as an afterthought around the store, mixed in randomly among the major furniture items or as a limited range of accessories in the kitchen and bathroom departments. In Bed Bath & Beyond in the USA, this category has been pulled together and re-merchandised as an exciting totality. Bed Bath & Beyond's floor-to-ceiling display prompts consumers to re-think all their potential needs and uses for storage and containers, and the potential for these products to contribute to the overall style and organisation of the home. IKEA's range and display achieves a similar result, although somewhat more fragmented around different sections of their self-service warehouse area.

Our third example, from the USA, is taken from outside mainstream retailing, but provides an excellent model for what can be done with a retail category. The *coffee* sold in diners and cafés in the USA was, until recently, one of the world's worst culinary experiences. Weak and tasteless, it was retailed as a bulk commodity in styrofoam buckets, at 50 cents or less a cup. Coffee drinking in the USA has been revolutionised over the last five years by the national expansion of Starbucks and its Seattle-based competitors. The category has been transformed into a gourmet, aspirational lifestyle experience. Starbucks offers dozens of varieties of freshly-brewed, espresso-based coffee, and has introduced Americans to delights such as caffè latte and mocha cappuccino, selling for up to $3 per cup. Consumers debate the pros and cons of different chains' bean choice, or which chain delivers the best latte. As with wine in the UK, consumers are now confident and interested enough to have preferences between varieties of Kenyan and Columbian, and new bean types attract the same media coverage and consumer interest as a new award-winning cabernet. Around the core coffee offer, Starbucks retails a range of accessories and lifestyle merchandise which reinforce the coffee mystique: their own beans, home percolators and espresso systems, bean grinders, service sets, even their own label jazz CDs to play during the home coffee ritual. *Per capita* consumption and average price paid have soared, as has Starbucks' stock price.

Our fourth example is from *beauty and personal care*. Body Shop transformed the traditional stance of the cosmetics and personal care industry by offering a product range based on natural ingredients and an environmentally-friendly stance on sourcing and packaging. The stance was almost inverse-aspirational, convincing consumers that they need not sign up to the artifice and mystique of conventional cosmetics. Under this brand positioning umbrella, Body Shop re-defined and added new values into many sub-categories, such as soaps and shampoos based on natural fruits and herbs. The product offer was in harmony with the 'green' ambience of the stores.

Our final example is again from UK grocery: the development of the *chilled foods* cabinet in UK supermarkets. M&S was the pioneer and innovator in this development, in the late 1970s. The concept was to deliver fresh chilled product to the consumer through a supply chain in which temperature was held virtually constant, so that product freshness and hygiene was maintained through to point-of-sale. Compared with the frozen delivery system, the chilled chain preserved food in a much fresher state. Initially developed for relatively unprocessed fresh product such as chicken pieces, the full potential of the chilled system has been realised in the development of ready-meals (entrées and desserts), which can now match freshly-prepared home and restaurant cooking in their quality. As dual-income consumer households have become more pressed for time, the demand take-up of high quality, chilled ready-meals has soared. The same chilled system has supported the growth of pre-packaged fresh sandwiches, another major growth market over the last 10–15 years.

The chilled chain has been a major contributor to the growth in brand power on the part of UK grocers. Chilled is a category that has been primarily developed and continues to be dominated by the retailers and their store brands. Consumers' preference between chains is strongly affected by their preference for a chain's store brand chilled offer. It is a development that has required significant, long-term investment on the part of the retailers. Chilled cabinets and chilled distribution and warehousing are expensive. Quality control requirements are rigorous. Production sources often have to be developed from scratch. Product design and development, including packaging, are primarily the retailers' responsibility.

As an aside, UK store brand penetration in chilled ready meals is 94%, while in frozen ready meals it is only 29%. Frozen ready meal run lengths are much longer, generating economies of scale and margin advantage for the brand leader, which in this instance have been reinvested in heavy marketing spend. Chilled ready meals are shorter shelf-life products, with short run lengths and little scale economy. Producers find themselves with no margin to invest in marketing.

US grocery retailers are currently very keen on developing 'meal solutions', a concept which has similarities with the development of the chilled chain in the UK. At its centre is the idea that American consumers no longer have the time, or even the ability, to plan and prepare the traditional home-cooked family meal, and are spending more of their food dollar on eating out. Retailers and producers alike want to halt, or slow, the switch to eating out, which represents an absolute loss of market for both. 'Meal solutions' would present consumers with products organised around meal occasions, with everything needed for (say) an Italian dinner – starter, entrée, dessert – merchandised together as a unit, with different meal menus offered for different days of the week. However, most US grocers have not yet made the investment in the chilled chain necessary to deliver freshness and quality comparable to a good eating-out alternative, and 'meal solutions' as currently conceived is a more a merchandising tactic than a real new value-added consumer proposition. Most importantly, it continues to leave the retailers in thrall to the producer brands, rather than developing retail brand leadership and differentiation.

One Store Brand or Sub-brands?

Retailers with strong store brands have to choose whether to maintain one store/fascia brand across all own-label products, or whether to start developing different sub-brands for particular product categories, such as Sainsbury's Novon in detergents.

There are several arguments made in favour of sub-brands: that they can enable different consumer segments to be more effectively targeted within the same store; that they can increase consumer perception of choice and quality; and that they can increase the premium and return that a retailer can earn from investing in store brand development. It can also be argued that they reduce brand risk for the retailer, by not linking every own-label offer to the overall fascia brand. The temptation to sub-brand is stronger the more successful a retailer has been at bringing store brand quality up to a level that matches or exceeds producer brands. Sainsbury's feels that the quality of their Novon detergent product (made by McBride) is every bit as good as the P&G or Unilever product, and can therefore earn a similar standing and even a brand premium.

However, in our view there are strong arguments against sub-branding. A retail brand covers the whole range of products and in-store service experiences of the consumer. Consumers understand that, and they can accept that a store brand can and should embrace a wide range of categories and price/quality positions. If product quality really does match that of leading producer brands, not using the store brand loses a major opportunity to strengthen overall consumer loyalty and preference. In many cases, the use of sub-brands reduces rather than increases the consumer's perception of choice and quality, by presenting her with shelves stocked with the equivalent of unknown, unmarketed third-tier producer brands – many sub-brands simply imitate producer brands and do little to advance consumers' perceptions of the retail brand. Finally, there is a danger that retailers will get drawn into managing these sub-brands like real producer brands: making directly-allocatable investment in sub-brand marketing campaigns, moving into the wholesaling of sub-brands to other retailers, and adding complexity and over-head cost into the business.

M&S is an excellent example of a retailer that has consistently refused to go into sub-brands, despite being in the retail sector – fashion – where the arguments for segmented range and brand targeting are strongest. Its range of men's business shirts provides a good example of how different quality and price points can be clearly identified but marketed under the one store brand umbrella: $10 to $40 price points, clearly correlated with choices around the quality of material and finish, from polyester through to fine cotton.

Moving into sub-brands can take a retailer too far along the path of becoming like a producer brand, and ignores the differences in the function and role of retail and producer brands. Broad differences in price/quality positioning can still be signalled, through packaging and presentation and through the use of store brand 'tags' ('Select', 'Basics'), while still staying within a store brand umbrella. Monoprix, probably the most credible and value-added grocery store brand in France, uses the Monoprix brand over its three 'tag' sub-brands of Gourmet (luxury foods), La Forme (light/healthy foods) and Vite Pret (ready meals), with the Monoprix name prominent.

Investing in the Supply Chain and in Long-term Supplier Relationships

Dealing with suppliers of generics and of cheap/copycat own label, the retail buyer operates as an aggressive trader, frequently switching suppliers to find the lowest cost source, negotiating hard on every individual contract, and minimis-ing investment, risk and long-term commitment. But building a supply chain and a supplier base for quality and leadership store brands requires a completely different approach.

First, there needs to be a relatively *open information flow* between the retailer and the supplier. Retailers and suppliers need to debate and agree the objectives for a product line and for a category. Suppliers need to understand retailer economics, including the performance required from a store brand line versus competing producer brand ranges. Retailers need to understand supplier economics: fixed and variable costs, run lengths, packaging, stock-holding and distribution. In day-to-day operations, stock and re-order information and management need to be transparent and integrated between retailer and supplier.

There needs to be *joint investment in product development and quality control*. The retailer needs to invest adequately in resources to work with its supplier partners. Responsibility for product development and setting out the parameters for quality control lies primarily with the retailer, although the supplier will be responsible for operational execution (see Case Study 9.2).

Case Study 9.2 Early Learning Centre

The Early Learning Centre (ELC) provides an interesting example of investment in store brand development. ELC, now owned by the John Menzies Group, is UK market leader in educational and developmental toys for children under five years old. Where the vast majority of the toy market, as merchandised by Toys 'R' Us, is dominated by global producer brands, ELC has developed a high value-added store brand niche, and its offer is 75% own-label. Despite its small scale (sales of under $200 million, through small high street stores), ELC has invested heavily in in-house design, product development and sourcing. It has three tied designers working on store brand ranges, and its own engineers and merchandisers based in Hong Kong working with Far Eastern suppliers. ELC's investment in value-added product development has paid off. While most toy retailers fight it out on low margin producer brand ranges, ELC has consistently earned pre-tax margins of 10–15%, and is one of the most recognised, respected and trusted retail brands in the UK, on a par in consumers' minds with Boots and M&S.

There needs to be some level of *risk-sharing* between retailer and supplier. Investment in production and distribution equipment may remain the supplier's responsibility, but in a long-term partnership the retailer will 'under-write' the risk with a commitment to minimum order levels. Similarly, if supply-chain stocks are being managed as a totality to optimise costs, cash flow, stock-outs and write-downs, the retailer must assume joint responsibility for demand fore-casting and production and delivery scheduling.

Open information flows, joint investment and risk-sharing are possible and practical only if there is some level of *long-term commitment* from the retailer to the supplier. This commitment could be contractual, but more often will be informal and established by custom and practice over a long period. For example, if a particular new product line does not work, the retailer may work with the supplier to find new product opportunities to use spare capacity and production investment. (A retailer's long-term commitment with its suppliers need not be to specific production facilities. In the fashion industry, garment production moves very rapidly from one country source to another, changing within a year or even a season, chasing exchange rates and labour productivity. One of the roles of fashion suppliers is to manage those rapid changes in the production base, often by ruthlessly minimising their own commitment to specific factories and workforces.)

The question of *exclusivity* is often raised in this context of long-term commitment. If a retailer and a supplier have invested in and built up a strong, close, proprietary relation-ship, there is normally the assumption that the retailer will not take detailed product specifications and production processes to a competing supplier, and that the supplier will not offer the results of new product development to a directly-competing retailer. Contractual exclusivity is, how-ever, often hard to enforce, and may be illegal in the context of local legislation. In practice, a reasonable level of mutually-satisfactory exclusivity can only evolve over time from the development of long-term partnerships and mutual trust, and from an open discussion, in advance, of situations which might cause either partner concern.

Finally, there needs to be open and sensible recognition of the need for *attractive long-term financial returns for both sides.* While the retailer cannot and should not take on responsibility for the financial performance and survival of its suppliers, the retailer should not expect to extract all the 'super-profits' from a successful long-term partnership. The supplier needs to receive an adequate reward and return on its investment and risk in developing the partnership. M&S's relationship with several of its core suppliers provides a good example of a balanced, sustainable approach to relative financial returns (see Exhibit 9.4).

Over the last ten years, M&S and Dewhirst, its key UK-based clothing supplier, have both delivered an average return on capital of 22%. Dewhirst's returns have been more volatile: in the recession of the early 1990s, M&S pushed more of the short-term pain on to its supplier base, and managed to hold its own return on capital steady. In the 'good times', M&S is comfortable with its key suppliers earning a higher return.

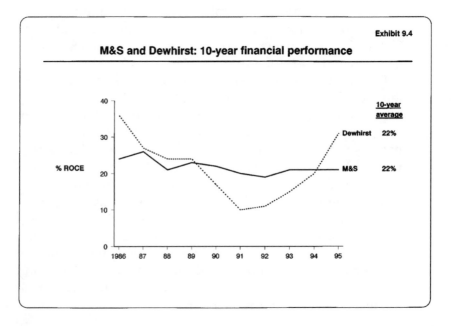

Exhibit 9.4

M&S and Dewhirst: 10-year financial performance

Balancing Store Brands and Producer Brands

In most retail businesses, store brands have to be kept in balance with producer brands. As store brands have grown in quality and market share, this balance has been moving in favour of store brands, with weak second- and third-tier producer brands bearing the brunt of market share loss (see Exhibit 9.5).

Even very strong, well managed retail brands can go too far, too fast, in developing store brand penetration and reducing the presence and choice of producer brands. Strong producer brands still command high levels of consumer loyalty, and retailers need to be careful that they are not crossing a threshold of consumer acceptance.

A useful way of thinking about the balance between store brands and consumer brands is around consumer switching propensity and switching cost. Faced with the absence (intended, rather than an unintended stock-out) of a preferred producer brand, consumers will either accept a substitute producer or store brand or go to another store to

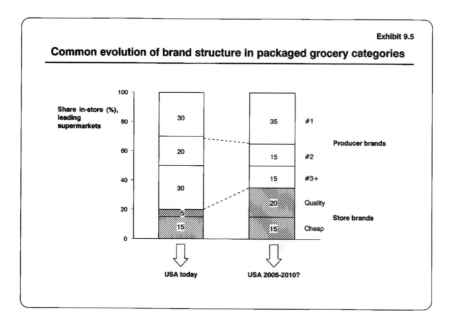

Exhibit 9.5

Common evolution of brand structure in packaged grocery categories

find their preferred brand. This effect or choice is cumulative: consumers may accept substitution on a few brands and products, but switch when they are faced with too many substitutions. Consumer propensity to accept a substitute or to switch is a good indicator of a brand's strength, and varies considerably across brands and categories.

From a retailer's perspective, there are two types of switching risk. Taking the example of the weekly grocery shop; if a consumer is intensely loyal to one or two particular producer brands that the retailer no longer stocks, she may continue to do her primary weekly shop at the original retailer but take on the extra time and effort needed to top up with her two favoured brands at another store. The retailer loses some small revenue but retains the majority of consumer spend and loyalty. Far worse is the situation in which the absence of preferred producer brands triggers a switch in the primary weekly shop. The timing and probability of this switch is much harder to estimate from consumer research, as consumers themselves will find it hard to articulate the point at which their overall retail loyalty switches due to an accumulation of frustrations.

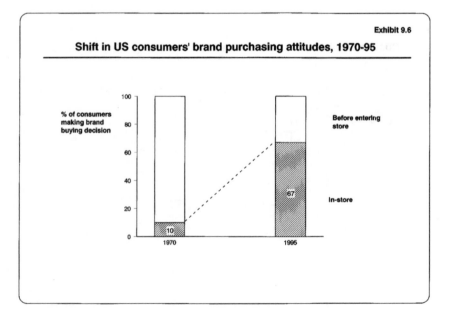

Exhibit 9.6

Shift in US consumers' brand purchasing attitudes, 1970-95

The balance between store and producer brands will always be in tension, and constantly evolving. The stronger the development of quality store brands, the stronger the retail brand's overall relationship with the consumer, and the greater the store switching cost; but producer brands will be fighting hard to make brand switching cost exceed store switching cost. Overall, consumer attitudes are moving in the retailers' favour. In 1970, most US consumers had decided which brand they were set on buying before they entered a grocery store; by the mid-1990s only 1 in 3 had made this decision in advance, while 2 in 3 were making their brand choice in-store, influenced by shelf display, promotions and store brand offer (see Exhibit 9.6).

Quality and Leadership Store Brands at Maturity

At maturity, quality and leadership store brands operate similarly to producer brands. Initial price discounts versus producer brands are reduced and store brands may achieve a premium versus producer brands.

This phenomenon can be seen in the relationship between the retail-producer brand price gap and store brand market share in the French grocery market (see Exhibit 9.7).

At low levels of market share, store brands struggle to be viable alternatives to producer brands, and have to compete on a heavy price discount (30–50%) with a generic or cheap/copycat offer. As their market share increases, this price gap diminishes, until at levels of around 50% share and above store brand pricing is at parity with producer brands. Cause and effect are interwoven: increased quality leads to higher market share and a reduction in the level of price discount, and/or high levels of discount preclude quality store brand development and limit market share potential.

This relative price/relative volume relationship is the exact opposite of what has been argued to exist by many industry experts, particularly in the USA. It is still common to find business articles taking as a given that the greater the price advantage of store brands, the greater their market share. In

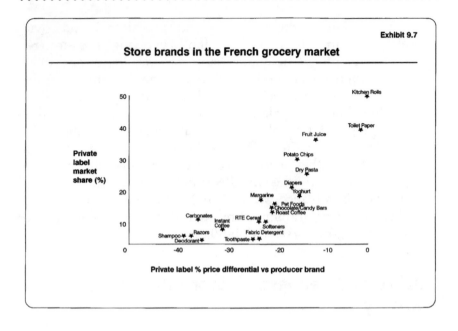

Exhibit 9.7

Store brands in the French grocery market

fact a 'counter-intuitive' inverse relationship occurs with branding, as producer brands have known for decades.

A further 'counter-intuitive' aspect of quality store brands at maturity is the skew in their consumer appeal. Many observers have also believed that store brands should appeal more to less affluent, price-sensitive consumers. This is partly true for the earlier cost- and price-based stages of store brand development. But quality and leadership store brands, if their market share by consumer group is skewed at all, will be more likely to have greater appeal to more affluent consumer groups, who will be more confident in their own taste and judgement in abandoning heavily advertised producer brands for higher or equal quality store brands. Producer brand loyalty and need for brand reassurance is typically stronger among less affluent consumer groups.

Quality and leadership store brands at maturity are therefore a rich prize, akin to the strongest producer brands. Market share and relative price levels move in tandem rather than in opposite directions, and store brand preference and loyalty will be particularly strong among more affluent consumer groups.

Investing in the Brand– Customer Relationship 10

After investment in quality store brand development, the next most important and effective brand investment a retailer can make is in building the brand–customer relationship. Mass marketing, as with producer brands, can and is used to communicate and position the brand with consumers; but retailers have a greater capacity than producers to use an even more powerful tool, namely the building of direct customer relationships.

Mass Marketing: The Growth in Retail Brand Advertising Spend

Until the 1980s, most retailers, even those with strong brand franchises, resisted spending heavily on advertising. In-town, 'high street' retailers had their prime high street frontage and fascias to achieve the same effect as advertising in keeping their brand name in the public eye; 'location location location' in traditional high street retailing not only maximised passing traffic but also gave brand visibility. Premium rents for prime space performed the same function in the cost structure as above-the-line media spend for producer brands. Many leading high street retailers, including M&S, still adhere to this philosophy.

But this situation is rapidly changing, and many retail brands are becoming heavy advertisers. The change is due to the growth of out-of-town large-store destination retailing, and to the emergence of mature competition between strong, quality store brands.

Category killers like Circuit City, Toys 'R' Us and IKEA need to draw customers out to them rather than rely on capturing passing traffic. They use advertising as part of the marketing mix to do this, with A/S (advertising/sales) ratios at up to 5% – well above the historically negligible ratios of high street retailers, although still a long way from the 10–15% or more of producer brands. (There are exceptions to this trend. French hypermarkets are prevented, by long-standing regulation favouring small shop-keepers, from advertising on TV, and have had to concentrate their mass marketing on billboards, print and home leafleting.)

In response to the advertising spends of category killers, many high street retailers are having to start spending on advertising also, to fight for the high street's survival versus out-of-town. This is a new, disconcerting and expensive experience for them, at a time of severe overall margin pressure.

The growth in media spending in the UK grocery sector is a good example of the increased use of advertising in the competitive battle between strong, mature retail brands. Advertising spends by leading grocers in the UK have now matched and surpassed those of most producer brands, and are continuing to grow at far faster rates.

Mass Marketing: Limitations for Retail Brands

Although retail brand advertising spends are increasing, there are limitations on the value of mass marketing in building the retail brand–customer relationship.

One limitation is retailers' own expectations of the payback on advertising investment. Much retail advertising is focused on short-term promotions and price positioning. Many retailers advertise only during their major seasonal sales.

Most retailers have an *expectation of short-term payback* on advertising investment, in the form of immediate sales up-lift. In contrast, leading producer brands focus on the long-term brand-building value of advertising in creating subliminal consumer associations, preference and loyalty. They look to the long-term payback of maintaining market share and brand premium versus competitors (see Exhibit 10.1).

Another limitation is the difficulties that retailers seem to face in developing a *compressed brand image and message.* Producer brands have learnt how to use the 30- or 60-second TV commercial to hammer home one message and one image about their (single) product brand. Retailers want to convey their offer of thousands of product lines, price positions and service elements. Given the difficulty of compressing that message, their strap-lines tend to be highly functional (even banal) statements such as 'good food at fair prices'. There are few examples in retail advertising of powerful abstract images, with minimal commentary, that create brand personality and quick visual association, such as the cowboy and western landscapes give to the Marlboro brand.

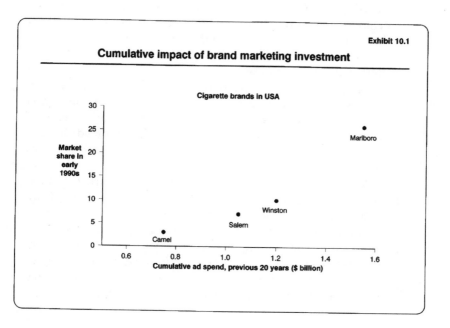

Exhibit 10.1

Cumulative impact of brand marketing investment

These empirical difficulties in retail brand advertising are inter-related. Producer brand advertising, even in very functional product categories, delivers compressed images of brand association and aspiration, with the goal of long-term brand-building. Retail advertising tends to focus on concrete promotions and price positioning with the goal of short-term sales increases, and rarely uses compressed messages and abstract imagery.

There are a few exceptions in retailing, almost exclusively in the fashion sector. The best-known example is Benetton (see Case Study 10.1).

Case Study 10.1 Benetton

Benetton's advertising images are among the most controversial and distinctive of any consumer brand, producer or retailer. The theme of 'United Colours of Benetton', originally stemming from the company's focus on simple colour-block statements in their core knitwear ranges, has evolved into a set of images increasingly abstracted from the product – but still serving to send and reinforce the unique brand identity. The 'colours' theme was first expanded into images of multi-racial harmony, and was maintained in the campaign showing multi-coloured prophylactics. The theme of multi-racial harmony then provided a platform for the campaigns to move away from any tangible association with the product offer, into images of AIDS, pollution and war. The thread of connection was maintained by the distinctive and immediately recognisable nature of a Benetton campaign, reinforced by the controversy and press coverage that was almost always generated.

Benetton remains a rarity among mass market fashion brands in the abstraction and radical nature of its advertising – although images of comparable power are found in adverts for designer brands such as Calvin Klein. It has also been consistent in maintaining its level of investment in marketing, at between 4% and 6% of sales, even in the difficult trading of the early 1990s. Marketing has played a vital part in Benetton's growth from a local Italian fashion brand, as recently as the

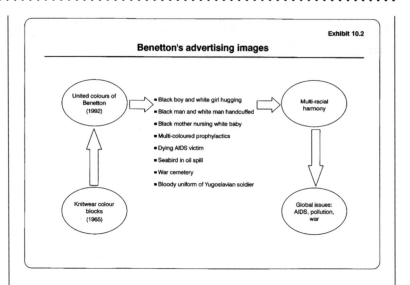

Exhibit 10.2

Benetton's advertising images

United colours of Benetton (1992)

- Black boy and white girl hugging
- Black man and white man handcuffed
- Black mother nursing white baby
- Multi-coloured prophylactics
- Dying AIDS victim
- Seabird in oil spill
- War cemetery
- Bloody uniform of Yugoslavian soldier

Multi-racial harmony

Knitwear colour blocks (1965)

Global issues: AIDS, pollution, war

late 1970s, to its current position as one of the leading global fashion brands, operating out of 120 countries and generating high returns for its family and outside shareholders.

It should be said that Benetton's recent, most radical advertising campaigns have generated many negative as well as positive reactions. In Germany, Benetton's second biggest market, consumer research in the early and mid-1990s showed big increases in brand awareness but a decline in 'likeability' versus other fashion brands. Several Benetton retailers in Germany boycotted the campaign, and a German court ruled against some of the advertising. The Group attributed some of its sales decline in 1994 to controversy over the adverts.

Outside the fashion and home lifestyle sectors, mass marketing investment is unlikely to be as effective for retail brands as it is for producer brands, given the greater breadth and complexity of the retail offer and the difficulty of honing it down effectively to a powerful compressed strap-line and image. Mass marketing also does not play to retailers' own strengths, and to their structural advantages over producers, which lie in the ability and opportunity to build strong direct customer relationships.

Building Direct Customer Relationships: The Retail Brand Advantage

Mass marketing projects brand awareness and positioning, through mass media, to a large number of consumers. The focus of direct customer relationships is to get as close as possible to a one-to-one direct relationship between the retailer/retail brand and the individual customer (see Box 10.1).

Box 10.1   Direct Customer Relationships

We use the term 'direct customer relationships' rather than 'direct marketing'. Direct marketing is a well established sales and marketing approach, used by specialists in mail order, telephone or personal selling, and used as part of a broader sales and marketing mix by many other businesses. The term 'direct customer relationships' emphasises the two-way nature of the brand–customer contact, rather than a one-way sales and marketing effort from the producer/retailer to the consumer.

Retail brands have several structural advantages over producer brands in their ability to develop direct customer relationships.

The first is *frequent direct contact with the customer*. While producer brands have to work through the intermediaries of their distribution channels, retailers deal directly with their customers in frequent transactions.

This frequent direct interaction gives retailers an advantage in the *breadth and immediacy of consumer information*. Retailers have access to information on how consumers behave within and across wide product categories. This information comes to them as part of day-to-day operations, rather than as a result of planned commissioned market research, and it comes to them on a daily basis, rather than with the lag inherent in producers' market share statistics and consumer research.

Compared with producers, retailers have a greater *capacity for quick, flexible experimentation*. Retailers can experiment easily and quickly with changes in range, pricing, promotions and store layout, with minimal cost. They can also vary and control the experiments over a number of stores to find the most effective approach. For producers, experimenting with changes to a brand, including new product introductions, is a far more expensive and lengthy process.

Finally, retailers have a greater opportunity for *tailoring the brand to local demand*. Store ranges, pricing and layout can be flexed to meet the preferences and demographic composi-tions of local markets. Such 'micro-marketing' is the antith-esis of the philosophy and economics of power producer brands, which work off national and even global homo-geneity and economies of scale.

There are several components to the building of direct customer relationships. Customers' individual characteristics and needs, likes and dislikes, and purchase behaviour need to be understood, in as much detail as possible. Retailers need to determine which customers and customer groups to prioritise and target, with what marketing and service programmes, with what levels of resources and investment, and with what short- and long-term objectives. There must be open, positive two-way communication between retailer and customer. We will explore each of these in turn.

Understanding the Customer

Understanding customers involves piecing together informa-tion on their behaviour in a retailer's own stores, on the background profiles of the customers, and on their behaviour in competitors' stores.

Understanding customer behaviour in own stores requires the ability to match and track individual customers against individual point-of-sale transactions. Customers need to be given the incentive of store loyalty or payment cards in order for this matching to be achieved. A store card system that captures even 30% of sales will start to be a powerful tool for customer understanding. Even with extensive store card take-up there will still be a sizeable chunk of store sales – to infrequent or accidental shoppers, to customers who simply cannot be bothered or persuaded to take up the store card, and to store card holders paying with cash – that will not be captured within the store card database.

Store card systems can also provide background profiles on the consumers themselves. When matched with catchment area databases, incorporating postal code demographic information down to street level, a retailer can track customer and spend penetration by customer group and within catchment area bands, and monitor changes in sales performance.

Matching individual customers against point-of-sale transactions opens up extensive opportunities for targeting and experimenting with the retail offer. Customer response to changes in range, layout and display, pricing, promotions and service initiatives can be tracked by line item and individual customer, and aggregated up to category and consumer groups.

Obtaining data on consumer behaviour in competitors' stores is far more problematic. Third-party research firms typically provide aggregate data on market share trends, often down to major category level, and aggregate U&A ('usage and attitude') surveys. These need to be supplemented by periodic in-house field surveys, around a sample of stores, of competitive activity on range, pricing, etc. and periodic consumer exit or catchment area interviews to monitor shifts in attitudes and shopping behaviour.

Customer Targeting

Once a retailer has a database that enables sales performance to be tracked by individual customer and customer group, management can begin to determine which customers or consumer groups should be targeted for development, and in what ways. Targeting can be structured around the innate characteristics of consumer groups, and/or around their competitive shopping behaviour.

Innate characteristics could include income, age, family status, sex, interests, employment, attitude to product categories . . . the potential list is long. The choice of where to target against innate characteristics is a logical extension of a retail business's strategy and brand positioning.

Targeting against *competitive shopping behaviour* involves a more complex set of choices. Consumers within Store *A*'s catchment area could be classified into primary loyal users, the core customer base who already use the store as first choice in the relevant product range; secondary or competitive users, whose primary loyalty is to another store or to no store, but who still shop more than occasionally at Store *A*; occasional users, who shop at Store *A* very infrequently; and non-users, who never shop at Store *A*. There are arguments for targeting any or all of these groups. The greatest potential new sales growth opportunity can obviously lie in attracting and converting non-users, but this may be difficult and very expensive. Much recent management literature has emphasised the value of keeping core customers, and the high cost of getting new customers or recovering lost ex-customers, which would support targeting primary loyal users first (see Exhibit 10.3).

Exhibit 10.3

Customer base segmentation and targeting

User group	% of population	% spend penetration	% of sales	% of total profit
Primary loyal	20	70	54	75
Secondary	35	30	40	25
Occasional	30	5	6	.
Non-user	15	.	.	.
Total/Average	100	26	100	100

The concentration of a retailer's sales and profitability within a small heavy user sub-set of the customer base can be quite extraordinary. McDonald's announced in 1995 that its principal marketing focus would be on increasing consumption among current customers. It gave the statistic that 77% of its sales were derived from 'super-heavy users' (probably in both possible senses): males aged 18–34 who eat at McDonald's between three and five times per week, spending $15–20 per week. Somewhat staggered by that fact, we checked its feasibility and were amazed to find that it made numerical sense.

To refine consumer targeting, innate characteristics of consumer groups (age, income, family status, etc.) need to be matrixed against competitive shopping behaviour (primary/secondary/occasional/non-users). Retailers can map current market and competitive profiles, and trends/volatility of market shares, onto this matrix. They need also to assess and test potential response, by cell, to new investment by the retailer. In total, this process will clarify a retailer's choices around which consumer groups to target with what level of investment.

Once target consumer groups have been identified, retailers can experiment with ways of increasing share or loyalty in those consumer groups. Range, pricing, store layout and in-store services can be modified and sales results tracked precisely by customer group, backed up by qualitative consumer research. Sales promotions and loyalty discounts can be targeted at small groups or even at individuals. Service levels can also be targeted: it may be economic to provide loyal, high spending, low credit risk customers with fully or partly pre-picked shopping baskets, pre-ordered by phone or interactive terminal, for pick-up in-store (with walk-through automated check-out charged to the store card) or for home delivery.

One of the most powerful uses of customer information databases and of direct customer relationships is *targeted life-cycle marketing*. Financial services provides one of the best examples. Consumers' needs for, and willingness to buy, financial services evolve in fairly consistent and predictable patterns as they age and as their family and employment situations change. Early simple needs for banking facilities evolve into needs for credit, mortgages, insurance, investment products and pension plans. A solid customer database and a strong direct customer relationship enables a financial services competitor to target marketing on the right products for the right lifestages, and to do so in a way that comes across as value-added customer care rather than as an intrusive hard sell.

Several other retail sectors are strong candidates for life-cycle marketing. Electrical retailers can target customers based on hardware life-cycles and service patterns, particularly if they maintain and nurture after-sales service contact with their customers. Retailers of children's goods can target parents based on their children's ages, the pattern of the school year, and the structure of the school curriculum.

Customer Communication

A further key element of building direct customer relationships is developing a process and culture of customer communication.

Retailers need to communicate the *intentions and benefits* of their direct customer relationship programmes and value-added services to the target customer groups. Customers need to feel that such communication is targeted and tailored specifically for them as individuals, and not simply part of a mass mail-out campaign. Databases on customer characteristics and sales history need to be integrated with the databases for mail-outs and telephone sales and service.

Communication must include a large element of *customer recognition*. One of the things that people value most in any service relationship is simply that the service provider recognises the customer's importance and values his or her loyalty. Again, such recognition needs to be tailored and individualised.

Communication can and must be a *two-way street*. Customers should be actively solicited and encouraged to give objective feedback as to what is working or failing in the retail offer and in the direct customer relationship programmes.

Customers need to feel that the retailer is not only willing to listen to feedback, both positive and negative, but is actively seeking it and using it to improve the retail proposition.

Building Direct Customer Relationships: The Investment Mentality

As with the development of quality store brands, the development of strong direct customer relationships requires the retailer to have a long-term investment mentality. Investment can take several forms, some more obvious and apparent than others.

The most obvious investment is in *databases, systems and research*. Collecting, processing and making practical use of the information that underpins direct customer relationship programmes is expensive, and payback periods can be long. But declining IT costs are making the maintenance of extensive customer databases more and more justifiable: the cost of keeping information on an individual customer is estimated to have come down from $1.00 in the 1960s to $0.01 in the 1990s.

Another fairly transparent investment is the cost of *rewarding loyal customers*. Loyalty incentives not only reward and promote customer loyalty, they encourage customers to participate in developing the customer information base and the two-way communication process. Loyalty incentives can show up in direct cost, such as cumulative points on a store card with trade-in value, or special discounts and promotions. They can also show up in the indirect cost of special services offered at no extra charge or at subsidised prices, such as pre-picking or home delivery.

A less obvious investment is deliberately *exceeding service expectations*. The relationship between a customer and a retail brand is one that combines product and service satisfaction. Successful service businesses know that consumers often only notice service failure, and that to create positive brand awareness and appreciation the service business has occasionally to surprise the customer with an unexpected gesture or personal touch, or an unusually high level of service. This is particularly important with the core base of loyal customers.

A final, and far from obvious, investment is *not viewing the tools of direct customer relationships as profit centres.* In the early days of store cards, many retailers viewed them primarily as a way of raising prices and profits via the high interest rates charged, without this being too obvious to price-sensitive consumers. Similarly, many electrical retailers view and use warranty contracts (a powerful source of customer information and long-term relationships) as a way of extracting 'hidden' profit on thin-margin hardware sales. Both approaches can deliver short-term profit enhancement, but run a significant risk of undermining long-term loyalty, particularly among the most loyal customers who may be the most exploited by high interest rates and over-priced warranties.

This last point applies also to the re-selling of consumer databases to third parties. This can be a profitable exercise with no negative impact on the customer: mail order companies, such as GUS in the UK, have earned large profits from the sale of consumer credit information. However, if the customer ends up being swamped with unwanted and unselective sales solicitations, or if expectations of privacy and confidentiality are breached, he or she may opt out of the database and the retailer will lose a cornerstone of that long-term direct customer relationship.

Lifetime Customer Value

Retail transactions are often individually of small value, consumers may give little evidence of retail brand loyalty in their search for best prices, and retailers themselves are often very focused on short-term sales performance. This combination tends to make retailers transaction-focused, and makes them lose sight of the potential lifetime value of customer loyalty.

Grocery retailing is a good place to start in any discussion of retail customer value. The value of a customer in grocery is high. Take a customer household over a core family-rearing period of 25 years, assume an average weekly spend of $120, with the main weekly-shop grocer getting and holding two-thirds of that or $80 per week. Sales value per customer household held throughout the 25 years works out at $104 000, and marginal contribution (at say 12.5% of sales) is $13 000. High income groups, and very loyal or longer-lasting customers, are obviously more valuable. Among other retail sectors, only automobile dealers can attribute such potential value to customer relationships and customer loyalty. The lifetime value of a grocery customer, combined with the high frequency of the grocery shop, make grocery retailers the natural centre in retailing for building long-term direct customer relationships and targeted marketing and service delivery, based on an unrivalled database of buying behaviour.

Customer value is not as high in other retail sectors as in grocery, but it is still significant. Value is driven by a combination of annual spend per spending consumer or household, the life-cycle of that spend, and the share of customer spend that a retailer might hope to achieve (see Exhibit 10.4).

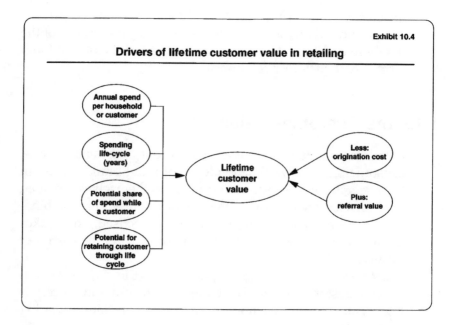

Exhibit 10.4

Drivers of lifetime customer value in retailing

Category killer markets such as home, DIY and electrical score highly on all counts: annual spends are significant, life-cycles are long, and consumers are potentially fairly loyal to a primary retailer. Within proximity retailing, customers may be very loyal to their local pharmacy, and customer lifetime value is high, from a combination of fee income and product margin. Toys and baby products have shorter life-cycles, although annual spend within the life-cycle can be high – and there is 'brand referral' value from one generation of child-rearers to the next. Fashion repertoire retailers would not expect to capture as high a proportion of even a loyal customer's total annual fashion spend.

Recognising the lifetime value of customer relationships can help retailers determine how much and where to invest in building direct customer relationships – although there is no automatic formula for deciding how much of that lifetime value to invest in capturing and keeping a customer. The lifetime value concept also helps to strengthen the organisational commitment to long-term brand-building and to outstanding customer service.

Investing in Brand Integrity 11

The title of this chapter may sound rather odd. How can a business invest in brand integrity?

It is an unusual concept of investment, but nonetheless very real and vital when applied to brands. Often it involves a long-term brand-builder *acting positively* in making and sticking to investment plans in the face of intense short-term pressure to cut corners and costs. Less obviously, it requires a brand-builder *deciding against acting* in ways that might enhance short-term revenue and profits but which would endanger long-term brand integrity and value. Both types of situation involve investment, either in actual or in opportunity cost, and both situations are acid tests of the brand-builder's mettle.

We will explore four aspects of investing in brand integrity in turn: product quality, pricing, staff motivation, and brand exploitation.

Product Quality

A brand-building retailer must stand behind its product range, whether producer brand or store brand/private label. Any customer problems are as much the responsibility of the retailer as the producer.

One clear manifestation of a retailer's commitment to product quality is a *no quibble returns* policy. If a customer has any problem with a product, including simply 'not liking it', the retailer commits, within a reasonable timeframe and provided it is in reasonable condition, to accepting the product back and making a full refund.

An unequivocally generous stance on returns means that customers can purchase in total confidence of being able to return if they are not satisfied, and their confidence in and loyalty to the retail brand shoots up. An ungenerous returns policy makes customers feel that a retailer is only interested in them up to the point at which they part with their money, and any problems after that are tough luck.

Like many investments in brand integrity, the costs can be measured quite precisely but not the benefits. The cost of a no quibble returns policy is that of customer abuse: some customers will use the product for several weeks then return it (a particular problem for fashion retailers). However, experience suggests that only a tiny minority will abuse the policy to any material extent, and the costs of this abuse will be many times offset by the positive loyalty creation.

The authority to make decisions on product returns needs to be delegated right down to shopfloor sales staff. Nordstrom is a famous example: shopfloor staff have the right to make any decisions regarding a customer's product satisfaction or dissatisfaction, the only exception being that they cannot say 'no' to a customer!

There are useful analogies outside product retailing. From its introduction, American Express knew that its policy of immediate, no-questions-asked replacement of lost travellers' cheques created an opportunity for fraud among a small minority of its customers, but it traded off that cost against the brand loyalty that that policy generated among the vast majority of its customers.

Retailers, just as producers, need to take a strong stance on dealing with *product failure*. If a store brand product turns out not to meet its performance specification, and even more so if the product failure involves any kind of risk to consumers, retailers must act decisively and publicly in recalling the product and assuming the costs of recall. Producer analogies are many: the Tylenol and Perrier recalls were extremely costly but essential for the long-term survival of the brand.

Dealing with product failure is an extreme example and manifestation of a retailer's commitment to product quality. On a day-to-day basis, this commitment needs to be manifested in the quality of every store brand product, and in the retailer's selection of producer brands.

Pricing

Pricing integrity is crucial in retail brand-building. It sends strong signals to customers about the quality of the retail offer and the integrity of a brand's relationship with its customers.

EDLP ('Every Day Low Pricing') is now common in consumer goods, with retailers and producers. Both sides have realised that constant promotions and discounting undermine brand loyalty, add costs to the total value chain, and create little if any real competitive sales gains. Brand value is reinforced by steady, consistent, fair pricing.

The corollary of EDLP is a *highly selective, controlled use of sales and promotions*. Sales should be limited to a very few seasonal clearances, at regular and consistent periods and with strictly-controlled duration. Promotions outside of sales periods should be clearly distinguishable from regular pricing, should not be too broad or frequent, and should represent a real price cut versus regular prices that have been held prior to the promotion for a reasonable period of time. (This last aspect is in fact now regulated in several countries.) Most producer brand item promotions in many retail sectors are now instigated and funded by the producers, and this can be highlighted rather than presented as a retailer-inspired price cut.

Most retailers would say that they subscribe to the principles of EDLP and limited sales/promotions. But faced with a slump in consumer demand or intense competitive pressure, leading to a dive in sales performance, one often hears the classic retail euphemism from senior management: 'we need to invest in price' (i.e. cut prices). In fact, for a long-term brand-builder, by far the more productive 'investment' is to *hold price in tough market conditions despite short-term sales loss*. Consumers remember which retailers discounted earliest and deepest, and their brand perception of those retailers will be undermined for years. As soon as they have money again in their pockets, they will return to the retail brand that maintained its values throughout.

Even simple moves such as *rounded ticket pricing* can help to send the message of pricing integrity. Ticket prices such as

'$14.99' are an affront to consumers' intelligence. Fashion retailers such as The Limited and M&S reinforce brand solidity and quality with '$15' rounded ticket pricing.

It is important to emphasise that *pricing integrity is compatible with price competitiveness.* If anything, the two reinforce each other. An EDLP retailer can still maintain a 'never beaten on price or your money back' guarantee, and consumers can be sure that an EDLP retailer's regular price is very competitive, not just its pricing during sales periods or on promotion.

Taken together, these elements of pricing integrity create and reinforce the consumers' perception of value pricing. Perception is as important as reality, and the two can diverge considerably. Among French hypermarkets, within the same real pricing band, LeClerc and Intermarché are perceived as much lower-priced than they really are, while Continent, Auchan and Carrefour are perceived as higher priced. Casino and Franprix are actually higher priced, but Casino is seen to be while Franprix gets away with a much lower price perception (see Exhibit 11.1).

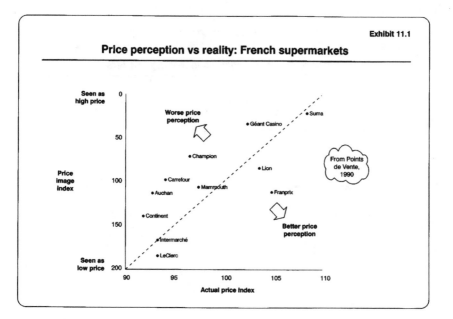

Exhibit 11.1

Price perception vs reality: French supermarkets

Staff Motivation

We observed in earlier chapters that one of the particular challenges for a retail brand-builder is to find ways of pushing commitment to brand values right down through the organisation, particularly to the thousands of front-line in-store staff whose interactions with customers form a vital part of customers' experience of the brand. To repeat a line mentioned twice before, the retail Chief Executive needs to be able to 'get a sound night's sleep without worrying that the bad attitude of a $6/hour checkout operator has just wiped out 15 years of careful loyalty-building with 100 customers in Dayton or Leeds'.

The chances of getting the right level and consistency of commitment from the front-line in-store staff are considerably increased by investment in a very broad-based performance and profit-related pay scheme. It is rare to find a long-term successful retailer in the UK that does not have some kind of pay scheme that ties the fortunes of its store staff to the fortunes of the company, or that does not go to great

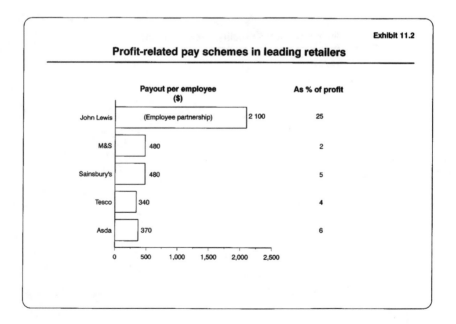

Exhibit 11.2

Profit-related pay schemes in leading retailers

	Payout per employee ($)	As % of profit
John Lewis	(Employee partnership) 2 100	25
M&S	480	2
Sainsbury's	480	5
Tesco	340	4
Asda	370	6

lengths to create a positive shared culture among its thousands of store-level staff (see Exhibit 11.2).

In the USA many leading retailers have pay and stock option schemes that build a sense of partnership right down the organisation. Many of Wal-Mart's employees, from senior management down through store managers to manual warehouse workers, have made hundreds of thousands of dollars, and often become millionaires, through their participation in Wal-Mart stock options. At the extreme, retail businesses can even work as employee-owned cooperatives. John Lewis is an excellent example of a successful retail cooperative, with a very tight and loyal 'family' culture.

It is not just front-line store staff who need to be 'bought in' to brand performance. The whole B&M team, the vital engine room of a retail business, needs to have a strong financial stake, with a significant part of their remuneration tied to category team and overall business performance.

Brand Exploitation

Owners of strong brands constantly face the question of how and how far to exploit the brand franchise. Brand value can take decades to build up, but can be 'milked' quickly and effectively over a few short years. A committed retail brand-builder needs to turn down short-term brand exploitation opportunities that will undermine long-run brand value. These are 'opportunity cost investments' in brand integrity.

Factory outlets are a classic example. They were originally conceived as clearance outlets for obsolete branded product, particularly fashion, located next to factories and in off-the-beaten-track locations: Rockport in Maine, Clarks in the UK. By the late 1980s, the high volume traffic being generated by the few original factory outlets prompted many retailers and producers to start viewing the format as a market opportunity in its own right. Many started opening 'factory outlets' in major urban markets, far away from factories, and began to produce new ranges, under their brand name, purely for those outlets. Even high quality retailers with strong brand franchises, like Nordstrom, were drawn into the factory outlet euphoria. But factory outlets, expanded beyond their initial narrow clearance role and remote locations, rapidly start to undermine the price and quality positioning of the core business. Consumers see no reason to pay a brand's normal price levels if the brand is conveniently accessible at knockdown prices. The initial rapid sales and profit boost from factory outlet volumes is easily offset by the long-run downward pressure on prices and volume in the core business, and recovering brand integrity is, as always, lengthy and expensive. After the initial hype in the early 1990s, interest and activity has died away.

Franchising or licensing of a brand, particularly into foreign markets, can generate short-term profits for near-zero investment – but brand owners need to keep a tight grip, with an eye on long-term global potential. Business partners need to be rigorously screened. Clear, tight parameters need to be set around how the brand can be used and what quality standards need to be maintained. Long-term brand property rights need to remain with the brand owner. Franchises and licences need to be for a finite period, with option to renew on both sides. Unless the brand owner is confident that all these conditions are being met, franchising and licensing options should be turned down, regardless of how much easy short-term money is on the table.

As argued in Chapter 3, retailers need to be wary of *wholesaling store brands* into other competing retailers, whether in domestic or foreign markets. Such wholesaling leverages a retailer's investment in-store brand development and its volume economies with suppliers, and can generate substantial extra profits on a short-term marginal or cash basis. But store brand exclusivity is destroyed, and the most compelling element of brand differentiation in the retailer's own stores is seriously undermined. Any short-term benefits will be offset long term by this reduction in core own-store brand differentiation and value. The retailer also becomes confused about whether to manage the business as a retail brand or as a producer brand.

Excessive or over-rapid category extension involves a similar set of short- versus long-term trade-offs. A strong fashion brand can be leveraged across a wide range of product categories, including clothing, footwear, accessories and jewellery, and home lifestyle – but the brand needs to retain a consistency of quality and positioning. Next in the UK was a prime example, having before its near collapse created over 25 brand and fascia variants straddling various product categories and consumer segments.

One of the analogous 'opportunity cost investments' for strong producer brands is to turn down private label contracts. The short-term contribution and profit impact of a big private label contract can be very tempting: production costs are marginal, and no extra investment is needed in sales, marketing or overhead. But accepting a big private label contract is one step down a very slippery slope for a producer brand, particularly a category leader, sowing the seeds for a long-term erosion of brand value.

Summary of Part III: Managing Retail Brands

Managing Multiplicity: The Detail in Retail

Retail brands differ from producer brands in the sheer multiplicity of brand attributes, arising from the combination of thousands of product lines and millions of in-store customer experiences. They also differ in the rate of change of these attributes. The need to manage the 'detail in retail' creates real difference in emphasis and priority versus the more centralised and controllable environment of fmcg brand management. It is here that the fmcg-experienced manager has to make the greatest changes in mindset.

Retail management has to lead by example in mastering and managing the details of the business, and in 'getting their hands dirty' out in the field. The key tools are range reviews, store visits, customer interaction, supplier meetings, and employee interaction and communication. Retail managers must also accept, value and encourage experimentation within brand strategy, and be ready let the brand evolve in response to unforeseen successes and opportunities.

Given the mountain of detail involved in retail management, effective management and decision support systems ('DSS') are an absolute necessity. Most retailers' information systems needs to be supplemented and honed to provide a more effective set of tools for retail brand management.

Organising for Retail Brand Management

A strong Marketing function is needed in any retail business committed to brand-building. As well as managing large

176

investments in mass marketing, promotional activity and direct customer relationships, a strong Marketing function should operate as the 'flag-carrier' for long-term brand strategy, championing the integrity of a brand's values in the face of short-term trading pressures.

The key interaction in retail brand management is between Marketing and B&M. B&M is already facing significant change, as its activities are unbundled into Range Management, Supplier Management and Stock Management, each with a distinct set of skills. B&M now needs to adjust to sharing its power over the retail proposition with Marketing, particularly at the core intersection of category management, where the two functions need jointly to review and develop overall category and store brand strategies.

Unlike in fmcg producer businesses, the Marketing function cannot be the king or queen of brand management. Brand strategy and brand management must necessarily remain a more complex team effort, driven by the inner circle of market-facing functional heads: the Chief Executive and the heads of B&M, Marketing and Store Operations. This inner circle must have a clearly articulated and shared idea of the long-term brand-building objective.

Investing in Store Brands

There are five stages in the development of store brands, roughly matching the stages of maturity and power of the retail brand. The first three stages – generics, cheap/copycat, and re-engineered low cost store brands – require little or no investment by the retailer. The last two stages – par quality and leadership – move from being cost- and price-based to being based on quality and innovation, and require extensive investment by the retailer in design and development, quality control, and close long-term supplier relationships.

Retailers can view the strategic purpose of store brand development as either short-term margin enhancement or long-term brand-building. Retailers who concentrate on generics and cheap/copycat store brands usually focus on margin enhancement and miss the greater brand-building opportunity. Retailers whose strategic purpose is long-term brand-building will behave and invest in a very different way, even in the early stages of store brand development.

Retailers cannot hope to develop strong store brand positions across all categories simultaneously. They must target and prioritise their effort and investment, either by targeting weak producer brands or by re-merchandising a category, examples of which range from wine, coffee and chilled foods through to storage and health and beauty care.

Moving into sub-brands can take a retailer too far along the path of becoming like a producer brand. Broad differences in price/quality positioning can be signalled through packaging and presentation and through the use of store brand 'tags' ('Select', 'Basics'), while still staying within a store brand umbrella.

Building a supply chain and a supplier base for quality and leadership store brands requires an investment-oriented approach, characterised by open information flows, joint investment in product development and quality control, some level of risk-sharing and long-term commitment, and recognition of the need for attractive long-run financial returns for both sides.

Even very strong, well managed retail brands can go too far, too fast, in developing store brand penetration and reducing the presence and choice of producer brands. Strong producer brands still command high levels of consumer loyalty, and retailers need to be careful that they are not crossing a threshold of consumer acceptance, particularly where the absence of preferred producer brands triggers a switch in primary shopping loyalty.

At maturity, quality and leadership store brands operate similarly to producer brands. As their consumer acceptance, quality and market share grows, initial price discounts versus producer brands are reduced and store brands may achieve a premium versus producer brands. Strong store brands may often, rather counter-intuitively, have greater appeal to and greater share in more affluent consumer groups, who will be more confident in their own taste and judgement in abandoning heavily advertised producer brands.

Investing in the Brand–Customer Relationship

Although retail brand advertising spends are increasing, there are limitations on the value of mass marketing in building the retail brand–customer relationship. Producer brand advertising, even in very functional product categories, delivers compressed images of brand association and aspiration, with the goal of long-term brand-building. Retail advertising tends to be more banal and crude, focusing on price and promotion with the goal of short-term sales up-lift, and rarely uses compressed messages and abstract imagery.

Mass marketing also does not play to retailers' own strengths, and to their structural advantages over producers, which lie in the ability and opportunity to build strong direct customer relationships. This retail advantage derives from their frequent direct contact with the customer, the breadth and immediacy of their consumer information, their greater capacity for quick, flexible experimentation, and their ability to tailor their brand and offer to local demand.

Building direct customer relationships has three key elements: customer understanding, customer targeting, and customer communication. Each requires investment in systems and resources, and overall investment is required in loyalty schemes that give customers reason to participate in the databases and in the relationship with the retail brand. This investment can be supported, and focused more effectively, by using the concept of lifetime customer value.

Investing in Brand Integrity

Investing in brand integrity can involve acting positively in making and sticking to investment plans in the face of short-term pressure to cut corners and costs, or deciding against acting in ways that enhance short-term revenue and profits but endanger long-term brand value. Both types of situation involve investment, either in actual or in opportunity cost, and both are acid tests of the brand-builder's mettle. As with every element of brand-building investment, commitment is only truly evidenced, and brand benefit accumulated, over many years.

There are several ways in which a retailer's commitment to brand integrity can be manifested. A 'no quibbles' returns policy is a powerful statement of a brand's commitment to and confidence in its product quality, and aligns the retailer solidly with the customer's interests. Pricing integrity – EDLP, limited sales and promotions, and holding the line on price in difficult trading conditions – sends the right message to consumers as to the brand's sense of its own worth, and strengthens rather than conflicts with a stance of never being beaten on price. Broad-based profit-sharing and performance-related pay can bind staff in to the brand culture, increasing motivation and commitment right down through the organisation. A committed retail brand-builder will turn down short-term brand exploitation opportunities that run the risk of undermining long-run brand value.

*   *   *

Our focus so far in the book has been on product retailing, and the challenges facing product retailers wishing to build strong retail brands.

In *Part IV* of the book, we switch perspectives for a moment. We look at the relevance of our theme to financial services retailing, and we 'switch sides' to take the producer perspective on the growth of retail brand power.

Part IV

Different Perspectives

The Financial **12**
Services
Supermarket

In product retailing, the main focus of this book, production and retailing are generally performed by different firms. In the past brand power has resided predominantly with the producer brands, while retailers have competed as cost-efficient distribution channels.

In service retailing, the tension between production and retailing, and between producer and retail brand power, is largely absent. Consider eating out and hotels. In these categories, the retail service is all or the largest part of the 'product' that the consumer purchases, and this 'product' is generally consumed at point-of-retail-sale. The producer/retailer split does not apply, and the retail service business has always taken on the brand-building role. These categories provide many examples of very strong brands, such as McDonald's, but they have limited relevance to the challenges facing product retailers.

Retail financial services, however, could be more analogous to product retailing (see Box 12.1). The 'product' includes service interaction at point-of-sale, but the majority of consumption and value occurs later. There is, or at least could be, a producer/retailer split – although that may be obscured, as it is in banking, by the historical legacies of regulation and vertical integration. Financial service retailers could in theory act similarly to supermarkets, offering consumers a range of choices of producer brands and of store brand product. There are examples of brand-building strategies, successful and unsuccessful. Finally, the sector provides an example of the threat of branch or store disintermediation, with broad implications for product retailers as interactive home shopping develops in the twenty-first century.

Box 12.1   Retail and Consumer Business

'Retail' and 'consumer' are used interchangeably in financial services, to distinguish that business from the 'wholesale' market and from trading and investment activity. 'Branch banking' is still almost synonymous in many managers' minds with 'retail banking', despite the growth of ATMs and phone banking.

The Context

Consumer financial services embraces a wide universe of institutions and products. A top-level classification could be as in Exhibit 12.1.

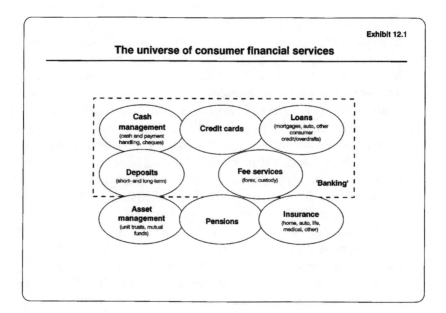

Exhibit 12.1

The universe of consumer financial services

Banks, and bank-type institutions such as savings and loan associations in the USA and building societies in the UK, have historically provided the core range of consumer services: chequeing accounts and cash handling, consumer credit (from mortgages and auto loans to general overdraft facilities), consumer deposits, and fee-based services such as foreign exchange and custody. Specialist institutions have provided insurance, asset management and pensions.

The very use of the term 'institutions', rather than 'firms' or 'competitors', reflects an historical context. Regulation has driven structure and strategy in the sector for the best part of the twentieth century, particularly since the depression of the 1920s. Regulation has constrained which businesses institutions could be in, which geographic markets they could operate in, how much credit or deposit business they could take on and at what rates, and what capital ratios they were required to maintain. The strategic issues and plans at the top of most senior managers' agendas have centred on where and how to work within regulatory constraints, or to get round them, or to lobby for keeping them, or to anticipate changes in them. Many institutions have been and still are fully or partly publicly owned; as recently as 1980 one of the first actions of President Mitterrand's new socialist government in France was to nationalise the major banks, many of which still remain in the state sector, accumulating ferocious losses.

Over the last 20 years the general trend in financial services world-wide has been one of de-regulation, sometimes at a rapid and dramatic rate, as in the City of London's 'Big Bang' of the late 1980s. National governments have found themselves unable to contain and manage wholesale markets in the face of new technology, the removal of fixed exchange rates and currency controls, and the general globalisation of industry, trading and money flows. Although regulation remains pervasive and very significant in the industry, financial 'institutions' have become, or are becoming, financial services 'competitors'. In the process they are re-assessing and re-defining the strategy, structure and economics of the sector: unbundling businesses and processes that were formerly inter-woven, such as wholesale and retail banking; forming new combinations that were previously prohibited, such as banking and insurance; shifting their attention from regulators to customers and competitors; and shifting their measures of success from asset size and credit rating to profitability and return on shareholder equity.

The Consumer Financial Services Value Chain

The retail financial services value chain can be broken down into three main elements, of which the first two can be characterised as 'production' and the last as 'retail distribution' (see Exhibit 12.2).

The key element of 'production' is the identification, evaluation and management of different types of risk: credit and interest rate risk for banks, investment risk/return for asset managers, and actuarial risk for insurers. Competitors win or lose depending on their ability to understand and implement risk management, and on their ability to unbundle and price that risk effectively to attract profitable customers. Risk management, in our definition, includes the capital base (or allocated capital) necessary to support the relative

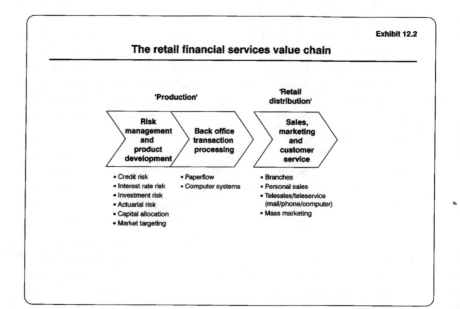

Exhibit 12.2

The retail financial services value chain

volatility of different types and levels of risk. Often risks are combined. US savings-and-loans (S&Ls) historically funded long-term fixed rate mortgages with short-term floating rate consumer deposits, combining credit and asset value risk (the mortgage and the underlying property) with interest rate risk (the mismatch between fixed long-term and floating short-term interest rates). The level of mismatch and asset value risk was often underestimated or understated, and the capital base insufficient to support it, leading to the S&L crisis and government bail-out of the late 1980s.

The back office transaction processing element of the value chain is straightforward. Many financial services products involve extensive 'paperwork' (paper-based and computerised), and back office operations are administrative factories for financial services providers. ATMs, in our definition, would fall under this area of transaction processing.

Retail distribution (often called 'origination') involves the acquisition and maintenance of customers, whether via the branch networks of banks and S&Ls, the personal sales forces and independent broker–distributors of insurers and pension funds, or telesales and teleservice via mail, phone and computer.

The Prospects for Financial Services Supermarkets

Given our definition of the retail financial services value chain and the distinction between 'production' and 'retailing', can we expect to see real financial services supermarkets?

There are frequent articles in the European and American press under headlines such as 'banks becoming like supermarkets'. The thrust of these articles is that banks are casting off their discreet, staid, conservative traditional image. They are starting to compete hard and publicly for customers, with aggressive promotions, free gifts and discounts to new customers, and increased spending on mass marketing of their brand.

While this is true, it does not make retail financial services providers into supermarkets. Banks are not starting to sell five varieties of deposit product from different producers, or ten brands of insurance. We do not believe that financial services supermarkets, offering a range of store brand and producer products, will become a reality, for several reasons.

One reason is the infrequent nature of 'shopping' for financial services products, and the related inertia of customer–supplier relationships. Once a bank account has been established, the consumer has to be given a strong positive reason to think about shopping again to switch supplier or open up an additional account. House, auto and personal insurances are usually on automatic annual renewal, and often are only actively 'shopped for' when a new house or car is bought. Mortgages and pensions are bought and forgotten for years, and often locked-in via high switching costs. As all financial services firms know, acquiring a new customer from an established relationship with a competitor is extremely expensive and difficult to achieve, unless a significant price or service advantage can be offered.

Outside of credit, consumers want, above all, security of deposits or investment funds and security of claims or pension payout. After security, they want smooth, reliable service. If possible, many consumers would put all their financial services business through one supplier, minimising the hassle and paperwork. Financial services offer little consumption pleasure, but choosing the wrong provider carries a serious financial risk. Hence the cautious, conservative and risk-avoiding stance of many consumers, which underpins inertia and infrequent comparison shopping.

This is a valid but not wholly convincing argument against the prospects for financial services supermarkets. Although customer inertia in retail financial services is still high, it is declining, particularly in products where switching cost and hassle is low, such as interest-earning deposit accounts or credit cards, or where markets have become much more competitive and open, such as mortgages. Consumers are becoming more knowledgeable and confident, and willing to shop around and switch suppliers. There may be no strong, long-run innate barriers to financial supermarkets solely from the perspective of consumer needs and behaviour.

A second and more convincing reason is the weight of vertical integration. The huge existing networks of bank, S&L and building society branches, and the formidable personal sales forces of insurers and pension providers, were created as tied, exclusive distribution channels for selling own-brand product. Citibank is as likely to start selling Bankers Trust CDs as Shell is to start selling Exxon petrol. Competitive innovations can, in general, be copied quickly and launched as own-brand product through these captive distribution channels. This vertical integration may have been created by history and regulation, but its result is that financial services 'retailers' already have one of the key characteristics of strong retail brands. They are 100% store brand businesses.

The third factor operating against the emergence of real financial services supermarkets is the trend towards disintermediation of branches and distributors.

Disintermediation of Branches and Distributors

Of all financial services providers, banks and bank-type institutions could have the greatest potential for becoming like grocery supermarkets. They have extensive store/branch networks, which many of their customers still visit physically and frequently, principally to pay in and withdraw money. Banks have the primary service relationship and most frequent service contact with customers in the financial services sector. It is easy to imagine supermarket 'shelves' in bank branches, merchandising insurance or asset management products, either own brands or independent producer brands.

But physical bank branch networks are facing the threat of long-term redundancy. The cash/chequeing deposit and withdrawal activity that accounts for the majority of day-to-day branch transactions is being taken over by unmanned ATMs. ATMs have lower operating costs, and can be located in more sites closer to customers, such as workplaces and supermarkets. All other elements of the banking relationship can be handled more economically, and with less inconvenience for the consumer, by mail, phone and electronic banking. Non-branch banking is one of the fastest growth sectors in consumer financial services. In the UK, it is estimated that one-third of banking customers will bank by telephone by the year 2000, up from around 10% in 1995 and around 1% in 1990. ('Bank by telephone' is defined as using a dedicated telephone banking service for over 50% of transactions apart from cash withdrawals.) The fastest growing bank in the UK is Midland's First Direct, which started in 1989 and by 1995 was opening 10 000 new accounts per month, the equivalent of opening two or three new branches. First Direct's customers carry average balances ten times higher than a normal branch customer, while operating costs per client are under 40% of those of a branch.

Disintermediation is even more pronounced and rapid in the insurance sector. Traditionally, most consumer insurance – house, auto, personal – was sold through insurance broker–distributors. These agents do look and operate like insurance supermarkets, selling a range of products from various producers. The recent growth in direct marketing of insurance, particularly phone selling and service, has transformed the distribution structure of the industry, particularly in auto, led in the UK by the growth of Direct Line (see Exhibit 12.3).

The future for the distribution of asset management products, such as mutual funds and unit trusts, is harder to call. Many are sold and serviced directly to the consumer, through print and mail-shot marketing and mail or phone servicing, with consumers 'shopping' in the investment pages of newspapers and financial journals. Charles Schwab, the leading US discount broker, began in 1992 offering a service called OneSource, whereby consumers could deal with one sales and service point to access and trade more than 500 no-load mutual funds from various suppliers; in five years this service has made Schwab into the third largest mutual fund distributor in the USA. But assembling a personal investment portfolio is still a daunting and complex task for most consumers, and many prefer to delegate the task to third-

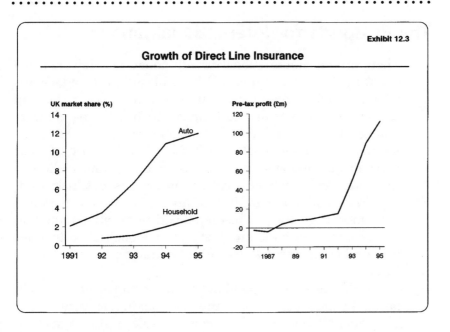

Exhibit 12.3

Growth of Direct Line Insurance

party financial advisors, who do act as a kind of personal supermarket for a range of asset management producers.

Branches and distributors will not disappear overnight. Consumers are still very attached to the symbolic security of bricks and mortar. Charles Schwab initially operated without branches, offering no-frills cut-price stockbroking over the telephone. But it discovered that its market share in Sacramento, California had doubled when it opened one physical branch in the area, and Schwab now has a policy of maintaining bricks-and-mortar branches in every major market. Bank branch networks will also continue to be valuable assets for their owners while they continue to hold a sizeable customer base – the number of bank branches is declining steadily, but at a slow rate.

Over the long run, however, the growth of non-branch sales and service in consumer financial services will militate against the development of financial services supermarkets. Consumers will prefer the efficiency and convenience of mail, phone and computer shopping and service interaction, certainly for most banking and insurance products, and possibly for asset management.

The Prospects for Internationalisation

There are few international brands today in retail financial services. American Express, VISA, MasterCard and Diners Club are global credit card brands. A few banks are leading retailers in more than one country, such as Hong Kong & Shanghai in Asia. Asset management firms are often international, piggy-backing off the global activity of their investment banking owners. Banks have sometimes followed their domestic customers overseas, into tourist destinations or expatriate communities. But competition in retail banking, insurance and pensions has remained primarily national, in stark contrast with the rapid, extensive globalisation that has occurred on the wholesale side and in trading and investment banking.

The rationale and potential for internationalising branch-based businesses is poor. Branch banking is very like a proximity retail format. Economies of scale, at store and chain level, are generally low. There are scale economies in back office processing, but this can increasingly be contracted out to a high volume third-party provider. Local market knowledge is critical for developing profitable business, particularly in consumer credit. Customer inertia and resistance to switching, high enough between two domestic competitors, are increased when faced with the choice of a new foreign brand: strong incentives, in 'price' and service level, need to be given to prompt a switch.

The growth of non-branch-based propositions could open up the opportunity for internationalisation. International direct sales/service competitors can offer substantial price and service advantages over traditional local branch-based firms, and can obtain economies of scale at an international as well as national level. Direct insurance and asset management, including pensions, could be prime candidates for such internationalisation – although overcoming taxation and regulation differences between countries has proven to be a major barrier in the development of pan-European competition in pensions and life assurance. Banking may be harder, given the strength of customer relationships, the still considerable differences in regulation between markets, and differences in language and culture between countries.

Brand–Customer Relationships

In Part III, we identified the key elements of retail brand-building as store brands, the brand–customer relationship, and brand integrity. Most retail financial services providers are already store brand retailers. Brand integrity is a strong part of many institutions' culture, given the fiduciary nature of the customer relationship. Mass marketing spends are high across the sector. The big remaining brand-building opportunity centres on direct customer relationships and life-cycle marketing.

The lifetime value of a customer in financial services is high, particularly for a competitor who can offer a broad range of products, from banking through insurance to asset management. This value can justify large investments in the databases needed to support direct customer relationships and life-cycle marketing. As well as making these investments and learning how to use them effectively, firms need to look at how their organisation is structured to manage long-term customer relationships.

Financial services competitors are still in the process of unbundling a formerly integrated business into discrete profit centres, with separate management and full P&L accountability. In the process of this unbundling, they have lost sight of the need for an integrated sales and service contact with their customers. Customers are frustrated by having to talk to different divisions and profit centres as if they were completely different firms, with no knowledge of the overall customer relationship and customer history. The local branch often provided a focal point for the customer relationship; this has not yet been replaced for customers who have converted to non-branch banking, and now only interact with their provider via phone, mail or computer. The customer-oriented financial services competitor of the future, dealing with non-branch-based customers, will need to find a way to re-integrate product profit centres and customer relationship management. First Direct is making considerable progress on this front, and its phone-based service and customer relationship management is superior to that of most branch-based banks.

Mayonnaise and Mutual Funds

Product retailers are themselves increasingly bundling some elements of financial services activity into their transactions and consumer offer, either to enhance their product retailing brand or as profit centres. The most obvious example is consumer credit. The majority of 'big ticket' retailing now comes with the offer of credit provided by the retailer: auto (via the vehicle manufacturer's financing arm), electrical, furniture. Most large department stores and many fashion retailers offer store credit cards. Mail order companies bundle extended credit into their pricing and payment terms, and in many countries are the prime source of consumer credit ratings.

Some retailers are now going beyond offering consumer credit. Consumer research in the UK indicates that consumers trust their supermarkets more than they trust their banks. UK supermarkets, holding the central shopping relationship with consumers, are taking on large parts of branch banking services: cash withdrawal as an added option at the check-out, the maintenance of cash balances on quasi-'chequeing' accounts, and the provision of ATMs. (Banks are, in fact, sometimes happy to see those traditional branch banking activities switch over to the supermarkets; many of their low-balance current accounts are loss-making on a fully-costed basis, and they do not charge for cheque cashing and cash withdrawals.) M&S has gone further. It now sells its own-store brand unit trusts, PEPs, life assurance, and consumer loans, earning almost $100 million in operating profit from its financial services activities (see Exhibit 12.4).

In late 1996, Sainsbury's announced a partnership with the Bank of Scotland to launch the Sainsbury's Bank in 1997. Sainsbury's intends to begin by offering debit and VISA cards and savings accounts, followed later by the full range of consumer financial services, including current accounts, mortgages and insurance. The new bank will be a telephone service along the lines of First Direct, with its own ATMs in Sainsbury's stores. A spokesperson for Sainsbury's said 'what we're doing is not an add-on to a loyalty card . . . it will be a fully-fledged bank'.

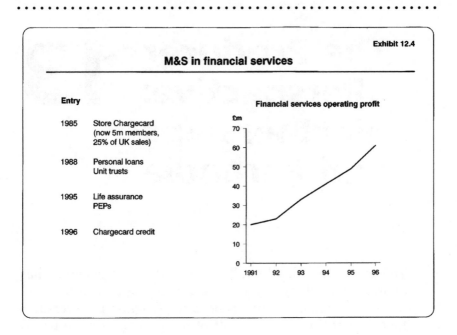

Exhibit 12.4

M&S in financial services

Entry

1985	Store Chargecard (now 5m members, 25% of UK sales)
1988	Personal loans / Unit trusts
1995	Life assurance / PEPs
1996	Chargecard credit

Financial services operating profit

The Producer Perspective: Partnerships and Paranoia 13

The growth of retail brand power, actual and potential, has enormous implications for the strategy and prospects of producer brands. Producers need to recognise the pressures that they will face as a result of the growth of retail brand power, and determine how they will respond to these pressures.

Retailers need to understand the producer perspective. They need to know where and how they can work with producers – either as branded category leaders or as store brand suppliers – in a mutually beneficial partnership. They also need to know where and how they can target and exploit weak producer brand positions to help build retail brand strength and quality store brands. The relationship between brand-building retailers and producers will be a balance of 'partnership and paranoia'.

The Historical Context: Producer Brands in the 1980s and 1990s

Producer brands have had a roller-coaster ride over the last decade. The *mid- and late 1980s was a peak period*, particularly in packaged grocery goods, a period in which the strength of 'power' brands was increasingly apparent in the economic returns they delivered to their owners. Costs of new brand development escalated, and the probability of new brand

success declined. The retail trade began aggressively rationalising second-tier brands. Leading power brands (number
one or a strong number two in a product category) increased
market share, became increasingly global in scale and scope,
and pulled away from the second-tier pack. 'Intangible'
brand assets became recognised, even on their owners'
balance sheets, as as valuable and long-lived as more
'tangible' assets such as technology and production capacity.
In most cases, the brand leaders in major packaged goods
categories in the USA and the UK were the same in 1985 as in
1925. Meanwhile, the US auto industry seemed to be
collapsing under the attack of foreign competition, and IBM's
mighty technology and installed base were being side-lined
by PCs, Microsoft and Intel.

A power brand came to be viewed as a uniquely defensible
asset. Like a Van Gogh painting, there was no material threat
of new entrants or substitutes. Brand value could be
increased by global distribution and extension onto new
products and variants. In the mid-1980s' boom, higher prices
and gross margins could be extracted from loyal consumers.
In the second half of the 1980s, power brand values – stock
market ratings and acquisition premia – soared. A wave of
global mega-deals, at p/e multiples in the mid-30s and over,
surged through the fmcg sector.

However, even as power brand euphoria and multiples
reached their peak, there were already several *developments
undermining the value of producer brands*. Producers were
shifting marketing investment from above-the-line advertising spend into below-the-line promotional spend. The shift
was rapid and significant: a 2:1 ratio in favour of above-the-
line spend in the early 1980s was reversed by the early 1990s.
Even the strongest producer brands were in practice selling
the majority of their product on one kind of promotion or
other: consumer coupons, special trade deals, multi-buys,
trial incentives, cross-product promotions, regional and
seasonal promotions. List prices, which were dutifully
increased at inflation-plus every year, were in practice a
fantasy. Net sales gains from much of this promotional
activity were dubious at best. Consumers and retailers
deferred purchase, or shopped around between stores and

regions, waiting or looking confidently for the promotional deal. The shift to promotional spend increased consumer price awareness and sucked away funds from advertising.

Producers were also drawn into brand extension and product proliferation. Given the high costs and low hit-rates of new brand development, coupled with the high costs and asset values of existing brands, producers found it far easier and cheaper to introduce new products under an existing brand umbrella, or to proliferate product varieties of existing brands. An OC&C study found that the advertising and promotion costs needed to convince customers to try out a new product were, on average, 36% less for a 'stretched' brand than for a new brand. Likewise, for one particular multinational, only 30% of new brand products were still on the shelf six years after launch, versus 50% of products that leveraged a pre-existing brand.

Some brand extension efforts were logical and successful: for example, the extension of Coke into Diet Coke or the Mars confectionery franchise into ice-cream bars. Kellogg's hyper-segmentation and preemptive filling of new demand opportunities in the ready-to-eat cereals market has contributed to overall category growth. Colman's, the worthy but rather unexciting brand leader in English mustards, has been extended over a new category of flavoured and speciality mustards and condiments, as well as into cooking sauces.

But many lacked any real rationale other than minimising investment and risk, and diluted the original brand franchise: for example, McVities in the UK, a biscuit brand which has now been extended over pizzas and frozen foods. And many simply added cost and complexity, reduced category profitability for all competitors, and confused the consumer – most notoriously the competitive proliferation in soap powders which culminated in Unilever's hasty withdrawal of Persil/Omo 'Power' after it was accused of reducing garments to shreds. Both Unilever and P&G now accept that the rate of product, pack and sub-brand churn needs to be reduced if credibility with the consumer is not to be further undermined.

The growing power of retailers was also starting to weaken producer brand values. In most cases, producers still felt this power simply as value-chain power: the negotiating clout of an increasingly concentrated and sophisticated retail sector. But value-chain power was already starting to evolve into retail brand power and competition from quality store brands, providing a price/value benchmark for the consumer that made it increasingly hard for producers to carry on extracting their historical brand premia.

Finally, the consumer boom of the 1980s was giving way to the world-wide consumer recession of the early 1990s. Premium luxury brands were particularly badly hit as consumers reined in discretionary spending, even in markets like Japan that had seemed to have an endless appetite for high-priced aspirational brands such as Louis Vuitton and Johnnie Walker. Across the board, consumers were seeking value and switching spending away from high priced brand leaders.

All these pressures eventually burst through and produced a significant, abrupt *downwards re-rating in the early 1990s* of the value of producer brands. The trigger point was Marlboro Friday in early 1993. Philip Morris announced a 20% across-the-board cut in the list price of Marlboro, to stem loss of market share. Analysts reacted with horror and wiped billions of dollars off the stock price of Philip Morris, and off the value of the Dow–Jones Consumer Goods Sector Index. Marlboro Friday was followed by similar moves by other fmcg giants such as P&G in the USA and BSN (now Danone) in Europe. April 1996 brought 'Grape Nuts Monday' in the USA: Philip Morris's Post and Nabisco divisions cut the list prices of Grape Nuts and other branded cereals by 20%. Ready-to-eat cereals had been one of the most heavily marketed and branded of fmcg categories; some estimates put the cost of advertising, sales and marketing, overhead and profit at over two-thirds of total branded producer cost, versus only one-third for actually making the product. Two months after Grape Nuts Monday, Kellogg's, the world's biggest and most profitable cereal maker, cut its list prices on many brands by almost the same amount. This re-rating, combined with the growth in market share of store brands and private label in the grocery sector in the USA, produced many analyses and articles hailing 'the death of brands'.

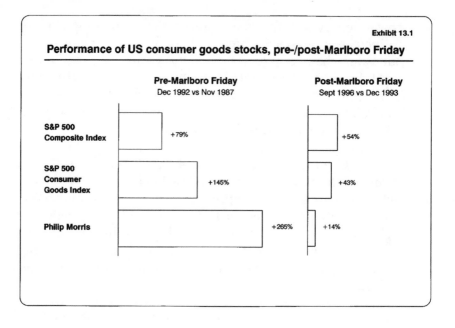

Exhibit 13.1

Performance of US consumer goods stocks, pre-/post-Marlboro Friday

	Pre-Marlboro Friday Dec 1992 vs Nov 1987	Post-Marlboro Friday Sept 1996 vs Dec 1993
S&P 500 Composite Index	+79%	+54%
S&P 500 Consumer Goods Index	+145%	+43%
Philip Morris	+265%	+14%

But after the trough of the mid-1990s, producer brands have recovered to today's *more balanced position*. Cutting list prices has allowed leading brands to start to recover market share and to reduce their dependence on promotions, re-establishing pricing integrity. Producer brands are now re-emphasising investment in the core elements that underpin long-term brand value: value-added product development rather than cosmetic product proliferation, and above-the-line marketing rather than promotions. Store brand market share growth has slowed, and consumer spending has steadily recovered, at least in the USA and the UK. Fmcg stock prices have also recovered, although not to the premium levels of the 1980s (see Exhibit 13.1).

Producer Attitudes to Retail Brand Power

Given this recent recovery, many producers and analysts outside the UK are now sounding complacent about the threat from retailers and retail brands. Store brands are dismissed as a cheap alternative for hard-pressed consumers.

Their market share growth is dismissed as cyclical, a function of the 1990s economic downturn, that is now being, or about to be, reversed as the consumer feel-good factor returns. Retailers are dismissed as incapable of understanding and investing in long-term brand-building at the same level and quality of leading fmcg producers. The UK model of strong retail brands is dismissed as an aberration that will not be repeated elsewhere.

This is partly wishful but honest thinking. Some producers, particularly in the USA, do believe that retail brands pose no significant long-term threat to producer brands. But it is also partly deliberate policy. Many producers recognise that, although producer brands are far from dead, there has been a structural shift in the balance of power between retailers and producers. If retailers seize the opportunity to build real retail brand power, this structural shift will be multiplied many times over. While publicly arguing against the rationale and likelihood of such a shift, behind the scenes these producers are assuming that it could happen, and are making plans accordingly: where and how to try to fight and hold the line, and where and how to work with retailers on store brand development.

The first step in developing a strategic response to retail brand power is an objective assessment of a producer's brand portfolio and the potential threats against it from retail brands. Strategy and tactics will be very different depending on whether a brand is a leader (number one or two in market share) or a follower in its product category.

Producer Brand Response: Category Leaders Reinvesting in Brand Value

Store brand penetration varies widely across categories. In grocery, penetration can range from virtually zero in health and beauty care or chewing gum, up to two-thirds of the market in pasta and ready meals (see Exhibit 13.2).

The reasons for this variation are complex and interconnected, but one of the most important is the strength, strategy and inclination to invest of the producer brand category

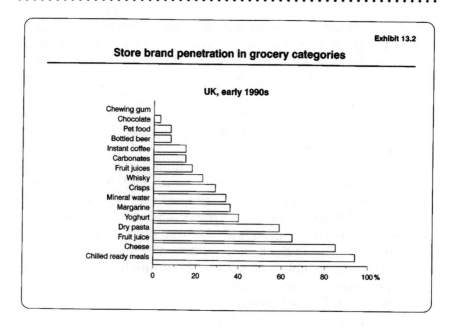

Exhibit 13.2

Store brand penetration in grocery categories

UK, early 1990s

leader. Store brand penetration levels, in the UK, the USA and other markets, show a strong inverse correlation with levels of producer brand investment in innovation and marketing (see Case Study 13.1).

Case Study 13.1   Nestlé in Coffee vs UB in Biscuits

Soluble coffee and sweet biscuits are similar-sized markets in the UK, both with brand leaders with around a 50% market share: Nestlé and UB. Nestlé has followed a positive category leader strategy. It has invested heavily in marketing and innovation, and refused to supply private label. As a result, few consumers rate store brands; private label share is only 19% and is trending slightly down. In contrast, UB has focused on low-cost volume production, under-invested in marketing and innovation, and gone into full co-production of private label. UB's branded franchise has been heavily eroded. Many consumers view store brands as offering comparable quality and better value. Private label share in the category is 50% and growing (see Exhibit 13.3).

Exhibit 13.3

Category leader strategies: Nestlé vs UB

	Soluble Coffee	Sweet Biscuits
UK market size (£m)	600	600
Leader	**Nestlé**	**UB**
Market share	48%	50%
A/S ratio	8%	1-2%
Innovation	High	Low
Attitude to private label production	Refuse	Full co-production
Consumer attitudes: Private label better value/comparable quality	16-17%	32-35%
Private label share	19%	50%

UB went into full co-production of private label many years ago, as a way of maintaining factory volume and short-term profits. The long-run effects of that strategy take time to emerge, but can now be seen rather clearly. From 1988 to 1994, operating margins halved and return on capital declined from 24% to 10%. In 1995 the business went into heavy loss (see Exhibit 13.4).

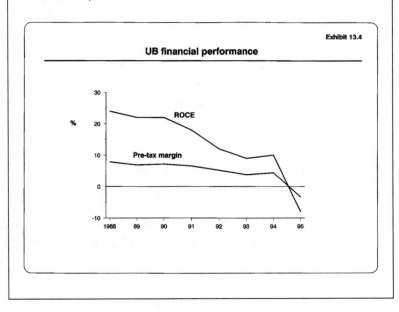

Exhibit 13.4

UB financial performance

The biscuit category is not a rare exception in the weakness of its producer brands. Brand leaders need to assess objectively the level of threat that retail brand power presents in their category. A useful technique is to take the perspective of an aggressive retailer. How vulnerable is the category and your brand to store brand penetration? How would you go about attacking the category if you were a retailer? Current relative rates-of-sale and retail price levels provide indications of strength or weakness: a strong brand needs to do well on both counts. Category and brand characteristics can also be evaluated: consumer potential, levels of marketing and innovation, technological difficulty, capacity utilisation, product life-cycles. Owners of producer brands need to do this evaluation themselves before a retail brand-builder does it for them.

The Nestlé/UB story in Case Study 13.1 emphasises how category leaders need to invest pre-emptively to defend their brand value, in product development, quality, production processes, technology and above-the-line marketing. Pernod–Ricard in France is another excellent example: with major marketing investment behind their Ricard and 51 brands, and a refusal to produce own label, they have rejuvenated a declining pastis market and built brand value and profitability. PepsiCo in the snacks market provides another example (see Case Study 13.2).

Most fmcg brands today are part of large portfolios, like Nestlé, Unilever and Philip Morris. These portfolio owners need to evaluate the situation of each individual brand and category, and then to concentrate resources and investment behind current or potential category leaders.

Lost causes or sub-critical mass brands in the portfolio may need to be milked or chopped. Unilever recently went through a major rationalisation of its brand portfolio, pruning out weak brands to concentrate resources behind the possible long-term big winners.

Perhaps the most difficult question of all for brand leaders is whether to join the opposition and produce store brands. For clear category leaders, the right answer is usually

Case Study 13.2 PepsiCo

PepsiCo entered the UK Savoury Snacks market in 1989 through the acquisition of Walkers/Smiths in the post-Nabisco/KKR auction, paying 30 times earnings. While the challenge of earning out the acquisition premium was substantial, the UK snacks market offered an excellent opportunity to drive category growth. Consumption *per capita* was only two-thirds that of the US level. Savoury snacks accounted for only 20% of total snack consumption in the UK, against 30% in the USA.

Avoiding the growing niche segment at the top-end, PepsiCo turned its attention on the large but stagnant standard crisp market. Efforts went on improving product quality, with substantial investments in plant technology and potato breeding. At high cost, a switch was made to foil bags to keep air out, and later nitrogen-filled bags were introduced. Consumers noticed the extra freshness. Inroads were made into the premium segment as consumers decided that a good standard crisp would do instead.

Marketing investment was focused behind the Walkers brand, with the poorly perceived Smiths brand withdrawn entirely. Marketing investment was increased by 25%. A new salesforce was recruited to secure improved distribution. The combined Walkers/Smiths infrastructure was extensively reengineered to reduce costs.

The achievements have been substantial. The UK savoury snacks market has grown by 5% per annum since 1990. Walkers' share has increased from 33% to 44%. Trading profit margin has expanded by 5 percentage points. Store brand share has fallen.

straightforward: don't do it. This is the purist position exemplified by global power brand producers such as Kellogg's, Coke and Pepsi, P&G, Nestlé in coffee, or Gillette.

For producer brands that are number two or three in their category, the question is much harder to answer – and there is certainly no general 'right' answer. Powerful arguments can be advanced in favour of producing store brands. It is a large and growing segment. Number two or three brands possess manufacturing and distribution scale economies, raw material sourcing advantages, and product and process competencies that are transferable to store brand production. It may allow closer, improved trade relationships. And there is the familiar refrain: 'If we don't do it, someone else will.' Such arguments are used to justify a variety of strategies for store brand production. Some use it as a tactical capacity-filler. Some use it as a means of 'market control', particularly in small categories where one producer brand and one store brand supplier can fill demand. UB in the UK and Besnier/President in France (which, unlike UB at present, has a highly profitable volume business in dairy products) are more unusual examples of full co-production.

However, there are also strong arguments against store brand co-production. It can be difficult to price into retailer accounts, particularly given that retailers work closely with their store brand producers and contracts do not change frequently – the risk of precipitating a price battle is significant. Bargaining power on the brand may be weakened, and account managers may be placed in the impossible position of justifying a trade price premium for the producer brand that has neither superior product specification nor higher rate of sale. The values of a category may be undermined, reducing overall producer returns.

Managing both producer brands and store brand production within the same business and organisation structure can lead to organisational schizophrenia and confusion over goals and priorities. The producer brand mentality of long-term investment and differentiation is at odds with the store brand production mentality of short-term flexibility and low cost. Store brand production should be run, as far as possible, as a totally separate unit, with different account managers focused solely on the needs of the retailer. This can minimise, although not eliminate, organisational conflict and business risk.

Producer Brand Response: Category Followers Becoming Store Brand Suppliers

Category followers (number 3, 4, 5 or worse market share positions) can choose to work proactively with retailers as suppliers of quality store brands. Although unlikely to deliver as high a return as a category-leading producer brand, focusing on supplying store brands can be an effective and profitable strategy. Northern Foods, the major foods supplier to M&S, has enjoyed strong sales growth and earned an average 24% return on capital over the last 8 years. Freiberger, based in Berlin, has become the largest frozen pizza producer in Europe, solely on the basis of retail own-label contracts. It outsells the McCain, Nestlé and Findus producer brands combined.

Being a profitable store brand supplier is tough. The overheads and investments associated with trying to stay in the branded producer game – consumer research, consumer marketing, and much of the salesforce – need to be stripped out. The business must be very disciplined in its cost control but flexible enough to cope with a wide variety of product and short runs. There will be a constant danger of excessive proliferation across too many product lines. Customer pressure for exclusivity will be constantly at odds with the need for multiple customers over which to amortise product development and fixed production costs.

The Cott Corporation provides an example of both the opportunity and difficulty of this business focus (see Case Study 13.3).

Case Study 13.3   Cott

In the late 1980s, Cott was a regional Canadian bottler of soft drinks, with sales around C$10 million. In 1989 Cott sold the idea of premium store brand cola to Loblaw's, the leading Canadian grocery retailer, which had already pioneered the development and penetration of quality store brands in North America with its President's Choice range. Cott found its source for cola syrup in RC (Royal Crown) Cola, the lagging third player in the US cola market, and tied up a long-term contract for exclusive supply and technical support. The President's Choice Cola, backed by Loblaw's store brand franchise and by a product quality equal to Coke and Pepsi, was an enormous success: by 1993, it was out-selling Coke and Pepsi, and Cott-supplied store brand products held 20% of the Canadian soft drinks market.

On the back of its success in Canada, Cott moved rapidly into other markets. In 1992 it obtained a contract with Wal-Mart to supply the same product under the Sam's American Choice label in the USA; the Wal-Mart contract was followed by supply agreements with other large US grocers. In 1993, the first contracts in Europe were obtained, with Continente (owned by Promodès) in Spain and with Sainsbury's in the UK. The early 1994 UK launch of Sainsbury's Classic Cola was a spectacular success, and within a year Cott was supplying the majority of the leading UK grocers (for more details, see Case Study 6.1, p. 92).

Cott's success shook one of the mightiest bastions of fmcg producer brands. The cola sector, and the Coke and Pepsi brands, had previously been considered all but impervious to attack by store brands. Coke and Pepsi poured billions of dollars into marketing and product development, and were confident that their product quality and taste could not be matched by a mere store brand offer. The impact of Cott on Coke in Canada was dramatic: Coke lost $200 million in Canada in 1992–3, as it slashed prices and rationalised production.

The result for Cott was a transformation from a tiny C$10 million sales company into a C$1 billion business by 1995, with 1997 sales forecast at C$1.5 billion. In the 5 years between 1991 and 1996, sales grew at a compound rate of 79% per annum. Between 1991 and 1994, pre-tax profits grew from close to zero to C$63 million (see Exhibit 13.5). Cott became the flag-bearer of the 'brand tax revolution' against over-priced producer brands, and its fastest growth period coincided with Marlboro Friday in the USA (see Exhibit 13.1, p. 200).

Although some analysts had already expressed concerns over cash flow and capitalisation of initial contract costs, Cott's success through 1994 was unarguable and spectacular. But in 1995, despite a 55% sales growth, profits fell from C$63 to C$56 million – and in 1996, despite a further 21% sales gain, the

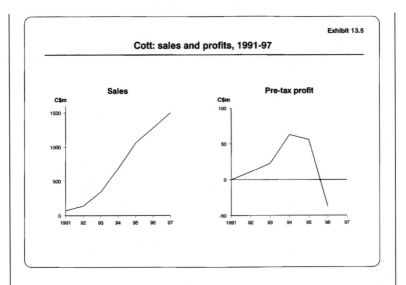

Exhibit 13.5

Cott: sales and profits, 1991-97

company plunged into a C$37 million pre-tax loss. The stock declined from a high of around $50 in 1993 to a low of around $7 in late 1995.

Part of this collapse in profitability was attributed to the rate of international expansion, and the costs and low prices involved in developing initial contracts in markets as far afield as Japan (Ito Yokado), Australia (Coles), Indonesia (Hero), and all across Continental Europe. Diversification into product areas outside soft drinks may have contributed, and these non-cola activities have now been pruned, leaving the company focused on soft drinks for over 95% of its world-wide sales.

The main factors appear to have been pressure on gross margins and a failure to squeeze operating costs and investments to the bone. From the peak profit year of 1994 to the trough of 1996, gross margins declined from 17.7% to 11.6%, while the total of SG&A, amortisation and interest charges increased from 8.5% to 11.6% of sales, wiping pre-tax margin (before restructuring charges) from 9.2% to zero (see Exhibit 13.6).

For 1997, Cott is forecasting a recovery in gross margins to around 15%, and expects the effects of the 1996 restructuring to flow through in lower SG&A and other costs. This could enable the company to recover to a pre-tax margin of 4% or more. The stock price has recovered from its 1995 low, but is still a long way off the heady heights of 1993.

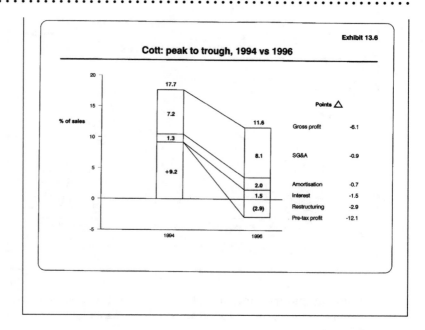

Exhibit 13.6

Cott: peak to trough, 1994 vs 1996

Points △	
Gross profit	-6.1
SG&A	-0.9
Amortisation	-0.7
Interest	-1.5
Restructuring	-2.9
Pre-tax profit	-12.1

For a short period, Cott looked as though it had found a licence to print growth and profits. The sales opportunity was real, but making premium returns from supplying store brands was never going to be as easy as Cott made it look until 1995. Big branded producers will fight back hard, as Coke did. Leading retailers will be aggressive in pricing negotiations, particularly in markets that are relatively undeveloped in terms of store brands and where success in taking on producer brand leaders is far from guaranteed. Operating costs and investments have to be stripped to the bone and tightly managed. Management has to stay focused on a narrow range of products and resist fragmenting its efforts.

Summary of Part IV: Different Perspectives

The Financial Services Supermarket

There are analogies between retail financial services and product retailing. There is, or at least could be, a producer–retailer split – although that may be obscured, as it is in banking, by the historical legacies of regulation and vertical integration. Financial service retailers could in theory offer consumers a range of choices of producer brands and of store brand product. There are examples of retail brand-building strategies, successful and unsuccessful.

However, it is unlikely that financial services supermarkets will become a reality. One reason is the infrequent nature of 'shopping' for financial services products, and the related inertia of customer–supplier relationships. A second and more convincing reason is the weight of vertical integration. Thirdly, the growth of mail, telephone and computer-based propositions is causing a disintermediation of branches and distributors. Consumers will prefer the efficiency and convenience of non-branch-based shopping and service, certainly for most banking and insurance products, and possibly for asset management.

The growth of non-branch-based propositions could open up the opportunity for greater internationalisation of retail financial services. International direct sales/service competitors can offer substantial price and service advantages over traditional local branch-based firms, and can obtain economies of scale at an international as well as national level. Direct insurance and asset management could be prime candidates for such internationalisation.

211

The lifetime value of a customer in financial services is high, particularly for a competitor who can offer a broad range of products, from banking through insurance to asset management. This value can justify large investments in the databases needed to support direct customer relationships and life-cycle marketing. The customer-oriented financial services competitor of the future, dealing with non-branch-based customers, will also need to re-integrate product profit centres and customer relationship management.

Product retailers are increasingly bundling some elements of financial services activity into their transactions and consumer offer, either to enhance their product retailing brand or as profit centres. Leading UK retailers with strong, trusted brands are now going beyond the most obvious example, consumer credit, and are offering quasi-banking services and mutual funds.

The Producer Perspective: Partnerships and Paranoia

Producers need to recognise the pressures that they will face as a result of the growth of retail brand power, and determine how they will respond to these pressures. The relationship between brand-building retailers and producers will be a balance of 'partnership and paranoia'.

After a peak in the 1980s and a trough in the early 1990s, the perception and value of producer brands have settled at a more balanced level. Some producers and analysts are now sounding complacent about the threat from retailers and retail brands. This is partly wishful thinking and partly deliberate policy. Most producers recognise that, although producer brands are far from dead, there has been a structural shift in the balance of power between retailers and producers.

The threat of retail brand power will strengthen producers' focus on and commitment to their category leadership positions. Producers will need to re-invest heavily in these category leaders – in innovation and quality, in above-the-line marketing and in speed-to-market – to preserve a distance and premium between them and quality store brands.

Category followers can choose to work proactively with retailers as suppliers of quality store brands. Although never delivering as high a return as a category-leading producer brand, focusing on supplying store brands can be an effective and profitable strategy.

*   *   *

In *Part V* of the book we return to our main perspective, that of product retailing.

Building strong retail brands is one of the top three strategic issues facing product retailers as they move into the next century. The other two are the internationalisation of retailing and the potential growth of interactive home shopping, or the virtual mall. Large retailers will also be facing the temptation and challenge of diversification. Part V addresses each of these issues, looking forward to how they might impact retailing in the future. The theme of retail brand power is connected to each, and gives us new ways of thinking about them.

Part V
Looking Forward

Retailing Without Frontiers **14**

Retailing has always been considered a business that doesn't travel well. Many historical efforts at taking retail formats across borders have failed. The number of truly successful international – particularly intercontinental – retailers is still very small. However, the conditions for retail internationalisation are changing, and we believe that retailers can and will become as international as fmcg producers over the next 30 years, albeit with many failures and reversals along the way. Before we give our reasons for that view, we will begin with a brief review of the poor history of retailing efforts at internationalisation.

Retail Internationalisation: Why so Little Until Recently?

Retailing until the 1980s was a relatively fragmented and localised industry, even within national borders. Few product sectors had consolidated into the mature, concentrated structures already typical by then of much producer brand national competition. Within the UK, market shares and presence still varied widely between the North and South of England, and between England and Scotland. The same variation and patchy presence was even more characteristic of other major European markets such as France and Germany, and is still characteristic of many retail sectors in the USA. Only small geographic markets such as the Netherlands, Sweden or Switzerland were consolidated at a national level.

The priority for retailers until the 1980s was therefore competition and consolidation within their home markets. In its store expansion programme in the USA, Wal-Mart always moved into adjacent territories rather than leaping ahead into the big urban markets and back-filling, thereby maximising distribution efficiency and limiting the risks of not under-standing new local markets.

In the past it was also unclear what advantages an international retailer might have over a strong local player. Small local stores predominated; decision-making was often still de-centralised to store-level; retailers were only just beginning to make large-scale investments in supply-chain and point-of-sale systems. Local market conditions (consu-mer behaviour, competition, regulation) differed widely between countries. An international retailer seemed to have little if any advantage in economies of scale, and faced a steep learning curve in matching the local market experience of established domestic competitors.

Actual experience of efforts at internationalising retailing seemed to bear out this diagnosis. Many non-US retailers have failed in their efforts to enter the USA, including the four major French hypermarket groups, Carrefour, Auchan, LeClerc and Euromarché, all of whom entered in the mid- to late 1980s and withdrew by 1993. Carrefour also failed in its early expansions into Germany and the UK. Boots had a disaster with its venture into Canada; M&S was failing in its overseas stores; Habitat's US operation managed to lose 50% on sales at its worst moment. US retailers, apart from efforts into Canada, hardly bothered to try to internationalise; Woolworth's, one of the earliest examples of international retailing, was sold off to local owners outside the USA.

Retail Internationalisation: The New Opportunity

In the 1980s, and continuing today in the 1990s, structural changes have opened up the potential for retail internationa-lisation. National markets have become concentrated – and in some cases saturated. While retailers still need to fight for market share in their core domestic markets, international growth has moved up the management agenda. Within the European continent, prime candidates for next-store opening are now as likely to be in another adjacent country as in the home market, and intra-European distribution is now no more complex or costly than distribution within a home market.

Several factors now work to give international players economic advantage over smaller local players. International retailers have buying clout with global producers that can be transferred from one market to another. Investment in retail systems has become more expensive and complex, and can be both transferred and amortised across international markets. Large-scale, out-of-town category killers work off store-level economies of scale and standardised business systems that are hard to compete with and hard to replicate quickly.

The sophisticated, centralised decision-making and decision support systems of large-scale retailers can now cope with differences in consumer demand between countries – as they can between regional markets and individual stores within the home country. Consumer demand itself is now becoming less distinct between markets, as consumers everywhere show a willingness to experiment with a variety of tastes, fashions and brands, and as powerful retail propositions such as McDonald's and Burger King win over consumers regardless of differences in cultural heritage and habits.

Finally, the growth of store brands, particularly in fashion and home lifestyle, has enabled retailers to think of and manage themselves internationally like global producer brands. Fashion retail brands such as Benetton, Gap and Laura Ashley are as international in scope as many leading global producer brands.

International Portfolio Owners versus International Brands

An international retailer may be a *portfolio owner*, acquiring and maintaining a portfolio of separate retail brands across different countries. Some portfolio owners may be very passive managers, acquiring and owning retail businesses as financial investments, without intending or attempting to transfer value-added or realise synergies across the portfolio. Others may be very active, applying a common value-added philosophy and strategy, and attempting to extract operational synergies.

There are several examples of the 'portfolio owner' approach to international retailing in the mail order sector. Otto, Quelle and La Redoute dominate mail order in Continental Europe, and all have strong presences in the USA and Japan. In country markets outside their domestic base, their presence has generally been established via the acquisition of a strong local brand, and that local brand name has been maintained. The companies attempt to obtain synergies across the country businesses in buying and merchandising and in systems development.

The same 'portfolio owner' approach is characteristic of much internationalisation in the grocery sector. European grocers have entered the American market by acquiring and maintaining existing US grocery brands, and are attempting to transfer the value-added store brand development that has been successful in Europe into the still relatively-undeveloped US market. Tesco and Sainsbury's have used the same approach in their entries into mainland Europe (see Exhibit 14.1).

At the other end of the spectrum, international retailing can involve the roll-out of an *international brand*, more or less consistently, across different country markets. In the context of our overall theme, we are more interested in this situation, which parallels the global roll-out of producer power brands such as Coke and Marlboro.

M&S has used a mix of the two approaches. Outside the USA, the M&S brand has been rolled out in Continental Europe, Canada and the Far East, where it is now slowly but steadily taking off after several false starts. In October 1996 it opened its first M&S store in Germany, in Köln. In the USA, however, development has been via acquiring and maintaining local brands: Brooks Brothers in fashion and Kings in grocery.

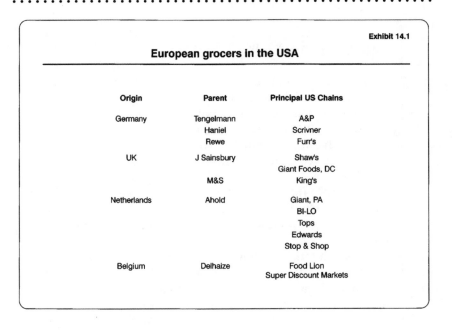

Exhibit 14.1

European grocers in the USA

Origin	Parent	Principal US Chains
Germany	Tengelmann	A&P
	Haniel	Scrivner
	Rewe	Furr's
UK	J Sainsbury	Shaw's
		Giant Foods, DC
	M&S	King's
Netherlands	Ahold	Giant, PA
		BI-LO
		Tops
		Edwards
		Stop & Shop
Belgium	Delhaize	Food Lion
		Super Discount Markets

Leading International Brands Today

The greatest number of strong international retail brands today are found in the *repertoire* sector. Fashion brands such as Benetton, Laura Ashley and Esprit are ubiquitous, with inter-continental coverage across North America, Europe and the Pacific, plus representation in many developing country markets. C&A gets almost 95% of its sales outside its home Netherlands home market. These are 100% store brand businesses, and look and operate very like global producer brands. IKEA is the epitome of an international brand in home lifestyle, combining, in its sheer size and range breadth, elements of both repertoire retailing and category killers (see Case Study 14.1).

There are other examples of international retail brands in home lifestyle, though none as convincing and powerful as IKEA. Courts, a UK furniture specialist, is an interesting example. Courts has quietly grown its international business to a level where it accounts for over two-thirds of sales and

Case Study 14.1   IKEA and Habitat

In an industry characterised by fragmented and local competition, IKEA has grown to revenues exceeding $5 billion through a global network of more than 100 stores. Less than 10% of IKEA's sales are now derived from its Swedish home market. The key elements of the IKEA proposition are now familiar to consumers world-wide: simple, high quality Scandinavian design; knockdown kits that customers transport and assemble themselves; huge stores with plenty of parking; amenities such as cafes and kids' play areas; massive range and low prices; products grouped together to provide designs for living.

IKEA is a family outing destination, and a visit is as much entertainment as shopping. Moreover, the customer enters into a unique bargain to perform certain of the tasks traditionally done by the retailer or manufacturer, such as transport and assembly. In return, IKEA makes it easy for the customer, through providing catalogues, tape measures and clear product information, and undertakes to share the value created with the customer through its low prices.

Alongside IKEA, Habitat is one of the few other large-format international retail brands in home lifestyle – but its fortunes provide an interesting contrast with IKEA. Habitat initially prospered in the UK based on Terence Conran's introduction of French and Mediterranean style into the English market. Expansion into the USA in the 1980s, under the Conran name (also used in the UK for a more up-market range than mainstream Habitat), was a disaster; at one point the US operation was losing 50% on sales. Performance in the core UK operation also declined badly.

Habitat's then-owner, Storehouse, finally lost patience in the early 1990s. The US operation was sold to local management, and Habitat UK and Habitat France were bought in 1994 by IKEA. Under IKEA, which keeps them completely separate from its main business, the UK is recovering and the French operation is prospering. Habitat's success in the French market is bizarrely based on selling an interpretation of French style, originally made for the English market, back to the French as a unique design statement.

profits, and has done so by focusing outside the classic markets of the West and on developing country markets in the Middle East, Africa and South Asia.

The *proximity* sector is not a strong candidate for international brand expansion (although it does encompass petrol/ gas station retailing, where the major oil companies have global brands that are carried through into their vertically-integrated retail outlets). Store brand development is generally low or non-existent, and the small-scale, simple nature of the business gives international players no economies of scale advantage. One of the few examples of international brand success in proximity retailing is Body Shop, which is unusual within the proximity sector, and could really be classified as a repertoire or fashion brand. It is 100% store brand, and offers a unique, strongly differentiated range. Boots, after its long failure in Canada, is now dipping its toe into international waters again: in 1997 it will open new stores in the Netherlands and Thailand, and expand its effort in Japan.

Category killers have the logic and potential to be global retail brands. IKEA, as discussed above, and Toys 'R' Us provide good models of global category killer brands (see Exhibit 14.2).

Despite its innate logic and potential, the international development of category killer brands is in its infancy. The emergence of category killers in domestic markets is a recent phenomenon, and most competitors still have a long way to go in consolidating their coverage and leadership positions in their home markets. Once those domestic positions are consolidated, category killer markets are prime candidates for internationalisation. Within Europe, Decathlon in the sports goods market is one of the prime candidates for such a move. It has an unrivalled dominance of its core French market, and has no competitors of equal stature in any of the other major European markets of Germany, UK, Italy and Spain. Its only competitors in the battle for international dominance along Toys 'R' Us lines are likely to be the US sports category killers such as Sports Authority, but those US competitors have a lot on their plate in consolidating their US market positions.

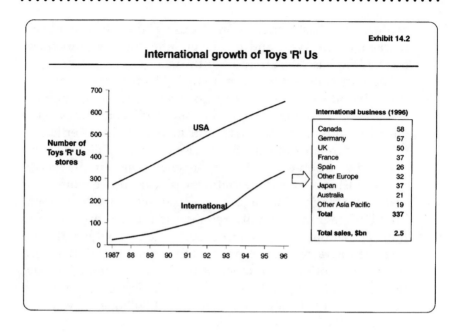

Exhibit 14.2

International growth of Toys 'R' Us

International business (1996)	
Canada	58
Germany	57
UK	50
France	37
Spain	26
Other Europe	32
Japan	37
Australia	21
Other Asia Pacific	19
Total	337
Total sales, $bn	2.5

Internationalisation of *grocery* brands is becoming a reality – but as yet on a regional rather than intercontinental basis. Regional pan-European retailing is not that different from pan-North American retailing, with the added complexity of greater language, regulatory and cultural differences between markets. Grocery internationalisation has been led by French hypermarkets and, more recently, by hard discounters such as Aldi. The major French hypermarket chains have moved into Spain (where Carrefour/Pryca, Continente and Alcampo are now the three largest retailers in the country, with Spanish operations that are more profitable than their overall business), Portugal and, to a lesser extent, Italy, as retail regulation has been relaxed in these immature markets. The pan-European expansion of hard discounters has been driven by competitors from the north of Europe – Aldi and Lidl from Germany, Netto from Denmark – who have expanded rapidly south over the last five years.

Inter-continental expansion by grocery retail brands is far more limited. The sheer size of the grocery market, its continuing national fragmentation in the USA, the low penetration of quality store brands outside the UK, and the importance of adjacent distribution, have all militated against intercontinental leap-frogging. European grocers expanding into North America have preferred to use the 'portfolio owner' route, acquiring and maintaining existing local grocery brands and attempting to add value – particularly quality store brands – into their proposition, along the lines that have been successful in Europe. As of 1996, Carrefour is probably the biggest player as an international grocery/ hypermarket brand – followed closely by Aldi, which has $6 billion sales in Europe outside its German home market, all under the Aldi brand (see Exhibit 14.3).

Outside product retailing, in retail *services*, fast food and hotels give us very strong examples of global retail brands: McDonald's and Burger King, Pizza Hut and KFC, Hilton and Hyatt. McDonald's is a retail brand that has become as omnipresent and iconic as Coke and Marlboro, and similarly a symbol of American culture and values. Sales outside the USA already account for around half total system sales, and are more profitable than restaurants in the USA. By the year 2000, non-US sales and operating profits should be climbing towards two-thirds and three-quarters of the total.

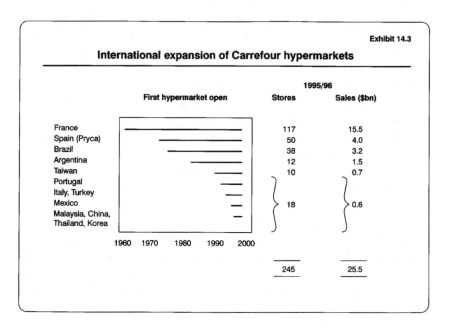

Exhibit 14.3

International expansion of Carrefour hypermarkets

	First hypermarket open	1995/96 Stores	Sales ($bn)
France		117	15.5
Spain (Pryca)		50	4.0
Brazil		38	3.2
Argentina		12	1.5
Taiwan		10	0.7
Portugal			
Italy, Turkey			
Mexico		18	0.6
Malaysia, China, Thailand, Korea			

1960 1970 1980 1990 2000

245	25.5

McDonald's business system and branding concept transformed the fast food industry and its potential for developing international brands. Before McDonald's, fast food businesses had even less rationale than proximity retailers for going international: markets and competition were highly localised, there were no economies of scale, consumer eating-out tastes and habits varied widely, and success depended heavily on the effort and creativity of individual restaurant owner–managers. In its early days of international expansion, McDonald's had to fight local country managers who wished to change the concept to increase its appeal to the local market. By and large, brand integrity and consistency have won and have proved to be the right choices.

Implications of Retail Brand Power for Retail Internationalisation

One of the benefits of building real long-term brand values in a retailer's core domestic market is that it provides a solid platform for taking a business and a brand international and global. Retailers without clear brand values, a strong brand culture and a consistent investment mentality will find it much harder to succeed in building international businesses, where the payback period can be long and the temptation to change a format and brand values to make short-term sales and profit targets can be even greater than in the core domestic market.

The retail businesses cited in the preceding pages as examples of successful brand globalisation are, in the main, also examples of the retail brand-building approaches and investment philosophy emphasised throughout this book. They are primarily or exclusively store brand businesses, investing heavily in quality store brand development and in long-term supplier partnerships; they invest in building the brand–customer relationship; and they are committed to maintaining brand integrity, in their product quality, pricing, staff cultures, and brand exploitation.

There is one area of exception to date. Category killers and large-space out-of-town hypermarkets can still today succeed in internationalising without being brand-builders, particularly if entering relatively immature markets dominated by small-scale retailers. Their advantage in size and economies of scale, category focus and buying clout is enough to beat local competitors. Toys 'R' Us is an example of a very successful international retailer which could not be classified as a brand-builder: store brand penetration is low, and the business is oriented overwhelmingly towards lowest cost high volume turnover of producer brands. (This does create problems for Toys 'R' Us, as evidenced by a drastic decline in profitability in the mid-1990s). The success of French hypermarkets in Spain has been achieved on a similar basis, in a market that was highly fragmented, small-scale and behind the times.

However, we believe that situation will change. As category killer markets mature, the need for brand-building will grow, and international competitors who last the pace will be those who have invested in and differentiated their brand offer. We would put Decathlon firmly in that camp.

Multi-business Retailing: Sum and Parts 15

The prospects of the growth of retail brand power, with retailers becoming real brand-builders on an international and ultimately global stage, opens up questions as to the structure of the retail industry over the next several decades. Will we see the emergence of large-scale multi-business conglomerates in retailing, along the lines of Nestlé or P&G, running a portfolio of global retail brands with a common brand-building philosophy?

This outcome is possible, but will require a fundamental change in the way multi-business retailers are managed. When we think of case studies of 'excellent retailing', what names come to mind? Internationally, Wal-Mart, Toys 'R' Us, Carrefour, IKEA and McDonald's would be among most people's first choices. In the UK, M&S, Sainsbury's and Tesco would be top of most lists. A common characteristic of these retailers is that they remain focused (80% or more of turnover) on one core business. Historically, in the mature markets of Europe and North America, our analysis shows that focused retailers have almost always out-performed multi-business retailers in terms of return to shareholders.

Is a Retail Portfolio 'Related'?

The question of whether focused firms systematically out-perform diversified or conglomerate corporations is far from unique to retailing. Much corporate re-structuring since the mid-1980s has been driven by the need to break up unwieldy conglomerates. In the USA and UK, many of the most diverse and unwieldy groups have now been broken up or have spun off their most unrelated businesses. Business analysts have come to distinguish between 'related' and 'unrelated' diversification: as long as a portfolio is reasonably 'related', as in large fmcg corporations like Unilever or industrial corporations like GE, the performance of multi-business groups can match that of single business firms, and 'related' businesses can add value to each other.

A portfolio of retail businesses is reasonably 'related' compared with the very broad-based conglomerates prevalent in the 1970s. Core skills and concepts are common across all retail formats: B&M, store operations, marketing, retail systems, location planning, logistics. There may well be a large overlap in customer base and in the nature of consumer shopping behaviour. In a relatively immature retail market such as Japan, this level of relatedness has been the basis for the creation of large diversified retail groups such as Daiei, Ito Yokado and Jusco (see Exhibit 15.1). These have been the most successful retailers in Japan, in terms of both sales growth and profitability.

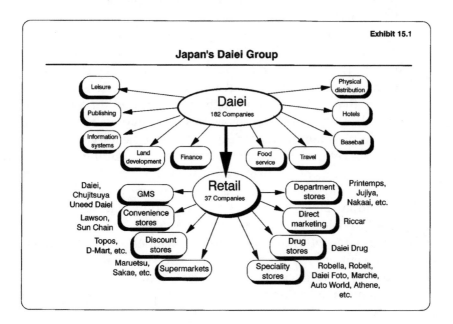

Exhibit 15.1

Japan's Daiei Group

There are degrees of 'relatedness'. Within each of our four product retail sectors, businesses can understand and learn from each other, regardless of product specialisation: a category killer in sports goods can add value to a category killer in electrical, and vice versa. Moving between sectors is more difficult: proximity retailers can find it difficult to understand the principles of category killer retailing, and vice versa. Every retailer coming from outside the repertoire sector seems to find fashion retailing, with its complex supply chain, intangible style values, demand unpredictability and markdown risk, particularly problematic to manage.

Although a retail portfolio can satisfy the need for businesses to be 'related', diversified retailers still need to avoid falling into the same traps that brought down large conglomerates in the 1980s. These traps are of three kinds: a portfolio management mentality, cost and bureaucracy created by the centre, and the pursuit of false synergies.

Avoiding the Portfolio Management Mentality

In the 1970s, senior management in the head offices of diversified conglomerates developed a portfolio management mentality. They came to think of their prime roles as being allocating investment and spreading risk, rather than maximising the value of individual businesses. They spent much of their time thinking about which businesses to sell or buy, rather than how to run existing businesses for profit and growth. They worked on ways to spread market and financial risk to maintain a smooth EPS growth trajectory. Divisional reviews centred on battles for corporate funding, with the centre imposing constraints based on targets for group gearing and cash flow. The performance and volatility of individual businesses were hidden from analysts in aggregated divisional and corporate accounts.

This concept of the portfolio management role of conglomerate centres was fundamentally discredited and rejected in the 1980s. Financial markets were recognised to be more efficient in allocating investment and spreading risk than individual corporations and corporate managers. Internal cash constraints imposed by the centre were often artificial and bore no relation to a business's ability to raise cash on the external capital market. Investors wanted to be able to invest as precisely as possible in individual businesses, and wanted management to concentrate on their main job of running those businesses.

Retailing offers a clear example of one of the biggest negative effects of the portfolio management mentality: a lack of commitment to sticking with, and realising the full potential of, a core business.

Analysts frequently argue that some retail proposition (McDonald's/Tesco/Toys 'R' Us/M&S/Wal-Mart – take your pick!) is reaching saturation and is about to go ex-growth, or is facing new competition or changes in customer needs that will make the proposition obsolete and unprofitable. The temptation, in the face of such analysis, is to reduce investment and effort in the core brand and to look for new businesses – or, for a multi-business retailer, to switch investment towards other businesses in the portfolio.

The great focused retailers have ignored that analysis and resisted that temptation, and continued to deliver steady growth and high profitability from their core business. They have understood that their investment priority is to maximise the potential of their core existing assets: their retail brand, their category-specific B&M expertise and clout, and their loyal customers. The closer to 'home' they stay, the greater the likelihood of success and the higher the return on investment.

For McDonald's, adding a successful pizza offer to the menu is a billion dollar growth opportunity; as is taking the McDonald's format to new markets such as Russia and China. For M&S, developing their offer and market share in footwear, kidswear or home textiles up to the level they achieve in general adult clothing is an enormous opportunity; as is slowly shifting the balance of their site portfolio from the high street to out-of-town; as is leveraging the strength of their retail brand into new areas such as financial services. (As also opening up a mail order sales channel would be, an avenue of growth which M&S has surprisingly not yet fully pursued.)

Or take Tesco. As Terry Leahy related, when he was Tesco's Marketing Director:

'[In 1980] the company was in severe difficulty. At that time it had a market capitalisation of just £200 million, low profit margins less than 2% of sales, 700 small and increasingly old-fashioned retail outlets, and little or no capital investment. Indeed, in 1980 the company was ripe for takeover . . . [but then] a new generation of managers led by Ian MacLaurin took control of the business. They decided to move Tesco's image upmarket. In addition they determined to invest in an entirely new chain of out-of-town food superstores and to close the majority of the company's existing stores.'

In contrast, because they are not committed to a core business, multi-business retailers often neither invest to push a fascia to its full potential nor defend it adequately against competition. The portfolio management mentality tends to conclude too early that a retail brand no longer justifies investment, either for growth (because coverage is 'saturated') or for defence (because competition has become tougher), and tends to focus on re-shuffling the portfolio via acquisition and divestment.

The Sears Group in the UK presents a classic example of this danger. Over the last 10–15 years it has entered and withdrawn from the menswear market; become market leader in sports goods with its Olympus chain, then divested it when market conditions got tough; in mail order, entered and withdrawn from Continental Europe, and not invested in the growth area of direct catalogues; and is still trying, despite its market leadership position, to re-vitalise its BSC footwear business. As of writing, it is in the final stages of selling Freemans, the mail order business it bought in 1986, and is rumoured to be on the point of closing or selling off at a knockdown price its entire shoe business.

Multi-business retailers need to recognise this danger. They need to be as capable as a focused retailer of sticking with, investing in and re-positioning their core brands and businesses. They need to avoid the trap of a portfolio management mentality.

Avoiding Cost and Bureaucracy Created by the Centre

Part of the reaction against diversification in the 1980s stemmed from recognition of the cost and bureaucracy inherent in conglomerate structures: large central staffs, a vast accumulation of paperwork and internal meetings, a slowdown in decision-making and market responsiveness, and an erosion of line management clarity and accountability.

For multi-business retailers, the direct costs of the centre are an important but not the major issue. These costs, like all overhead, can become too high and need to be tightly controlled. The more important issue is the indirect bureaucratic cost of the centre: the impact that it can have on the operating divisions, on their management focus and productivity, on responsiveness and on overhead costs. The basic problem for centre management is how to review and direct the strategy and performance of a portfolio of retail businesses. The centre, in its search for a value-added role, can create significant cost and confusion.

Earlier in the book, we discussed the differences in brand management between fmcg producer brands and retail brands, and we observed that the careful, centralised decision-making and control processes of an fmcg brand cannot work in retailing. We were thinking then of a single fascia business. The problem is even greater for the CEO and head office team of a multi-business retailer. How does the centre know that an agreed strategy is really being implemented, or even whether the operating division and the centre have the same understanding as to what the strategy is? How does the centre monitor operating performance, given the profusion and complexity of range and store data, without either regularly getting into line-item level detail, or retreating to the very abstract and potentially deceptive level of aggregate sales and financial ratios?

In practice the right balance is hard to achieve, and in practice centre management generally feel compelled to dive into the details of range and store performance. But without living day-to-day with those details, these interventions are rarely effective. They tend to create extensive duplication of activity and cost between the centre and the operating divisions. They muddy accountability for performance. Most dangerously, they cause an overall slowing of decision processes, particularly in B&M, which need to be speedy and responsive to constant small changes in the marketplace.

Multi-business retailers need to avoid creating this cost and bureaucracy. Centre management must be able to delegate day-to-day operational management down to individual businesses. Strategy reviews need to be confined to once a year. Monthly and quarterly performance reviews need to be tightly structured around a clear and consistent agenda, and MIS support for those reviews focused on exception reporting. Analysis and reports should not be duplicated between the centre and the operating divisions. Line authority and accountability must clearly lie with operating division management, and their time and staff resources should not be taken up with second-guessing the centre's next line of attack.

Avoiding the Pursuit of False Synergies

There are potential synergies to be had in the *support and overhead functions* of multi-business retailers. Warehousing and distribution can often be shared and unit costs reduced, subject to compatibility in physical handling characteristics and order/delivery patterns. (In the 1960s and 1970s, as Charles Clore acquired multiple shoe fascias and built up the British Shoe Corporation, he drastically reduced logistics costs by combining all their fragmented warehousing and distribution into one large complex at Braunstone in Leicester.) Pooling demand can support a higher level of in-house professional skills in areas such as property management: location planning, site acquisition and divestment, and contract negotiation. The costs of accounting, personnel administration and systems support can be shared.

It is legitimate for multi-business retailers to pursue these synergies, but they need to recognise and manage the risks involved. Divisional Managing Directors can be very protective about retaining full line business autonomy, and can fight hard to retain these functions under their direct control. They need to be fully convinced as to the logic and benefits of sharing centralised resources, or they can become distracted from their main task of managing the market-facing functions of B&M, store operations and marketing, and spend a disproportionate amount of their time fighting over the back-office turf.

The centre also needs to recognise that the value of these synergies is declining. Third-party contract options in warehousing and distribution, and in computer facilities management, have reduced the benefit of spreading these functional costs in-house across multiple businesses. Management information systems have been decentralised. Overhead support functions have declined as a percentage of retailers' overall cost structure, relative to the front-line costs of store operations, B&M and marketing. Coupled with the risk of distracting line management from the 'main game' of managing the retail proposition, this may lead the Centre to conclude that there are better uses for the organisation's limited time and energy.

We have seen several multi-business retailers experiment with *centralised operational functions* such as Marketing, Design, Customer Service or Supply Chain/Retail Systems. The centre may believe that standards and skills in these areas need to be raised and made more consistent across the various operating divisions. If kept small-scale, such experimentation can be effective: one or two experienced specialists at the centre, working as consultants or catalysts on specific projects with the operating divisions as their 'clients'. But in practice there is a big risk of cost and bureaucratic process mushrooming, both at the centre and in the operating divisions, to negative rather than positive effect. Senior operating division management end up committing more and more time and resources to group-wide working parties that simply document differences in status and practice across divisions, and expending energy on resisting implementation in their division of impractical group-wide programmes. Even more damagingly, creating such centralised operational functions can seriously muddy and erode line management's accountability for performance.

Multi-business retailers often attempt to extract synergy from *pooling buying power*, and will use a calculation of the benefit in their evaluation of acquisition candidates. Small proportionate gains can have a big impact for retail groups with several fascias in the same market sector, when a few percentage points off cost-of-goods-sold could double or treble the trading margin. But retailers need to distinguish two situations: producer brands and store brands.

There is a rationale for pooling the buying of *producer brands*. The large Continental European grocery buying groups exist and operate on this basis. The Metro Group, Germany's largest retailer, recently merged its cash-and-carry, Asko and Kaufhof businesses in order to increase buying power. But the benefits should not be over-estimated. Over a certain size threshold, retailers will not be able to squeeze out material increases in discount levels. Business focus and buying sophistication, including information on the range of discounts available to competitors, can be as effective as sheer purchase volume. Kwik Save, the leading producer brand discounter in UK grocery, achieved its market position from a standing start, without the benefits of higher volume line buying.

There is much less rationale, and greater dangers, from pooling buying power in store brands. This risks corrupting the key element of brand-building and of brand differentiation. To obtain unit cost benefits, the same store brand products end up being offered across different fascias. This is particularly damaging in fashion and homestyle markets, where each retail brand has to have a unique identity and earn a distinct place in its customers' shopping repertoire. The British Shoe Corporation, with its numerous look-alike shoe fascias selling interchangeable product, was for years a classic example of the danger. The Burton Group in the mid-1980s tried pooling B&M, split into menswear and womenswear, across its various market-segmented fashion multiples, and saw sales performance collapse (see Case Studies 3.1 and 3.2, pp. 59 and 63). If Habitat were to piggyback off the line buys of its recent acquiror, IKEA, it would soon lose its more up-market and distinctive appeal for its customer base (see Case Study 14.1, p. 222).

Multi-business retailers must avoid pursuing false synergies: centralised operational functions and store brand buying. Real synergies can be had from combining support and overhead functions and in pooling producer brand buying, but these should be pursued cautiously so as not to compromise line management's accountability and their focus on the 'main game' of the retail proposition.

Break-up: The Outcome for Under-Performing Multi-Business Retailers

The inevitable outcome for many diversified retailers is break-up. After years of under-performance, management and shareholders grow impatient with the pursuit of false synergies, the lack of focus and the inefficiencies inherent in running a diversified portfolio. Breaking up a group into smaller business units is often the quickest and most effective solution.

Melville in the USA was a classic under-performing multi-business retailer. Finally, in 1996, it was broken up into its constituent parts, by selling off businesses and by floating two new corporations out of the old Melville shell (see Exhibit 15.2).

In the medium-term, break-up is the likely outcome for several of Japan's highly diversified 'new wave' retail groups, as the Japanese market and corporate structures mature. Their profitability has been squeezed in the 1990s, and is low compared even to a low price, high volume, large-scale US retailer like Wal-Mart – despite the Japanese groups' continuing dependence on high gross margin convenience store retailing as a core business platform.

Retail Brand Management: A Basis for Multi-business Retailing?

The glue that holds together diversified fmcg groups such as Nestlé, Unilever, P&G and Philip Morris is a common philosophy of, and set of skills in, consumer goods brand-

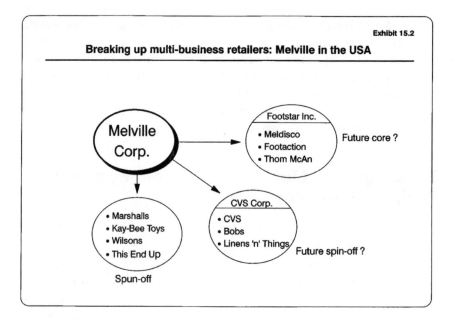

Exhibit 15.2

Breaking up multi-business retailers: Melville in the USA

Melville Corp.

Footstar Inc.
- Meldisco
- Footaction
- Thom McAn

Future core ?

- Marshalls
- Kay-Bee Toys
- Wilsons
- This End Up

Spun-off

CVS Corp.
- CVS
- Bobs
- Linens 'n' Things

Future spin-off ?

building. They may share certain resources across businesses, but in the main each business unit contains all the key functions and authority to compete as an autonomous entity. This has proven an effective basis for addressing market opportunities and competitors, and compelling as a rationale for investors and the financial markets.

Multi-business retailers are not currently set up on the same basis. In the mature markets of North America and Europe, they are largely the results of acquisitive financial strategies: for example, the UK financial markets in the early 1980s seriously under-valued retailers, and the time was ripe for the acquisitive strategy that produced the current Kingfisher portfolio. The highly diversified Japanese retail groups leverage operational retail skills (store management, retail technology, logistics and warehousing) across multiple retail formats.

Looking forward, brand-building could provide the same strategic glue for multi-business retailers as it does for fmcg groups. Retailers that understand how to invest in long-term brand-building and in brand differentiation, via quality store brands, direct customer relationships and brand integrity, and know how to build international and global retail brands, will be able to transfer that expertise and philosophy across different businesses within a retail sector, and even across retail sectors. This will be a stronger, more durable glue than consolidating distribution into one warehouse or combining payroll processing into one administration centre.

Home Shopping: From Mail Order to the Virtual Mall 16

The growth of interactive home shopping, or 'IAHS', will be one of the biggest developments in retailing as we move into the twenty-first century. IAHS will not explode overnight, and will not become the dominant form of retailing for the foreseeable future. Its impact will be limited to certain sectors of product and service retailing. However, it is a threat to traditional, store-based retailing, and it does give retail brand-building an extra impetus and urgency.

Early Home Shopping: Mail Order

Mail order was the earliest form of home shopping. The Sears Roebuck catalogue in the USA allowed consumers in the pioneering farming communities of the West to order products formerly only available on their infrequent trips to big cities. Mail order also provided credit to consumers who otherwise would have difficulty obtaining it. 'Agency' mail order, still the prevalent form in the UK, was based around agents selling to relatives, close friends and close neighbours. The agency network was both an effective sales vehicle and an efficient credit screen, as the agents could personally rate the credit-worthiness of their customers.

Early mail order was therefore mass-market, and skewed towards lower income consumers. The product range offered was very broad, matching the coverage of inner-city department stores, from the front-of-book focus on fashion to the back-of-book range in electrical, home and leisure products.

'New wave' mail order, the growth sector of the industry, is generally sold direct via catalogue mailings to consumers rather than via agents, and is targeted rather than mass-market. Fashion brands such as Lands' End, Racing Green and L.L.Bean are new wave direct mail order competitors. In the UK, Next uses direct mail order as an additional distribution channel, selling the same range as in its retail stores. N Brown targets older consumers with specific needs, for example for home healthcare and security.

One other form of mail order is classified as 'direct response': media-advertised products that the consumer orders by clipping a coupon or calling an 800 number. Direct response mail order provides a link to the early forms of interactive TV shopping that emerged in the 1980s: cable TV shopping channels, as exemplified by QVC and HSN.

Cable TV Shopping Channels

QVC and HSN in the USA have been the pioneers of dedicated 24-hour cable TV shopping channels. Merchandise is displayed and reviewed in revolving time slots, and consumers buy by calling up on 800 numbers and paying by credit card. To increase viewer draw and excitement, big name presenters are often used, as are a variety of formats, including limited-time-period offers and quasi-auctions. Both channels have grown rapidly in the USA, and are increasing their coverage in other countries, via satellite as well as cable distribution. However, they represent a very limited niche in the retail market. Their customer base, and the product groups that they have been successful in selling, are narrow. Jewellery and fashion accessories account for over half their sales – including $5000 fur coats, bought sight-unseen on impulse! Their share of total retail sales in the USA peaked in the early 1990s, at less than 0.2%, and HSN crashed into huge operating losses.

The potential of these shopping channels is limited by their non-interactive nature. Consumers cannot select what product groups they are interested in, at the time they wish to shop, and browse through a range of offers. They have to sit through whatever the cable broadcaster is running and see if anything grabs their interest. Apart from retired, wealthy TV addicts who have all day to sit on the sofa in front of the TV, these channels' prime function is impulse selling to a consumer who has switched to the channel for five minutes – hence the strong sales skew towards jewellery and accessories. Consumers cannot use such non-interactive TV channels as a practical substitute for more than a tiny minority of their shopping needs.

The Big New Opportunity: Interactive Home Shopping (IAHS)

IAHS will represent a step-change in potential versus home shopping channels such as QVC and HSN. With IAHS, consumers will be free to browse through a 'virtual mall', which will not only simulate the physical shopping experience but will provide a range of additional benefits.

Consumers will be able to specify broad parameters, such as price and style, and 'pre-screen' for options before exploring any in depth. Comparison shopping, on price, performance and features, will be easier and more efficient. Electronic payment will reduce 'check-out' time to almost zero. Interactive video merchandising will transform consumers' ability to shop for fashion and home lifestyle products: they will be able to ask to see items modelled in real-life situations, such as clothes on models or home decor options in a model room, and to play with colours and styles in real-time to find their preference. Music and image merchandising will be seamlessly and cheaply integrated with 'store' and product video merchandising. Many of the service elements that retailers now need expensive in-store staff to provide will be automated: a beginner in golf will be prompted towards one level of golf equipment, a low handicap golfer towards another.

There will still be the innate disadvantage of not being able to touch and feel the product. For some consumers and certain product categories this will be an insuperable barrier, at least for a generation. Colour and audio quality are also likely to be major difficulties for many years, certainly on PCs.

Five key technologies can be identified as central to delivering IAHS effectively. These technologies embrace both hardware and software, and combinations of the two.

Even in the six months taken to write this book, the status of these technologies has changed significantly – particularly in areas of overlap with development of the Internet. Our intention here is not to be technology forecasters, but merely to summarise the main technology elements, and to indicate that most of these are likely to be in place over the next 5–10 years at a level that can support the practical and serious development of IAHS.

The *server* is probably the least contentious of these technologies. The central computers needed to handle decentralised on-line interactive networks require enormous speed and capacity. IBM points to the shift away from desktop computers towards network servers as a vindication of its commitment to the mainframe, which it now calls a 'superserver'. Oracle argues that server hardware is relatively straightforward, and that the key technology is database management.

The second key technology is the *distribution medium*. There are several competing alternatives, from land-based telephone and cable TV pipes to air-based wireless and satellite transmission. In countries with large, established cable TV networks – primarily the USA, Canada and Germany – cable provides a high speed, high bandwidth medium for inter-activity. In the USA, @Home, a company partly owned by TCI, has just launched the first commercial Internet service via TV cable, in Fremont, California. @Home estimates that by the year 2000 half the homes in the USA could have cable Internet access. Outside these cabled markets, and even in them, telephone operators could compete, with high speed ASDL connections over phone lines. Outside the dense, wealthy markets of the West, the sheer cost of infrastructure investment may make land-based distribution a less attractive route than wireless or satellite. Teledesic, a joint venture between Microsoft and McCaw Cellular, plans to have a satellite network in orbit by 2002 that will duplicate the speed, capacity and responsiveness of land-based cable, opening up electronic interactivity in markets that lack even a basic telephone system.

The third key technology is the *network*. The Internet has exploded from a commercial nowhere only four years ago to revolutionise the software industry and transform the potential of the electronic marketplace. Network commercial services providers such as AOL and Prodigy are folding their fortunes in with the Net. On-line consumers in the future, with the Net as their basic network, will choose which commercial service providers to purchase for value-added services (such as navigation, editing, payment and security; proprietary databases and transaction services; specialised on-line communities).

The fourth key technology is the *home interface*. Here it seems likely that competing solutions will battle it out for some time, and may even co-exist in the long run, depending on the needs and preferences of the consumer. Between a third and a half of US households already have home computers, and penetration is climbing towards that level in European markets like the UK and Germany. The PC's computing capacity may make it the logical candidate for the home interface. Alternatively, the network computer or 'thin client', which does away with much of the PC's functionality and cost in favour of using the network, may come to the fore. And there are alternative interfaces for consumers who seek simpler IAHS applications; including TV set-top boxes, video game sets, cellular phones or even networked household appliances.

A further requirement is the creation of reliable rules and systems for *payment and security*, to guarantee the identity and integrity of buyers and sellers and their electronic transactions. Broadly speaking, the same principles that underpin credit card payment systems can underpin electronic transaction. Verisign in California is working with VISA on a system for authenticating credit card holders (buyers and vendors) over the Internet. An alternative to a credit card system in the open environment of the Net would be a transaction system limited to and managed by a commercial service provider, where subscribers and transactions would be easier to monitor and track, and consumers would be more confident of protection.

The dominant US model for IAHS delivery in the first decade of the next century could be the PC and the Internet, distributed down cable TV pipe. Server systems will be various, and several effective payment and security systems will be operative.

The Status of IAHS at end 1996

For all the excitement and coverage of the Internet and interactive electronic commerce, actual volume of on-line sales as of 1996 was negligible. Most estimates put actual consumer transactions (excluding the purchase of subscriber and other information services) at only $200–400 million, *world-wide* – in fact, almost entirely in the USA. Off this very low base, projections for the year 2000 range enormously, and with little foundation, from $2 billion to $30 billion, still mainly in the USA. Apart from sales, managers in all the many industries affected by the Internet have another big question: who if anybody will make money out of electronic commerce over the next ten years? The only businesses currently making material profits out of the Internet are companies selling products and services to help other companies build their own sites on the Net.

Although current volumes are negligible, many established retailers are experimenting with a presence – and several new firms have started up to focus entirely on electronic retailing. Retailers experimenting with the Net have three basic options for where to set out their cyber-store.

Commercial service provider malls offer virtual mall sites that allow merchants to showcase and, if they choose, sell product. All three main commercial service providers (AOL, Prodigy and CompuServe) offer this service. For an annual fee plus a small percentage on sales (generally $25– 50 000 plus 2–5%), the provider can design and maintain a retail offering, and promote the offer by directing traffic to the site. CompuServe's electronic mall includes JC Penney, Brooks Bros and Virgin Megastore; AOL offers FAO Schwartz, Eddie Bauer and Godiva Chocolates; and Prodigy has Lands' End and Hammacher Schlemmer.

Alternatively, a retailer can take space in a *Web mall site* – the open Internet version of the service provider mall. Leading Web mall site operators include DreamShop, eShop, SHOPPING2000, and marketplaceMCI. Lastly, vendors can choose to set up their own *Home Page on the Web*, equivalent to a freestanding retail store outside a mall environment. This last option gives more control but requires more investment in design ($100 000+) and ongoing technical support.

As in the real world, retailers will not limit themselves to one mall, but will have a presence in any and all locations that look promising traffic-generators. Sears Roebuck maintained an presence in the Prodigy mall, a Web mall site and its own Home Page, merchandising a limited selection of its Craftsman tools. OfficeMax has a presence in all the major electronic malls as well as its own Home Page.

Although many retailers have presences on the Net, the majority use it so far as a way of distributing information and marketing, rather than as a transaction medium. Wal-Mart and Kmart have Web sites but customers cannot purchase goods electronically. The number of businesses allowing actual transactions and doing any significant volume is so small that the press coverage has to resort to citing such low volume examples as 1–800FLOWERS ($7.5m online revenue) and Virtual Vineyards, a Web-based retailer of hard-to-find wines.

What Will Consumers Shop for in the Virtual Mall?

The IAHS marketplace today is in its very early stages of development, and its current status provides only limited clues to how rapidly it will grow and where it will have most impact. In assessing its long-term potential, it is more useful to go back to first principles of consumer needs and

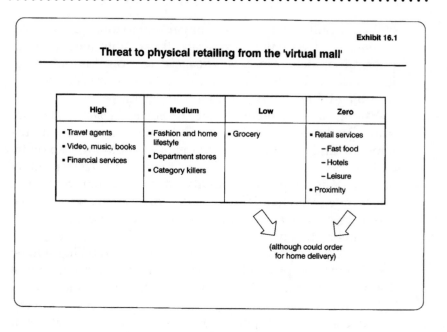

Exhibit 16.1

Threat to physical retailing from the 'virtual mall'

High	Medium	Low	Zero
▪ Travel agents ▪ Video, music, books ▪ Financial services	▪ Fashion and home lifestyle ▪ Department stores ▪ Category killers	▪ Grocery	▪ Retail services 　– Fast food 　– Hotels 　– Leisure ▪ Proximity

(although could order
for home delivery)

behaviour. What will consumers eventually shop for in the virtual mall? Which physical (branch- and store-based) retail formats are under the greatest threat (see Exhibit 16.1)?

Several retail services are highly vulnerable to IAHS, to such an extent that IAHS could rapidly become the dominant form of distribution – once the technology and access infrastructure are in place. The *travel agency* business is a prime candidate for switching. Vacation packages can be far more effectively merchandised via video than via brochures, and consumers can speed up the shopping process by specifying destination options, dates, number of people, price bracket, and facilities desired. Airlines and hotels will be keen to reduce the intermediary costs of travel agents, which run at 10–15% of sales and constitute one of the largest items of total cost for travellers. The entire *video rental* store network could become redundant inside 20 years as consumers switch to pay-per-view video-on-demand. Similarly, *music shops* could be made redundant as CD material can be down-loaded directly into the home, either on a pay-per-listen basis or as pay-to-own. (Both video and audio are likely to go through an intermediate stage, where retail branches still exist but no longer have to hold physical inventory.) IAHS will accelerate the disintermediation of physical branches in *retail financial services*. Shopping for insurance via IAHS will be as easy and consumer-friendly as shopping by telephone, and more efficient.

Among product retail sectors, *fashion and home lifestyle* are prime switching candidates. Consumers are already accustomed to and comfortable with the idea of buying fashion by mail order, without having to 'touch and feel' product quality. The potential benefits of the virtual mall and interactive merchandising, with consumers able to see products in situ and to play with colours and styles, will make interactive home shopping compelling.

At the other end of the spectrum, *proximity* retailing will be unaffected. The proximity consumer usually cannot, or will not, wait for home delivery, even if within the same day.

The impact on *grocery* is harder to assess. Grocery customers also need rapid product delivery; and, of all retail sectors, the need to see and feel product quality is strongest, particularly in fresh produce. However, there may be a large minority of grocery customers who could become comfortable with buying remotely, and who could find an interactive home shopping system the most efficient way of conducting their weekly shop with their principal retailer. For these customers, an IAHS link may be the most effective way of building and maintaining long-term direct customer relationships.

In the USA, one of the largest and most advanced trials of IAHS in grocery is the Peapod operation. Peapod operates on-line grocery shopping and delivery services on behalf of Jewel in Chicago and Safeway in San Francisco. The service is available via direct dial-up and the Net, with a current (end-1996) customer base of around 20 000 households. The consumer 'walks' through the Peapod system with a shopping basket. Promotions are highlighted. A default list of regular weekly/monthly items is created. The Peapod Personal Shopper, who picks the order, gets to know consumer requirements and preferences, and develops good enough relationships and understanding to make substitutions on out-of-stocks and suggestions on fresh produce.

Average weekly basket spends are high, $100–150 – these are valuable, affluent, time-pressed customers.

In the UK, Tesco is trialling an on-line CD-ROM grocery service, with a £5 delivery charge. Most of the major UK grocers and wine merchants already offer their mail order services on the Net. Channel 11, a new on-line food-and-drink network which went on-line at the end of 1996, will provide comparative shopping information including consumer tests and price checks.

The impact on *category killers* is the most difficult to assess – and gives us a logical point for raising a fundamental question. Where is the retailer in the virtual mall?

Only Strong Retail Brands will Survive in the Virtual Mall

IAHS poses a real threat for many traditional store-based retailers selling primarily producer brands. Consider electrical retailing. Producer brands such as Sony and Philips, which dominate the sector, can buy space in the virtual mall from the mall-owner. The mall-owner may charge 'rental' on the electronic space, but the fixed costs and charges will be lower than for a physical store network. There will be services in the mall (or at least in the network) to help consumers pre-screen and make their final choices, including price and performance comparisons from objective independent evaluators such as *Consumer Reports* in the USA or *Which?* in the UK. Sony and Philips may not like such aids to comparison shopping, but there will be little they can do to stop them. Once consumers have made their selections, order processing, product delivery and returns ('fulfilment', in mail order terminology) can be handled directly by producers or contracted out, on a cost-plus basis, to third-party service operators. The same arrangements can occur for installation, after-sales service, and the supply of parts and accessories.

Where is the role for Circuit City, Dixons or Darty in this version of the future? The economic need for the retailer intermediary has vanished. There are no store fixed costs and in-store labour to cover, and no store-level stocks and demand to manage. Consumers are better served by the absence of a retail intermediary. This is a threat for all retailers whose sales mix is skewed towards big ticket items and producer brands: department stores, non-store brand fashion and home lifestyle retailers, and category killers in furniture, sports and toys, as well as electrical.

The strongest long-run defence for these businesses is to build strong retail brands, particularly quality store brands, to become more like producers and less vulnerable to disintermediation. The threat from IAHS and the virtual mall reinforces, and makes even more urgent, the retail brand-building imperative which is the central theme of the book.

Shopping occasions which involve frequent purchases of low value items should be able to resist this threat. Even if they become virtual mall shoppers and even if they buy exclusively producer brands, consumers will probably not 'disintermediate' grocery retailers. Dealing directly with dozens of producers for the weekly grocery shop will be unpleasant and impractical. Grocery retailers will continue to play a valuable role in editing and acting as a single sales/service point.

Summary of Part V: Looking Forward

Retailing Without Frontiers

Retailing has behind lagged other industry sectors, including fmcg producers, in going international and global. Retailers have had too much of a job to do in competing in and consolidating their local markets, and traditional small-scale decentralised retailers have held no advantages over entrenched local players in foreign markets.

These conditions have now changed. Many domestic markets have consolidated, and retailers are looking abroad for further growth opportunities. Large-scale retail formats, including out-of-town destination retailers, have economic advantages that can offset the established presence and local market knowledge of local competitors.

We distinguish two types of retail internationalisation: portfolio owners, who maintain separate brands in different country markets; and international brands, which are rolled-out relatively consistently under the same brand name in different markets.

In the latter category, we can find today several examples of strong global retail brands in fashion and home lifestyle product retailing, and in retail services, primarily fast food and hotels; almost no examples in proximity retailing, which is the sector with the weakest rationale for internationalisation; a few examples among category killers, although mostly at a very early stage; and almost no global examples yet in grocery, although pan-European competition is developing rapidly.

The retail brand-building values argued for throughout this book significantly enhance a retail business's potential for going international and global. Outside of category killers, successful global retail brands to date are committed to investing in quality store brands and long-term supplier partnerships, brand–customer relationships, and brand integrity.

Multi-Business Retailing: Sum and Parts

Historically, multi-business retailers in mature markets have not performed as well as focused single-business retailers. Although a retail portfolio can satisfy the need for businesses to be 'related', diversified retailers need to avoid falling into the same traps that brought down large conglomerates in the 1980s.

Multi-business retailers need to avoid the portfolio management mentality. They need to be as capable as a focused retailer of sticking with, investing in and re-positioning their core brands and businesses.

They need to avoid the cost and bureaucracy that can be created by the centre, in particular the negative effect that the centre can have on management focus and productivity, on responsiveness and on overhead costs in the operating divisions.

They must also avoid pursuing false synergies across businesses, in centralised operational functions and store brand buying. Real synergies can be had from combining support and overhead functions and in pooling producer brand buying, but these should be pursued cautiously so as not to compromise line management's accountability and their focus on the 'main game' of the retail proposition.

Looking forward, brand-building could provide the same strategic glue for multi-business retailers as it does for fmcg groups. Retailers that understand how to invest in long-term brand-building and in brand differentiation, and know how to build international and global retail brands, will be able to transfer that expertise and philosophy across different businesses within a retail sector, and even across retail sectors.

Home Shopping: From Mail Order to the Virtual Mall

IAHS represents a step-change in potential versus home shopping channels such as QVC and HSN. With IAHS, consumers will be free to browse through a 'virtual mall', which will not only simulate the physical shopping experience but will provide a range of additional benefits.

The main necessary technologies are likely to be in place over the next 5–10 years at a level that can support the practical and serious development of IAHS. The dominant US model for IAHS delivery in the first decade of the next century could be the Internet, distributed down cable TV pipe, supported by various server systems, home interfaces, and systems for payment and security.

The IAHS marketplace today is in its very early stages of development, and its current status provides only limited clues to how rapidly it will grow and where it will have most impact. Although many retailers have presences on the Net, the majority use it so far as a way of distributing information and marketing, rather than as a transaction medium.

In assessing long-term potential, it is more useful to go back to first principles of consumer needs and behaviour, and ask what consumers will eventually shop for in the virtual mall. Several branch-based retail services are highly vulnerable to IAHS, to such an extent that IAHS could rapidly become the dominant form of distribution. Travel agents, video and music stores and financial services are prime candidates for substitution. IAHS is also a threat for all product retailers whose sales mix is skewed towards big-ticket items and producer brands: department stores, non-store brand fashion and home lifestyle retailers, and category killers in furniture, sports and toys, as well as electrical.

The strongest long-run defence for these threatened businesses is to build strong retail brands, particularly quality store brands, to become more like producers and less vulnerable to disintermediation. The threat from IAHS and the virtual mall reinforces, and makes even more urgent, the retail brand-building imperative which is the central theme of the book.

Summary and Conclusion

The Context

The Growth of Retail Power and the Brand-building Challenge

Retailing has become large-scale, concentrated, centralised and sophisticated. Retailers are well down the track of seizing value-chain power. The next major challenge and opportunity for retailers is the development of strong retail brands, that generate long-run consumer preference and loyalty and create sustainable differentiation between direct retail competitors.

The current status of retail brand development, and the future potential for brand-building, varies widely across countries and retail sectors. Strong retail brands are most advanced in the UK, including possibly the world's strongest brand in product retailing, M&S.

Are Retail Brands Different from Producer Brands?

We can see today that strong brands can be established in retailing. Internationally, many examples can be found in repertoire and service retailing. The UK gives us examples of strong brands in the grocery sector. Examples in the proximity and category killer sectors are harder to find, but we can point to Boots in the UK and Decathlon in France. Retail brands clearly can become 'The Real Thing'.

As with producer brands, differentiation is a central concept in retail brand strategy, and applicable across all retail sectors. We identify six key sources of retail brand differentiation: investment in store brands, investment in the supply chain and supplier relationships, mass marketing, the development of direct customer relationships, brand integrity and brand culture. Overall, segmentation is relevant in retail brand strategy, particularly in repertoire and service retailing, but it is less central than it is for producer brands. While there are examples of segmented propositions in product retailing outside fashion and home, lifestyle retailers often compete for maximum market share in their categories, across all customer groups within their catchment areas and across a wide range of price positions.

A real and important difference between most producer brands and most retail brands is the sheer multiplicity of retail brand attributes, and their high rate of change. The problems this creates around clarity of brand positioning are greatest in grocery and hypermarket or supercenter retailing, which need to work hard to create a broad umbrella brand assurance of quality, value and service, overlaid with unique store brands. The multiplicity of attributes of a retail brand also creates practical differences in decision-making, control and organisation relative to classical fmcg brand management.

Two intrinsic differences are often argued to exist between the economics of retail brands and producer brands: the level and nature of the brand premium, and the ability to invest in brand-building. For retailers with highly developed and high quality store brands, there is no fundamental difference in the potential for a volume and price premium; but retailers who mainly sell producer brands cannot extract any material long-run price premium, and must instead focus on volume advantage versus competitors. There is no innate difference between retail and producer brands in their ability to invest in brand-building: the high financial and operational gearing of many non-UK retailers is a choice rather than an inevitability and need not constrain productive investment; operating margins, thin or fat, are the result of strategy, not the cause.

Brand-building Strategies in Four Sectors

Repertoire Retailing: Fashion and Home Lifestyle

Brands in repertoire retailing, both fashion and home lifestyle, can be as strong as the strongest producer brands.

Fashion retailers can use the full range of segmentation and differentiation approaches and tools in their brand-building strategies. The most important and powerful is the development of a strong and distinctive store brand range, supported by investment in managing the complex fashion supply chain. Like producer brands, they have the opportunity of distribution through a mix of sales channels, although they must retain some exclusivity and competitive distinction for their core own stores.

By default, department stores are increasingly becoming large-space repertoire retailers, focusing on fashion and home lifestyle categories. They need to make this repertoire retailing role work, by meeting the challenge of brand-building as both a producer brand showcase and as a provider of quality store brands.

Home products occupy a position in the retail market that is a mixture of fashion repertoire shopping and the more functional shopping of category killers. Home lifestyle products can represent fashion choices for the home living environment, and brand-building strategies can be similar to fashion retailers.

Proximity Retailing

The chemist/drugstore market is unusual in proximity retailing: the health and beauty product core provides a strong platform on which to build brand loyalty and differentiation. Elsewhere across the sector, brand-building is a particularly hard challenge, unless a retailer is leveraging a strength in store brands/private label from a core position in another, large-scale retailing sector, such as Tesco with its Tesco Metro format.

Category Killers

Strong retail brands can be developed in category killer destination retailing, and will become the central driver of competitive performance and profitability as category killer markets mature. Defining the target product market, or 'which category to kill', and sticking to it, are key elements of a successful brand strategy. Developing a strong store brand/ private label offer is also key, and has been achieved by retailers of home products and sports goods.

Where destination retail sectors are dominated by producer brands, and there are real barriers to store brand development, category killers may have to depend on other sources of brand differentiation, particularly service and the creation of long-term direct customer relationships.

Grocery Retailing

The grocery sector is at the heart of the debate over the current and potential growth of retail brand power, and on the front-line in the battle with global producer brands for consumer preference and loyalty.

The UK provides a concrete case of how grocery retailers can become very strong differentiated retail brands. Their key differentiation strategy is based on the development of quality store brands/private label, supported by investment in the supply chain and supplier relationships. Another key weapon is the building of strong direct customer relationships, which supermarkets are in a unique position to be able to do, and which should prove even more effective long-run than investments in mass marketing.

There are no innate reasons why the UK grocery model of retail brand development cannot be replicated in other markets, including the USA, if leading grocery retailers make the necessary commitment to long-term brand-building investment. Arguments that the UK is somehow 'different' do not hold water. Several US grocers are making good progress in building their brands, and the recent growth in store brand/private label share will prove to be a secular rather than a cyclical trend.

Although most chains will continue to address the unsegmented general market, segmentation is possible in grocery retailing. As store networks are duplicated and reach saturation, more retailers may find it more attractive to pursue a segmented strategy, targeting limited sets of customer or product groups with clear positions on the price/quality spectrum, than to continue to go for maximum share of aggregate catchment area grocery spend.

Hypermarkets and supercenters face particularly tough brand-building challenges, caused by their combination of non-food (competing with category killers) and food (competing with local, close-to-customer supermarkets).

Managing Retail Brands

Managing Multiplicity: The Detail in Retail

Retail brands differ from producer brands in the sheer multiplicity of brand attributes, arising from the combination of thousands of product lines and millions of in-store customer experiences. They also differ in the rate of change of these attributes. The need to manage the 'detail in retail' creates real difference in emphasis and priority versus the more centralised and controllable environment of fmcg brand management. It is here that the fmcg-experienced manager has to make the greatest changes in mindset.

Retail management has to lead by example in mastering and managing the details of the business, and in 'getting their hands dirty' out in the field. The key tools are range reviews, store visits, customer interaction, supplier meetings, and employee interaction and communication. Retail managers must also accept, value and encourage experimentation within brand strategy, and be ready let the brand evolve in response to unforeseen successes and opportunities.

Given the mountain of detail involved in retail management, effective management and decision support systems ('DSS') are an absolute necessity. Most retailers' information systems needs to be supplemented and honed to provide a more effective set of tools for retail brand management.

Organising for Retail Brand Management

A strong Marketing function is needed in any retail business committed to brand-building. As well as managing large investments in mass marketing, promotional activity and direct customer relationships, a strong Marketing function should operate as the 'flag-carrier' for long-term brand strategy, championing the integrity of a brand's values in the face of short-term trading pressures.

The key interaction in retail brand management is between Marketing and B&M. B&M is already facing significant change, as its activities are unbundled into Range Management, Supplier Management and Stock Management, each with a distinct set of skills. B&M now needs to adjust to sharing its power over the retail proposition with Marketing, particularly at the core intersection of category management, where the two functions need to jointly review and develop overall category and store brand strategies.

Unlike in fmcg producer businesses, the Marketing function cannot be the king or queen of brand management. Brand strategy and brand management must necessarily remain a more complex team effort, driven by the inner circle of market-facing functional heads: the Chief Executive and the heads of B&M, Marketing and Store Operations. This inner circle must have a clearly articulated and shared idea of the long-term brand-building objective.

Investing in Store Brands

There are five stages in the development of store brands, roughly matching the stages of maturity and power of the retail brand. The first three stages – generics, cheap/copycat, and re-engineered low-cost store brands – require little or no investment by the retailer. The last two stages – par quality and leadership – move from being cost- and price-based to being based on quality and innovation, and require extensive investment by the retailer in design and development, quality control, and close long-term supplier relationships.

Retailers can view the strategic purpose of store brand development as either short-term margin enhancement or long-term brand-building. Retailers who concentrate on generics and cheap/copycat store brands usually focus on margin enhancement and miss the greater brand-building opportunity. Retailers whose strategic purpose is long-term brand-building will behave and invest in a very different way, even in the early stages of store brand development.

Retailers cannot hope to develop strong store brand positions across all categories simultaneously. They must target and prioritise their effort and investment, either by targeting weak producer brands or by re-merchandising a category, examples of which range from wine, coffee and chilled foods through to storage and health and beauty care.

Moving into sub-brands can take a retailer too far along the path of becoming like a producer brand. Broad differences in price/quality positioning can be signalled through packaging and presentation and through the use of store brand 'tags' ('Select', 'Basics'), while still staying within a store brand umbrella.

Building a supply chain and a supplier base for quality and leadership store brands requires an investment-oriented approach, characterised by open information flows, joint investment in product development and quality control, some level of risk-sharing and long-term commitment, and recognition of the need for attractive long-run financial returns for both sides.

Even very strong, well-managed retail brands can go too far, too fast, in developing store brand penetration and reducing the presence and choice of producer brands. Strong producer brands still command high levels of consumer loyalty, and retailers need to be careful that they are not crossing a threshold of consumer acceptance, particularly where the absence of preferred producer brands triggers a switch in primary shopping loyalty.

At maturity, quality and leadership store brands operate similarly to producer brands. As their consumer acceptance, quality and market share grows, initial price discounts versus producer brands are reduced and store brands may achieve a premium versus producer brands. Strong store brands may often, rather counter-intuitively, have greater appeal to and greater share in more affluent consumer groups, who will be more confident in their own taste and judgement in abandoning heavily advertised producer brands.

Investing in the Brand–Customer Relationship

Although retail brand advertising spends are increasing, there are limitations on the value of mass marketing in building the retail brand–customer relationship. Producer brand advertising, even in very functional product categories, delivers compressed images of brand association and aspiration, with the goal of long-term brand-building. Retail advertising tends to be more banal and crude, focusing on price and promotion with the goal of short-term sales up-lift, and rarely uses compressed messages and abstract imagery.

Mass marketing also does not play to retailers' own strengths, and to their structural advantages over producers, which lie in the ability and opportunity to build strong direct customer relationships. This retail advantage derives from their frequent direct contact with the customer, the breadth and immediacy of their consumer information, their greater capacity for quick, flexible experimentation, and their ability to tailor their brand and offer to local demand.

Building direct customer relationships has three key elements: customer understanding, customer targeting, and customer communication. Each requires investment in systems and resources, and overall investment is required in loyalty schemes that give customers reason to participate in the databases and in the relationship with the retail brand. This investment can be supported, and focused more effectively, by using the concept of lifetime customer value.

Investing in Brand Integrity

Investing in brand integrity can involve acting positively in making and sticking to investment plans in the face of short-term pressure to cut corners and costs, or deciding against acting in ways that enhance short-term revenue and profits but endanger long-term brand value. Both types of situation involve investment, either in actual or in opportunity cost, and both are acid tests of the brand-builder's mettle. As with every element of brand-building investment, commitment is only truly evidenced, and brand benefit accumulated, over many years.

There are several ways in which a retailer's commitment to brand integrity can be manifested. A 'no quibbles' returns policy is a powerful statement of a brand's commitment to and confidence in its product quality, and aligns the retailer solidly with the customer's interests. Pricing integrity – EDLP, limited sales and promotions, and holding the line on price in difficult trading conditions – sends the right message to consumers as to the brand's sense of its own worth, and strengthens rather than conflicts with a stance of never being beaten on price. Broad-based profit-sharing and performance-related pay can bind staff in to the brand culture, increasing motivation and commitment right down through the organisation. A committed retail brand-builder will turn down short-term brand exploitation opportunities that run the risk of undermining long-run brand value.

Different Perspectives

The Financial Services Supermarket

There are analogies between retail financial services and product retailing. There is, or at least could be, a producer–retailer split – although that may be obscured, as it is in banking, by the historical legacies of regulation and vertical integration. Financial service retailers could in theory offer consumers a range of choices of producer brands and of store brand product. There are examples of retail brand-building strategies, successful and unsuccessful.

However, it is unlikely that financial services supermarkets will become a reality. One reason is the infrequent nature of 'shopping' for financial services products, and the related inertia of customer–supplier relationships. A second and more convincing reason is the weight of vertical integration. Thirdly, the growth of mail, telephone and computer-based propositions is causing a disintermediation of branches and distributors. Consumers will prefer the efficiency and convenience of non-branch-based shopping and service, certainly for most banking and insurance products, and possibly for asset management.

The growth of non-branch-based propositions could open up the opportunity for greater internationalisation of retail financial services. International direct sales/service competitors can offer substantial price and service advantages over traditional local branch-based firms, and can obtain economies of scale at an international as well as national level. Direct insurance and asset management could be prime candidates for such internationalisation.

The lifetime value of a customer in financial services is high, particularly for a competitor who can offer a broad range of products, from banking through insurance to asset management. This value can justify large investments in the databases needed to support direct customer relationships and life-cycle marketing. The customer-oriented financial services competitor of the future, dealing with non-branch-based customers, will also need to re-integrate product profit centres and customer relationship management.

Product retailers are increasingly bundling some elements of financial services activity into their transactions and consumer offer, either to enhance their product retailing brand or as profit centres. Leading UK retailers with strong, trusted brands are now going beyond the most obvious example, consumer credit, and are offering quasi-banking services and mutual funds.

The Producer Perspective: Partnerships and Paranoia

Producers need to recognise the pressures that they will face as a result of the growth of retail brand power, and determine how they will respond to these pressures. The relationship between brand-building retailers and producers will be a balance of 'partnership and paranoia'.

After a peak in the 1980s and a trough in the early 1990s, the perception and value of producer brands have settled at a more balanced level. Some producers and analysts are now sounding complacent about the threat from retailers and retail brands. This is partly wishful thinking and partly deliberate policy. Most producers recognise that, although producer brands are far from dead, there has been a structural shift in the balance of power between retailers and producers.

The threat of retail brand power will strengthen producers' focus on and commitment to their category leadership positions. Producers will need to re-invest heavily in these category leaders – in innovation and quality, in above-the-line marketing and in speed-to-market – to preserve a distance and premium between them and quality store brands.

Category followers can choose to work proactively with retailers as suppliers of quality store brands. Although never delivering as high a return as a category-leading producer brand, focusing on supplying store brands can be an effective and profitable strategy.

Looking Forward

Retailing Without Frontiers

Retailing has lagged other industry sectors, including fmcg producers, in going international and global. Retailers have had too much of a job to do in competing in and consolidating their local markets, and traditional small-scale decentralised retailers have held no advantages over entrenched local players in foreign markets.

These conditions have now changed. Many domestic markets have consolidated, and retailers are looking abroad for further growth opportunities. Large-scale retail formats, including out-of-town destination retailers, have economic advantages that can offset the established presence and local market knowledge of local competitors.

We distinguish two types of retail internationalisation: portfolio owners, who maintain separate brands in different country markets; and international brands, which are rolled out relatively consistently under the same brand name in different markets.

In the latter category, we can find today several examples of strong global retail brands in fashion and home lifestyle product retailing, and in retail services, primarily fast food and hotels; almost no examples in proximity retailing, which is the sector with the weakest rationale for internationalisation; a few examples among category killers, although mostly at a very early stage; and almost no global examples yet in grocery, although pan-European competition is developing rapidly.

The retail brand-building values argued for throughout this book significantly enhance a retail business's potential for going international and global. Outside of category killers, successful global retail brands to date are committed to investing in quality store brands and long-term supplier partnerships, brand–customer relationships, and brand integrity.

Multi-business Retailing: Sum and Parts

Historically, multi-business retailers in mature markets have not performed as well as focused single-business retailers. Although a retail portfolio can satisfy the need for businesses to be 'related', diversified retailers need to avoid falling into the same traps that brought down large conglomerates in the 1980s.

Multi-business retailers need to avoid the portfolio management mentality. They need to be as capable as a focused retailer of sticking with, investing in and re-positioning their core brands and businesses.

They need to avoid the cost and bureaucracy that can be created by the centre, in particular the negative effect that the centre can have on management focus and productivity, on responsiveness and on overhead costs in the operating divisions.

They must also avoid pursuing false synergies across businesses, in centralised operational functions and store brand buying. Real synergies can be had from combining support and overhead functions and in pooling producer brand buying, but these should be pursued cautiously so as not to compromise line management's accountability and their focus on the 'main game' of the retail proposition.

Looking forward, brand-building could provide the same strategic glue for multi-business retailers as it does for fmcg groups. Retailers that understand how to invest in long-term brand-building and in brand differentiation, and know how to build international and global retail brands, will be able to transfer that expertise and philosophy across different businesses within a retail sector, and even across retail sectors.

Home Shopping: From Mail Order to the Virtual Mall

IAHS represents a step-change in potential versus home shopping channels such as QVC and HSN. With IAHS, consumers will be free to browse through a 'virtual mall', which will not only simulate the physical shopping experience but will provide a range of additional benefits.

The main necessary technologies are likely to be in place over the next 5–10 years at a level that can support the practical and serious development of IAHS. The dominant US model for IAHS delivery in the first decade of the next century could be the Internet, distributed down cable TV pipe, supported by various server systems, home interfaces, and systems for payment and security.

The IAHS marketplace today is in its very early stages of development, and its current status provides only limited clues to how rapidly it will grow and where it will have most impact. Although many retailers have presences on the Net, the majority use it so far as a way of distributing information and marketing, rather than as a transaction medium.

In assessing long-term potential, it is more useful to go back to first principles of consumer needs and behaviour, and ask what consumers will eventually shop for in the virtual mall.

Several branch-based retail services are highly vulnerable to IAHS, to such an extent that IAHS could rapidly become the dominant form of distribution. Travel agents, video and music stores and financial services are prime candidates for substitution. IAHS is also a threat for all product retailers whose sales mix is skewed towards big-ticket items and producer brands: department stores, non-store brand fashion and home lifestyle retailers, and category killers in furniture, sports and toys, as well as electrical.

The strongest long-run defence for these threatened businesses is to build strong retail brands, particularly quality store brands, to become more like producers and less vulnerable to disintermediation. The threat from IAHS and the virtual mall reinforces, and makes even more urgent, the retail brand-building imperative which is the central theme of the book.

In Conclusion: From Trading to Brand Leadership

Great retailers need to be great traders – but to build retail brand value, trading ability is not enough. Retailers need to overlay and institutionalise brand management skills, philosophy and reflexes. The two philosophies need to be in balance, or in a state of constant creative tension. A retail business that loses its trading edge, disregarding the need for short-term sales and profit, is a business at risk that may not survive to reap the benefits of long-term brand-building. But a retail business that has no long-term brand-building strategy and instincts will never build defensible competitive advantage, and will always be very vulnerable to competitive attack.

For a retail Chief Executive, making the change from trading to brand leadership involves recognising the difference; committing to the long-term goal of brand-building; developing the brand-building strategy; putting in place the necessary organisation structure and resources; translating the strategy into concrete medium-term programmes and priorities; and winning over the Board and investors.

Building strong retail brands will be a key to shareholder value creation in retail businesses. As well as higher operating margins, strong brands have higher growth prospects, greater sustainability, and reduced volatility of returns, all of which contribute to a much lower cost of capital. On a net present value basis, the value of a strong retail brand may be four times that of a retail trader with the same sales volume.

Shareholder value creation is the prize for successful retail brand-builders, and the beginning of the twenty-first century could be the era of retail brand power. Developing a strong brand franchise is one of the best defences against the intense competitive pressures of mature retail markets. Rolling out international brands will be one of the most effective forms of global retail competition. And strong brands provide the best platform for participating in the virtual mall and combating the risk of disintermediation.

Index